America's Children

Health Insurance and Access to Care

Margaret Edmunds and Molly Joel Coye, *Editors*

Committee on Children, Health Insurance, and Access to Care
Division of Health Care Services, Institute of Medicine, and
Board on Children, Youth, and Families,
National Research Council and Institute of Medicine

NATIONAL ACADEMY PRESS
Washington, DC 1998

NATIONAL ACADEMY PRESS • 2101 Constitution Avenue, N.W. • Washington, D.C. 20418

NOTICE: The project that is the subject of this report was approved by the Governing Board of the National Research Council, whose members are drawn from the councils of the National Academy of Sciences, the National Academy of Engineering, and the Institute of Medicine. The members of the committee responsible for the report were chosen for their special competences and with regard for appropriate balance.

The Institute of Medicine was chartered in 1970 by the National Academy of Sciences to enlist distinguished members of the appropriate professions in the examination of policy matters pertaining to the health of the public. In this, the Institute acts under both the Academy's 1863 congressional charter responsibility to be an adviser to the federal government and its own initiative in identifying issues of medical care, research, and education. Dr. Kenneth I. Shine is president of the Institute of Medicine.

This study was supported by the Robert Wood Johnson Foundation. The views presented in this report are those of the Institute of Medicine's Committee on Children, Health Insurance, and Access to Care and are not necessarily those of the funding organization.

Additional copies of this report are available for sale from the National Academy Press, Box 285, 2101 Constitution Avenue, N.W., Washington, D.C. Call (800) 624-6242 or (202) 334-3313 (in the Washington metropolitan area), or visit the NAP's on-line bookstore at **http://www.nap.edu.**

Library of Congress Cataloging-in-Publication Data

America's children : health insurance and access to care / Margaret Edmunds and Molly Joel Coye, Editors.
p. cm.
"Committee on Children, Health Insurance, and Access to Care Division of Health Care Services, Institute of Medicine, and Board on Children, Youth, and Families, National Research Council and Institute of Medicine."
Includes bibliographical references and index.
ISBN 0-309-06560-7 (pbk.)
1. Child health services—United States—Finance. 2. Health services accessibility—United States. 3. Insurance, Health—United States. 4. Medically uninsured persons—United States. I. Edmunds, Margaret. II. Coye, Molly Joel. III. Institute of Medicine. Committee on Children, Health Insurance, and Access to Care. IV. Board on Children, Youth, and Families (U.S.)
RJ102 .A387 1998
362.1'9892'000973—ddc21

98-25491

Printed in the United States of America

The serpent has been a symbol of long life, healing, and knowledge among almost all cultures and religions since the beginning of recorded history. The image adopted as a logotype by the Institute of Medicine is based on a relief carving from ancient Greece, now held by the Staatliche Museen in Berlin.

COMMITTEE ON CHILDREN, HEALTH INSURANCE, AND ACCESS TO CARE

MOLLY JOEL COYE (*Chair*),* Director, West Coast Office, The Lewin Group, San Francisco
IRENE AGUILAR, Primary Care Physician, Westside Family Health Center, Denver
BRIAN K. ATCHINSON, Second Vice President, Government Relations, UNUM, Portland, ME
STEPHEN M. BOROWITZ, Associate Professor of Pediatrics, University of Virginia Health Sciences Center
RICHARD BUCCIARELLI, Professor, Institute for Child Health Policy, and Associate Chair, Department of Pediatrics, University of Florida College of Medicine
PETER BUDETTI, Professor of Health Services Management, Preventive Medicine and Law, and Director, Institute for Health Services Research and Policy Studies, Northwestern University
THOMAS W. CHAPMAN, Senior Vice President for Network Development and Professor of Health Services Management and Policy, The George Washington University Medical Center
MARGARET C. HEAGARTY,* Director of Pediatrics, Harlem Hospital Center, and Professor of Pediatrics, College of Physicians and Surgeons, Columbia University
ROBERT B. HELMS, Resident Scholar, Director of Health Policy Studies, American Enterprise Institute, Washington, DC
VELVET MILLER, Deputy Commissioner, New Jersey Department of Human Services, Trenton
ARNOLD MILSTEIN, Managing Director, William M. Mercer, Inc., and Medical Director, Pacific Business Group on Health, San Francisco
PAUL NEWACHECK, Professor of Health Policy and Pediatrics, Institute for Health Policy Studies and Department of Pediatrics, University of California at San Francisco
DAVID S. WEINER, President and CEO, Children's Hospital, Boston
STEVEN H. WOOLF, Fairfax Family Practice Center, and Clinical Professor, Department of Family Practice, Medical College of Virginia

Institute of Medicine Staff

MARGARET EDMUNDS, Study Director
ELISE LIPOFF, Research Associate (March 1997 through June 1997)
ANNICE HIRT, Research Assistant (March 1997 through September 1997)
KATHLEEN NOLAN, Research Assistant (November 1997 through May 1998)
TRACY MCKAY, Project Assistant
JOHN BROTHERS, Graphics Consultant
CARINA WEI-YEE FUNG, Student Intern
MICHAEL DOMBECK, Student Intern

*Member, Institute of Medicine.

BOARD ON HEALTH CARE SERVICES
INSTITUTE OF MEDICINE

DON E. DETMER (*Chair*),* Senior Vice President, The University of Virginia
STUART H. ALTMAN,* Sol C. Chaikin Professor of National Health Policy, The Florence Heller Graduate School for Social Policy, Brandeis University
NANCY W. DICKEY, Private Practice, College Station, TX
B. KEN GRAY, Corporate Medical Director, Metroplex Emergency Physician Associates, P.A., Dallas
PAUL F. GRINER,* Vice President and Director, Center for the Assessment and Management of Change in Academic Medicine, Association of American Medical Colleges, Washington, DC
BRENT C. JAMES, Executive Director, Institute for Health Care Delivery Research, and Vice President, Medical Research and Continuing Medical Education, Intermountain Health Care, Salt Lake City
JACQUELINE KOSECOFF, President and Co-Chief Executive Officer, Value Health Sciences, Inc., Santa Monica
SHEILA T. LEATHERMAN, Executive Vice President, Center for Health Care Policy and Evaluation, United Health Care Corporation, Minneapolis
JOHN LUDDEN, Senior Vice President for Medical Affairs, Harvard Pilgrim Health Care, Brookline
BARBARA J. McNEIL,* Ridley Watts Professor, Department of Health Care Policy, Harvard Medical School
RUSSELL L. MILLER, Health Science Center, State University of New York at Brooklyn
MILDRED MITCHELL-BATEMAN,* Clinical Director, Huntington Hospital, Huntington, WV
MARY MUNDINGER,* Dean and Centennial Professor in Health Policy, Columbia University
UWE E. REINHARDT,* James Madison Professor of Political Economy and Professor of Economics and Public Affairs, Princeton University
MARY LEE SEIBERT, Acting Provost, Ithaca College
GAIL L. WARDEN,* President and Chief Executive Officer, Henry Ford Health System, Detroit

Institute of Medicine Staff

CLYDE J. BEHNEY, Deputy Executive Officer and Director, Board on Health Care Services

*Member, Institute of Medicine.

BOARD ON CHILDREN, YOUTH, AND FAMILIES
NATIONAL RESEARCH COUNCIL AND INSTITUTE OF MEDICINE

Preface

The Committee on Children, Health Insurance, and Access to Care was asked by the Robert Wood Johnson Foundation to address a series of questions about health insurance for children. In addition to evaluating empirical evidence about the relationship between health insurance and access to care, the committee was asked to identify key trends in insurance coverage and in the delivery of care for uninsured children. The committee was asked to pay particular attention to changes in the provider community that might have an impact on access to care for uninsured and underserved children.

The committee approached the study as an opportunity to evaluate the strengths and limitations of insurance as a means of improving children's health. From the beginning of their deliberations, the committee members took the position that several strategies potentially could increase the number of insured children and that their task was not to recommend one particular option. Rather, they decided to evaluate the advantages and disadvantages of a wide variety of approaches and to provide the best possible analysis of the various policies that might be considered, including some that have not yet been fully implemented or evaluated.

The timing of the study brought special challenges. The committee held four meetings and a public workshop between March 1997 and January 1998. From the beginning of 1997, President Clinton and members of Congress debated a variety of proposals about insurance coverage for children, including Medicaid expansions, block grants, vouchers, tax credits, and several other strategies. In August 1997, Congress passed the Balanced Budget Act of 1997, enacting a new State Children's Health Insurance Program (SCHIP) with provisions for Medicaid expansions as well as market-based approaches to reducing the number of uninsured children.

Because of the rapid rate of ongoing change in the health care system, particularly the increasing emphasis on Medicaid managed care, the committee intended for this report to present a general framework that would apply to several programs and strategies over time. The committee prepared a separate report entitled *Systems of Accountability: Implementing Children's Health Insurance Programs*, to focus on the evaluation of SCHIP and its impact.

The committee included clinicians, researchers, policy analysts, and administrators. This consensus report reflects compromises made by committee members with differing views in order to reach language that each member of the committee could accept. For example, some committee members were willing to recommend universal, comprehensive coverage for all American children, while others were reluctant to do so because they felt it was beyond the scope of the study, or because they questioned the availability of resources, political will, or feasibility of comprehensive approaches. In the end, the committee recommended that all children should have health insurance, but did not recommend a single set of benefits or a single source of financing.

This report, then, is intended as an overview of key issues in the organization, delivery, and financing of health care for children. The audience for the report is intentionally quite broad. It includes the study's sponsor, the Robert Wood Johnson Foundation, as well as other philanthropic organizations; members of Congress, congressional staff, and federal agencies; governors, state legislatures, and state agencies; the public health community; providers and the many provider associations representing them; employers; health insurers; parents; and children's advocates.

The committee hopes that this report will help a variety of policy makers and other decision makers to make more informed decisions about how to achieve their multiple—and often competing—objectives as the SCHIP program is implemented across the country. The committee hopes that over time its contribution will be useful in shedding light on the impact and possible consequences of choosing various policy options to expand health insurance coverage for children.

Molly Joel Coye
Chair

Acknowledgments

The members of the Committee on Children, Health Insurance, and Access to Care and the study staff appreciate the assistance and contributions from many individuals and organizations during the course of the study.

We express deep appreciation to all of the individuals and groups who contributed to the public workshop on June 2, 1997. Presentations were made by the following invited speakers: Maureen Ceidro, Julius Goepp, John Goodman, Jane Horvath, Dennis Johnson, Kay Johnson, Karen LaPlante, Charles LaVallee, John McDonough, Kim Monk, Diane Rowland, and Eugene Steuerle. Public statements were made by James Bentley, Stan Dorn, Steve Edwards, Samuel Flint, Shelly Gehshan, Catherine Hess, Ross Marine, and Kathleen Means. The committee and staff are particularly grateful to Patrick Chaulk and Carl J. Schramm, who served as moderators, and J. Michael McGinnis, who aptly summarized the day's proceedings.

We also would like to thank the speakers who made invited presentations at the committee's first meeting in March 1997. They are Pamela Dickson, Burton Edelstein, Paul Fronstin, Dan Hawkins, Laurence McAndrews, and Jacqueline Noyes.

We particularly appreciate the contributions made by Paul Fronstin of the Employee Benefits Research Institute, who analyzed and provided data especially for this study and was responsive to numerous requests for additional information. We also thank Mark Hall of Wake Forest University's School of Law and Bowman Gray School of Medicine for providing a background paper and glossary on private insurance. Jane Koppelman's insightful and helpful comments on an earlier draft of the report are gratefully acknowledged. Michael Hayes, copy editor, also made many useful contributions and suggestions to improve the report. Thanks also go to Jane Andrews, Ellen Bayer, James Crall, Shelly Gehshan, Shirley Girouard, Suzanne Hansen, Dan Hawkins, Joan Henneberry, Robert Isman, Barbara Lamb, Marjorie Shofer, Marina Weiss, and Pete Wilson for providing technical comments on draft sections of the report.

We are especially grateful to the members of the liaison panel for providing materials and public statements for the committee's consideration. The complete list of liaison panel members is included in Appendix D. Among those who were particularly active and helpful at various stages of the study are Sheila Avruch, Laura Camisa, Patrick Chaulk, Burton Edelstein, Donna Grossman, Elizabeth Hadley, Catherine Hess, Ed Howard, Ron Manderscheid, John McDonough, Kathleen Means, Ed Neuschler, and Eugene Steuerle.

The committee could not have accomplished its tasks without the steadfast and creative efforts of the Institute of Medicine staff, led by Margo Edmunds, the study director. Her thoughtfulness, foresight, and ingenuity in planning and managing the study were exemplary. Her efforts were supported by Elise Lipoff, research associate; Annice Hirt, research assistant; Kathleen Nolan, research assistant; Tracy McKay, project assistant; two summer interns, Carina Wei-Yee Fung and Michael Dombeck; and John Brothers, graphics consultant.

Several members of the staff of the Institute of Medicine and National Research Council made contributions to this report. Clyde Behney developed the idea for the study with the sponsor and provided guidance throughout the project. Kenneth Shine, Karen Hein, and Deborah Phillips also made several helpful comments at several stages of the project. Others who made contributions are Drusilla Barnes, Sue Barron, Mona Brinegar, Claudia Carl, Margo Cullen, Molla Donaldson, Jane Durch, Mike Edington, Robert Epstein, Marilyn Field, Kay Harris, Roger Herdman, Carrie Ingalls, Jeff Isenhour, Jim Jensen, Patricia Kaiser, Linda Kilroy, Michele Kipke, Jeffrey Koshel, Karen Kreiger, Marion Ein Lewin, Cathy Liverman, Luis Nunez, Constance Pechura, Deborah Phillips, Barbara Kline Pope, Dan Quinn, Barbara Rice, Kristen Robinson, Evelyn Simeon, Mary Lee Schneiders, Sally Stanfield, Michael Stoto, Kathleen Stratton, and Gooloo Wunderlich.

This report has been reviewed by individuals chosen for their diverse perspectives and technical expertise, in accordance with procedures approved by the National Research Council's Report Review Committee. The purpose of this independent review is to provide candid and critical comments that will assist the authors and the IOM in making the published report as sound as possible and to ensure that the report meets institutional standards for objectivity, evidence, and responsiveness to the study charge. The content of the review comments and the draft manuscript remain confidential to protect the integrity of the deliberative process. We wish to thank the following individuals for their participation in the review process: John Bartkowski, Sixteenth Street Community Health Centers, Inc., Milwaukee, WI; Judith Feder, Georgetown University Institute for Health Care, Public Policy, and Research, Washington, DC; Julius Goepp, Division of Pediatric Emergency Medicine, University of Rochester School of Medicine, Rochester, NY; Bernard Guyer, Department of Maternal and Child Health, Johns Hopkins University School of Hygiene and Public Health, Baltimore, MD; Mark Hall, Wake Forest University School of Law and Bowman Gray School of Medicine, Winston-Salem, NC; and Melvin Worth, IOM Scholar in Residence.

While the individuals listed above have provided many constructive comments and suggestions, responsibility for the final content of this report rests solely with the authoring committee and the IOM.

The study was undertaken with the support of the Robert Wood Johnson Foundation. The contributions of Foundation staff members Pamela Dickson, senior program officer, Robert Hughes, vice president, and Judith Whang, program officer, are gratefully acknowledged.

Contents

PART II: FINANCING HEALTH CARE FOR CHILDREN

BOXES, TABLES, AND FIGURES

Boxes

Tables

Figures

America's Children

Summary

BACKGROUND

In the summer of 1996, the Robert Wood Johnson Foundation asked the National Academy of Sciences to form a committee to examine the extent of health insurance coverage for children and to analyze evidence of the relationship between health insurance coverage and children's access to health care. The committee was asked to focus on safety net providers such as community health centers and children's hospitals that traditionally have provided care for uninsured children and their families, to examine trends affecting these providers, and to evaluate the potential effects of those trends on children's access to health care.

APPROACH TO THE STUDY

The study was a joint effort between the Division of Health Care Services of the Institute of Medicine and the Board on Children, Youth, and Families of the Institute of Medicine and the Commission on Behavioral and Social Sciences and Education, which is part of the National Research Council. The Board on Health Care Services and the Board on Children, Youth, and Families approved the proposal for the study and received regular updates on its progress and activities from the Institute of Medicine study staff. Nominations for potential committee members were sought from a wide range of sources, including Boards, members, and staff of the Institute of Medicine; national professional organizations; federal agencies; private policy research organizations; foundations; and other groups.

The Committee on Children, Health Insurance, and Access to Care met four times between March 1997 and January 1998. The committee included 14 individuals with expertise in health care financing and delivery, private indemnity insurance, managed care, Medicaid, and other public programs; health care delivery, both primary and specialty care for children and adults; health care policy; legislative policy, regulation, health law, and health economics; health services research; and epidemiology.

The committee convened a public workshop in June 1997 in Washington, D.C. In addition, a liaison panel was formed with nearly 200 representatives of state and federal government, national organizations, health care providers, and other groups. Members of the liaison panel attended the workshop and also submitted written statements for the committee's consideration.

Because of their different backgrounds and different views about health insurance, the committee members began their deliberations by developing a unifying set of beliefs about health insurance. The committee members agreed that a variety of strategies could be used to expand children's health insurance coverage, with funds for those strategies coming from several possible sources: federal and state budgets, employers, families, health plans, insurers, and communities. After discussion, they agreed that the ultimate goal of health insurance is to provide access to coordinated, efficient, and effective care and services when needed for all American children, including those who have preventable illnesses and injuries as well as those with chronic conditions and other special health care needs.

The timing of this study presented unusual challenges. During the months when the committee was meeting, children's health insurance took on national prominence as both political parties and the Clinton Administration presented a variety of proposals that were widely discussed by Congress, state policymakers, national professional organizations, the media, and the general public. Among the proposals were Medicaid expansions, block grants, vouchers, refundable tax credits for families, a tax credit for all children, family Medical Savings Accounts, and a new Children's Health Trust Fund.

It was unclear what, if any, national legislative approach would be taken until Congress passed the Balanced Budget Act of 1997 in August, with its provisions for the State Children's Health Insurance Program (SCHIP). The structure of the SCHIP legislation reflected the diversity of opinions about insurance strategies. Under SCHIP, states may choose to expand Medicaid, to design or expand state-sponsored or private programs, or to use a combination of strategies to improve insurance coverage for uninsured, low-income children.

The committee began the study with a decision to take an evidence-based approach to its examination of the relationship between health insurance and access to care. With the rapid rate of ongoing change in the health care insurance and delivery picture for children, the committee later decided to supplement the review of scientific and empirical evidence with an analysis of health care trends that are likely to affect the implementation of new children's insurance programs. Key sources of information included the following:

- analyses of the Current Population Survey conducted by the Employee Benefits Research Institute especially for this study;
- health services research findings published in peer-reviewed journals;
- publicly available descriptions of federal and state programs, and research findings and public statements by federal and state agencies;
- published materials and public statements submitted to the committee by national organizations;
- policy analyses, reports, newsletters, and news analyses by private organizations;
- published reports of philanthropic organizations, including the Annie E. Casey Foundation, the Kaiser Commission on the Future of Medicaid, the David and Lucile Packard Foundation, and the Robert Wood Johnson Foundation; and
- reports published by the Institute of Medicine and the National Research Council.

The committee's goal for this report was to draw a general set of conclusions about ways to help improve children's access to care that would apply to a variety of public and private insurance programs. The committee hopes this report will help to improve the evidence base for children's health and children's health insurance efforts and for efforts to improve the quality of children's health care. The committee's specific concerns about the need for data to evaluate the SCHIP program and its recommendations for designing a system of accountability for SCHIP are presented in a companion report entitled *Systems of Accountability: Implementing Children's Health Insurance Programs* (IOM, 1998).

TRENDS IN HEALTH INSURANCE COVERAGE FOR CHILDREN

The majority of American children have private insurance through their parents' employers. Over the past decade, the rates of employer-based coverage for children have been declining. With increasing health care costs, employers have been shifting a greater proportion of the costs of dependent coverage to their employees. Many working parents have low-wage jobs with small businesses that do not pay for their insurance coverage, and there are very few affordable insurance products for dependent coverage in the individual insurance market.

The declining rates in employer-based coverage have been partially offset by increases in Medicaid enrollment. Due to changes associated with welfare reform, however, Medicaid enrollment may begin to decrease. If these trends continue, the number of uninsured children is likely to continue to increase.

More than 11 million American children are uninsured. Most uninsured children live in families with working parents. Many are not eligible for Medicaid because their parents tend to work in low-wage jobs for employers that do not offer health insurance, and the parents cannot afford to purchase private insurance on their own. More than 3 million children nationally are eligible for Medicaid but are not enrolled for a variety of reasons.

Black and Hispanic children are more likely than white children to lack coverage. Nationally, one out of every six black children and one out of every four Hispanic children are uninsured, and one out of ten white children is uninsured.

State and regional variations in coverage rates are significant, in part because of differences in Medicaid coverage options for children used by each state, differences in state-sponsored programs and private initiatives, and also because of state and regional economic differences. Under the new SCHIP program, some of these coverage patterns will begin to change.

HEALTH INSURANCE AND ACCESS TO CARE

After reviewing evidence about financial and nonfinancial barriers to health care access, the committee has determined that insurance coverage is the major determinant of whether children have access to health care. This determination is based on the finding that is consistent across many studies: compared with children who have insurance coverage, uninsured children have many unmet health care needs. They are more likely to be sick as newborns, less likely to be immunized as preschoolers, less likely to receive medical treatment when they are injured, and less likely to receive treatment for illnesses such as acute or recurrent ear infections, asthma, and tooth decay.

Access to health care can influence children's physical and emotional growth, development, and overall health and well-being. Untreated illnesses and injuries can have long-term—even lifelong—consequences. For example, untreated ear infections can lead to hearing loss or deafness. Children who are unable to hear well can have trouble performing well in school and trouble interacting normally with their families and friends. Language or other developmental delays due to untreated neurological problems also can frustrate normal development and social interactions.

Uninsured children are the least likely members of society to have routine access to a physician. Without a regular source of care, low-income children are more likely to use publicly funded clinics for standard preventive services such as immunizations and are more likely to use emergency rooms for care for acute illnesses. Some aspects of the health care system also can create barriers to access, particularly the shortages of providers to serve low-income groups, lack of cultural sensitivity, and inconvenient scheduling.

Although children who are uninsured have less access to care, the presence of insurance alone will not eliminate all of the barriers to accessing appropriate health care services. Children are dependent on their parents to identify problems and seek treatment, and even insured and responsible parents may delay seeking care because of the cost of the out-of-pocket expenses or because it is difficult or inconvenient to schedule appointments. Delays in ambulatory care because of cost may result in diagnosis or treatment later in the course of illness or disease, when treatment may be more complex and more expensive.

SAFETY NET PROVIDERS

Safety net providers include those hospitals, clinics, community health centers, public health departments, school-based health centers, individual practitioners, and others who provide health care for uninsured and underinsured adults and children. These safety net providers are funded by the Medicaid and Medicare programs, Disproportionate Share Hospital (DSH) payments, the Maternal and Child Health Care Services Block Grant, federal research grants, state and local sources, private insurance payments, private donations, and patient payments.

Safety net providers and others have also provided care without any direct source of compensation. Until recently, many providers serving the general population could offset the costs of uncompensated care. As purchasers have turned to managed care for cost savings, however, the cross-subsidies and excess revenue sources that could support uncompensated care are shrinking. Purchasers have been negotiating deep discounts in contracts with mainstream hospitals and group practices, forcing many who formerly provided care for the uninsured to refer these patients to safety net providers. At the same time, some safety net providers have been entering into managed care networks so that they can continue to serve the same vulnerable populations or to maintain their financial viability by changing the mix of insured and uninsured patients whom they serve.

The mix of providers, sources of financing, and responsibility for care for the uninsured are different in every community. In a market-driven health care system, the impact of providing unreimbursed or partially reimbursed care is profound. No managed care organization will compete to care for uninsured individuals, and government subsidies to care for low-income and uninsured individuals are generally being reduced.

Not all safety net providers will be able to make a successful transition to the competitive health care marketplace. Success may be based on the degree to which providers can offer and market strong primary care services, can compete for Medicaid managed care contracts, and can negotiate payment arrangements that not only cover their costs but also contribute to their financial health.

MEDICAID

Medicaid is the largest single health insurance program for American children. The number of children enrolled in Medicaid has nearly doubled since 1985. In 1997, more than 22 million children—one out of every four children—were covered by Medicaid.

This increase in Medicaid enrollment has offset the simultaneous decrease in children's insurance coverage through private sources and has significantly reduced the disparities in access to health care for poor children enrolled in Medicaid. For some types of care, such as immunization rates and rates of professional treatment for injuries, access to health care for children with Medicaid coverage is comparable to that for privately insured children.

Medicaid has been successful in increasing rates of insurance coverage among children, but millions of children who are eligible for Medicaid have not been enrolled in the program. Because reimbursement rates have been lower than the rates in the private insurance market, provider participation has been lower than would be desirable. In addition, because of provider shortages in medically underserved areas, even children with Medicaid coverage may lack access to a regular source of preventive and acute care.

Several shifts in policy and legislation are changing the configuration of the Medicaid program. First, in an attempt to control costs, many states are converting their state programs from fee-for-service to managed care programs, so that the number of children enrolled in Medicaid managed care has increased sharply. Managed care may increase the level of access to preventive services and also may decrease the level of access to needed specialty services for children with special needs.

Second, the delinking of welfare payments from automatic Medicaid enrollment may lead to a decrease in the enrollment of Medicaid-eligible children. As more parents leave welfare and earn wages that are above the income threshold for Medicaid eligibility, states may consider approaching the insurance problem through the provision of subsidies to families or employers, the use of tax credits, or other strategies.

Based on the Medicaid experience with underenrollment, new state-sponsored and private SCHIP programs will have similar problems unless they can improve their outreach, enrollment, and eligibility determination procedures. States also must provide adequate reimbursement rates to maintain and improve provider participation, and quality standards must be enforced for all providers.

STATE AND PRIVATE INITIATIVES

Even before Congress enacted the State Children's Health Insurance Program (SCHIP), there were only six states without some type of public or private insurance subsidy program for children. In the past decade, states have taken a variety of steps to extend health insurance coverage to low-income children. Some have expanded Medicaid eligibility, some have developed state-sponsored programs which subsidize private coverage, and some have supported privately sponsored programs developed by insurers and health plans.

Income and age requirements for Medicaid eligibility, cost per child, the level of cost-sharing, the sources of financing, and Medicaid enrollment strategies vary widely. Most of the state program benefits are provided through contracts with managed care plans and are similar to the benefits offered to most privately insured individuals enrolled in managed care plans.

Although most of these programs have not been evaluated systematically, they have reduced the numbers of uninsured children in the United States. The variety of programs suggests that the problem of uninsured children can be approached in many ways. Comparisons of the different approaches could yield helpful information about what strategies and innovations are most effective for outreach and enrollment, cost-sharing, and other components of the programs.

CHILDREN'S HEALTH CARE NEEDS

Most children—approximately 70 percent, or about 50 million—are generally healthy. To help them stay healthy, these children need immunizations, regular preventive care, and professional treatment for acute illnesses and injuries.

Twenty percent of American children—about 14 million children—have such chronic problems as persistent ear infections, respiratory allergies, asthma, eczema, and skin allergies. These conditions may impose significant limitations on the children's ability to function effectively in school and at home. Children with chronic conditions require more frequent visits to primary care physicians, are more likely to visit emergency rooms, are more likely to need care from specialists, have greater needs for medications, and may also need hospitalizations during acute episodes. Their medical expenses, on average, are two to three times higher than those for the average healthy child.

The remaining 10 percent, about 7 million children, have one or more such severe chronic conditions as congenital heart defects, neural tube defects, juvenile diabetes mellitus, sickle cell disease, or human immunodeficiency virus (HIV) infection. This group accounts for 70 to 80 percent of all medical expenditures for children. Some of these children require extensive health care services (e.g., surgical procedures) requiring large expenditures primarily early in life. Others with severe medical conditions may require lifelong, intensive case management from primary care practitioners along with consultations from pediatric subspecialists, as well as services from allied health professionals to maintain or to improve their functioning.

Children with special needs typically also have additional, nonmedical needs. These include supplemental or adjunctive therapies; specialized transportation, supplies, and equipment; linkages with schools and other community-based organizations; and support for their families, including respite care and assistance with out-of-pocket (noncovered) expenses.

The most comprehensive and child-specific package of benefits is Medicaid, which offers a full range of medically necessary care for children, including children with special needs. Insurance coverage for children is variable and fragmented, and many controversial issues remain unresolved.

The committee recognizes that health care resources are not unlimited. However, as a matter of principle, the committee believes that all American children should have access to coordinated, efficient, and effective health care, including children who have preventable illnesses and injuries, chronic conditions, or other special health care needs.

THE STATE CHILDREN'S HEALTH INSURANCE PROGRAM (SCHIP)

The SCHIP program, enacted under the Balanced Budget Act of 1997, allows states to choose whether Medicaid expansions, state-sponsored programs, or state-private initiatives will be implemented. States may choose a combination of strategies and may implement different programs for different defined populations and regions.

The flexibility in SCHIP design appeals to most states because of the opportunity to provide coverage and services in ways that reflect the state's availability of insurance products and providers, geographic distribution of uninsured children, potential sources of financing, and many other factors. The structure of this legislation, with its flexibility and range of options, reflects the variety in current views about the government's role in a predominantly employer-sponsored insurance system.

With the new SCHIP programs, states that increase their Medicaid eligibility thresholds and otherwise subsidize coverage for previously uninsured children can raise the rates of insurance coverage and thus reduce the burden of providing uncompensated care among safety net providers. However, in order for SCHIP funds to make significant reductions in the numbers of uninsured children, states must draw down all of the available funds, actively pursue effective outreach and enrollment strategies, and also minimize the risk of replacing existing private coverage.

Over the next several years, it will be important to measure the extent to which the new children's health insurance programs alleviate the pressure on other sources of funding for uncompensated care. Unless better data systems are developed, this will be extremely difficult to measure. Thus, the advent of the SCHIP program offers a unique opportunity to track and measure changes in the number of uninsured children and to assess the program's effectiveness from its onset. Lessons learned from the evaluation of the program will have important implications for the likelihood and nature of future insurance expansions.

CONCLUSIONS

From the beginning of their deliberations, the committee members took the position that several strategies potentially could increase the number of insured children and that their task was not to recommend one particular policy option. The committee members agreed throughout their deliberations that the ultimate goal of these strategies is to provide access to coordinated, efficient, effective, and cost-effective health care for all American children, including children who have preventable illnesses and injuries, chronic conditions, or other special health care needs.

Based on its review of scientific evidence and analysis of current trends, the committee drew the following conclusions.

1. **All children should have health insurance.**
2. **Public and private insurers should be encouraged to develop affordable products that address**

the specific needs of children, including children with chronic conditions and special health care needs.

3. Nonfinancial barriers to care should be reduced through the provision of assistance with child care and transportation, through the provision of culturally appropriate services, and through the use of information technology.

4. Outreach and enrollment procedures and coordination efforts should be designed so that all programs achieve the highest enrollment possible, particularly when states offer multiple programs with different eligibility requirements.

5. Information generated from children's health care and insurance programs should be designed to be useful in evaluating short-term trends and making program adjustments, and should be made widely available.

REFERENCE

IOM. 1998. *Systems of Accountability: Implementing Children's Health Insurance Programs.* Washington, D.C.: National Academy Press.

Part I

Does Insurance Equal Access to Care?

1

Introduction and Overview

Since 1987, the number of American children covered by employer-based health insurance coverage has decreased. By 1996, more than 11 million children lacked insurance (Weigers et al., 1998). According to a recent national survey sponsored by the Robert Wood Johnson Foundation, 1 of every 10 American children were unable to obtain health care in 1994, and lack of insurance was the primary reason (Berk et al., 1995). Data from a 1996 federal survey showed that 1 of every 4 Hispanic children, 1 of every 6 black children, and 1 of every 10 white children were uninsured (Employee Benefits Research Institute, 1997).

Most uninsured children live with parents who are low-income workers (EBRI, 1997). In general, their parents tend to work for employers that do not offer health insurance. These working parents earn too little to be able to afford to buy health insurance on their own, and they earn too much to be eligible for public health insurance such as Medicaid. Among employers who do offer some form of health insurance coverage for full-time employees, a larger share of the costs of dependent coverage is being shifted to employees (GAO, 1996; Weigers et al., 1998).

Traditionally, uninsured children have received "charity care" from hospital emergency rooms, outpatient departments in public and teaching hospitals, state and local health departments, community health centers, and individual practitioners, all of which are known as "safety net providers." The availability of safety net services varies from community to community. Local economic and social environments are different, as are the mix of providers, the concentration of responsibility for uninsured children, and the availability of financing for unpaid care (Baxter and Mechanic, 1997). One common element among safety net providers has been their reliance on funding from the Medicaid program, which is the largest single source of insurance coverage for American children.

In recent years, state Medicaid agencies have been evolving into large-scale buyers of managed health care coverage. With the rapid expansion of Medicaid into managed care in the 1990s, states increasingly are using private-sector bargaining strategies to negotiate reasonable rates, while protecting Medicaid enrollees (Rosenbaum et al., 1997). At the same time that public subsidies for free and low-cost care have been reduced, the number of uninsured Americans has been increasing, and so has the demand for uncompensated care (Center for Health Economics Research, 1993).

Together, these changes have challenged safety net providers to adapt their strategies to the competitive health care marketplace. Safety net providers are taking a variety of steps to continue serving uninsured and low-income Americans, but this is a period of major transition (Baxter and Mechanic, 1997; Fishman and Bentley, 1997; Lipson and Naierman, 1996).

About a year ago we made a decision to close down five church-based immunization clinics because of funding cuts. Consequently, we had people come to the health department for immunizations for their children. We have subsequently seen a sharp decline in the immunization rates because transportation is a major problem, and we are unable to provide that service at this point in time.

Ross Marine
Jackson County Health Department, Kansas City, MO
Public Workshop, June 2, 1997

In addition to market forces, recent national legislation also can be expected to have a significant impact on the delivery and financing of health care for low-income Americans, and children may be particularly affected. The Personal Responsibility and Work Opportunity Reconciliation Act of 1996 ("welfare reform"), which was required to be in effect in all states by July 1, 1998, eliminates the automatic connection between welfare and Medicaid eligibility. In combination with other changes in Medicaid, this could dramatically change the flow of funding for safety net providers over the coming years.

In August of 1997, the Balanced Budget Act of 1997 (BBA) authorized $20.3 billion for a new State Children's Health Insurance Program (SCHIP) and $3.6 billion for Medicaid improvements (see Box 1.1). The SCHIP program was designed to help states cover uninsured children with family incomes that are too high for Medicaid but too low to afford private coverage. As of October 1, 1997, the SCHIP program will provide federal matching funds to states for new children's health care initiatives based on private insurance coverage, Medicaid expansions, and combinations of approaches.

In New York, we have had a long process of moving an entire AFDC [Aid to Families with Dependent Children] population into managed care programs. We are already experiencing a great deal of anxiety at the community level as the community health centers and a number of the essential community providers see themselves getting caught in a squeeze in terms of dollars. They are looking at their survivability, and unfortunately, if these folks can't be viable in the new health care landscape, then we're going to see a deficit of providers in poor communities. We are going to see a real loss for the residents of those communities as there will be no one rushing in to fill the vacuum. We have to be careful that in a rush to allow the market to work its magic, that as a by-product we don't end up losing some of the best providers we have for medically needy populations.

Dennis Johnson
Children's Health Fund, New York City
Public Workshop, June 2, 1997

Medicaid managed care in combination with new SCHIP programs could help to bolster the safety net, or could begin to replace it. Unless states specifically require safety net providers to be included in

BOX 1.1
Highlights of the State Children's Health Insurance Program

The Balanced Budget Act of 1997 provides approximately $24 billion in funding over five years to help states develop children's health care initiatives. Most of this funding will support the new State Children's Health Insurance Program (SCHIP), which was established as Title XXI of the Social Security Act. This is the largest allocation of funds for children's health since the Medicaid program was enacted in 1965.

As of October 1, 1997, the SCHIP program entitles states to block grants to expand or initiate health insurance programs for low-income uninsured children, with higher federal matching payments than under Medicaid. States may choose to expand Medicaid, support existing state or private programs, design new programs, or use a combination of these approaches.

Each state's allocation of SCHIP funds is based on the number of uninsured children in the state who live in families with incomes below 200 percent of the federal poverty level (FPL). States may cover currently uninsured children in families with incomes up to 200 percent of FPL, and states which already have programs for families at that level may increase eligibility to 250 percent of FPL.

States must submit a program plan for approval by the Secretary of the Department of Health and Human Services no later than June 30, 1998 for participation in the first funding cycle. By April 1, 1998, the Department of Health and Human Services (DHHS) had approved plans for 8 states that will cover more than 1 million children, and another 15 states had submitted plans for review and approval by DHHS.

Under SCHIP, states must screen all applicants for Medicaid eligibility and must enroll any eligible children in the Medicaid program. The law gives participating states the option of "presumptive" Medicaid eligibility to facilitate enrollment. It restores Medicaid coverage for disabled children who would lose their eligibility because of changes in the 1996 welfare law. It also gives states the option of guaranteeing Medicaid coverage for children for 12 months regardless of changes in their financial circumstances.

SOURCES: *Title XXI Summary from The Balanced Budget Act of 1997, Children's Health Insurance Program* by the Health Care Financing Administration at http://www.hcfa.gov/init/kidssum.htm and *Expanding Health Insurance Coverage for Children Under Title XXI of the Social Security Act* by the Congressional Budget Office at http://www.cbo.gov/showdoc.cfm?index=353&sequence=0&from=5

Medicaid and SCHIP managed care contracts, these providers—with the most experience in serving low-income populations—may not be included in the delivery of care. Under those circumstances, the quality of care and the scope of services for uninsured children could be adversely affected. If, however, states actively support the inclusion of safety net providers in SCHIP and enhance their efforts to coordinate enrollment and services across different programs and sources of financing, a seamless system of children's coverage could begin to emerge.

PURPOSE OF THIS STUDY

In the summer of 1996, the Robert Wood Johnson Foundation asked the National Academy of Sciences to conduct a study of the relationship between health insurance and access to care for children. In response to this request, the Institute of Medicine (IOM) Division of Health Care Services and the Board on Children, Youth, and Families of the National Research Council and the IOM, formed an expert committee to do the following:

• examine the extent of health insurance coverage of children,
• analyze evidence on the relationship between health insurance coverage and children's access to health care,
• identify safety net programs (e.g., community health centers, children's hospitals, and public health departments) that affect the degree of access children have to health care;
• examine available evidence on trends in the magnitude or availability of safety net programs, and
• consider the effects of changes in those programs on children's access to health care.

The Committee on Children, Health Insurance, and Access to Care included 14 individuals with expertise in health care financing and delivery. Collectively, these individuals had expertise in private insurance, managed care, Medicaid, and other public programs; health care delivery, including primary and specialty care in pediatrics and adult populations; health care policy, including legislative policy, regulation, health law, and health economics; epidemiology; and health services research.

The committee met three times between March and June 1997 and convened a public workshop in June 1997. Appendix C presents the workshop's agenda and participants.

The committee met again in January 1998 to discuss the new SCHIP program. The committee's recommendations about the SCHIP program are presented in a separate report, *Systems of Accountability: Implementing Children's Health Insurance Programs* (IOM, 1998).

To increase the input from a variety of stakeholders, the committee formed a liaison panel with nearly 200 representatives of national associations, provider groups, children's advocacy organizations, health policy organizations, and state and federal government agencies (see Appendix D). Members of the liaison panel were invited to make presentations at the public workshop and to provide written testimony and other materials for the committee's consideration.

Given the budget agreement, the challenge now is how to find political consensus on solutions, principally involving federal and state governments. So the challenge has shifted from where it was earlier this year, which was whether or not to take action, to how to take action.

Kathleen Means
Health Care Leadership Council, Washington, DC
Public Workshop, June 2, 1997

THE POLICY CONTEXT

The timing of this study presented an unusual set of challenges. The committee's deliberations took place over several months when children's health insurance and access were being debated by the U.S. Congress, the states, and the American public (see Box 1.2). At the beginning of the study, there seemed to be widespread support for incremental steps to reduce the number of uninsured children, building on activities that were already under way in several states.

During the course of the study, both political parties and the Clinton Administration presented a variety of proposals, including Medicaid expansions, block grants, vouchers, refundable tax credits for families, a tax credit for all children, family Medical Savings Accounts, and a new Children's Health Trust Fund. It was unclear what, if any, national legislative approach would be taken until Congress passed the Balanced Budget Act of 1997 in August, with its provisions for a flexible new program for states to expand children's health insurance (SCHIP) (see Box 1.1).

BOX 1.2
Headlines in *The New York Times*:
Children's Health Care Coverage, 1996–1997

November 11, 1996	New Approach to Overhauling Health Insurance: Step by Step
January 15, 1997	Health Insurance for Children Is Latest Hot Idea as Both Democrats and GOP Prepare Proposals
February 7, 1997	President Moves to Protect Half of Uninsured Children
February 7, 1997	135,000 Children to Be Struck from Disability Benefit Rolls
March 12, 1997	President's Plan to Rein in Medicaid Costs Draws Bipartisan Fire
March 14, 1997	Hatch Joins Kennedy to Back a Health Program
March 17, 1997	Children's Health Insurance: Sorting Through the Options
April 8, 1997	Insuring Children Sensibly (editorial)
April 12, 1997	GOP Fights Bill to Offer a Health Plan for Children
May 21, 1997	Citing Lost Cigarette Revenue, GOP Fights Child Insurance
May 22, 1997	Clinton Helps Kill Proposal to Raise Tax on Cigarettes
May 22, 1997	Child Health Plan Defeated in Senate
June 9, 1997	GOP Lawmakers Want $16 Billion for Health Plan
June 17, 1997	Capitol in Discord Over Plan to Aid Uninsured Youths
June 18, 1997	Senate Panel Rebuffs Clinton on Child Health Plan
July 2, 1997	Health Care Bills Don't Meet Goals, Budget Aides Say
July 20, 1997	Item in Tax Bill Poses Threat to Job Benefits
July 24, 1997	GOP Leadership Agrees on a Plan to Insure Youths
July 29, 1997	White House and the GOP Announce Deal to Balance Budget and Trim Taxes: Passage Is Likely—Plan Includes Tax Credit for Children and Cuts on Capital Gains
July 30, 1997	$24 Billion Would Be Set Aside for Medical Care for Children
August 3, 1997	Bills on Spending Are Moving Easily Through Congress: Few Partisan Disputes
August 15, 1997	Disability Checks of 95,000 Children Are to Be Cut Off
August 17, 1997	Workers Getting Greater Freedom in Health Plans: Flexibility for a Price
August 31, 1997	Welfare Mothers Prepare for Jobs, and Wait
September 3, 1997	Hospitals Serving the Poor Struggle to Retain Patients: Health-Care Changes Help Private Centers Lure Away Recipients of Medicaid
September 13, 1997	Disabled Children Get a Needed Review (editorial)
December 29, 1997	Clinton Ordering Effort to Sign Up Medicaid Children: About 3 Million Eligible
March 30, 1998	Health Insurance is G.O.P. Initiative for Election Year. Drafting Tax-Break Bill. Plan to Use Tobacco Revenue to Aid Uncovered Workers and Small Businesses

This issue concerns not just children without adequate access to health care, but also parents who get up every morning and go to work, pay their bills, pay their taxes, and still can't provide health insurance for their children. That is an important piece of the political dynamics here. This issue speaks more broadly than the question of uninsured children. It speaks to what it is like to be a working person in America today. How can you take care of your family's needs?

Stan Dorn
Children's Defense Fund, Washington, DC
Public Workshop, June 2, 1997

In the United States the primary way that we encourage people to get health insurance is tax subsidies. The problem with this system is that the greatest encouragement goes to the people who need it the least. We are giving six times as much help to families in the top fifth of the income distribution as we give to families in the bottom fifth of the income distribution.

John Goodman
National Center for Policy Analysis, Dallas, TX
Public Workshop, June 2, 1997

The tax subsidy is open-ended. It encourages excessive consumption of health insurance, which in turn encourages excessive consumption of health care, which in turn raises costs, which makes it more difficult to expand coverage and cover more people. The budget question is not one of whether we have enough money being spent in total, but rather to what extent can we reallocate that money to buy what we really think is best.

Eugene Steuerle
Urban Institute, Washington, DC
Public Workshop, June 2, 1997

In response to the charge from the Robert Wood Johnson Foundation, the committee's intention was to conduct a thorough review of the existing scientific evidence on insurance and access and to present and summarize the best available information as clearly and objectively as possible. With the rapid rate of ongoing change in the health care delivery system, the committee supplemented its review of scientific evidence with an analysis of other published information on health care trends that are likely to affect the implementation of new children's insurance programs (see Box 1.3).

BOX 1.3
Data and Information Reviewed for This Report

Large national, federally supported databases, primarily the Current Population Survey (U.S. Department of Commerce), the National Health Interview Survey (Centers for Disease Control and Prevention, U.S. Department of Health and Human Services [DHHS]), and the National Medical Expenditure Survey (Agency for Health Care Policy and Research, DHHS).

Additional analyses of the Current Population Survey conducted by the Employee Benefits Research Institute especially for this study;

Published health services research findings from national databases; state, local, and private information sources (e.g., medical records); national surveys; and original data collection;

Publicly available descriptions of federal and state programs, health policy research, health services research, and public statements by government agencies, including the Agency for Health Care Policy and Research, DHHS; Bureau of Labor Statistics of the U.S. Department of Labor; the California State Senate Insurance Committee; Congressional Budget Office; the U.S. General Accounting Office; the Health Care Financing Administration of DHHS; the State of Florida Agency for Health Care Administration; and the Social Security Administration;

Published materials and public statements submitted to the committee by national organizations, including the American Academy of Pediatrics, American Association of Asian and Pacific Islander Community Health Organizations, American Association of Health Plans, American College of Preventive Medicine, American Association of Maternal and Child Health Programs, American Hospital Association, Children's Defense Fund, Children Now, Children's Health Fund, Employee Benefits Research Institute, Families USA, Hewitt Associates LLC, Health Insurance Association of America, National Academy of Social Insurance, National Association of Children's Hospitals and Related Institutions, National Association of City and County Health Officials, National Association of Community Health Centers, National Association of Insurance Commissioners, National Association of Public Hospitals, National Conference of State Legislatures, National Governors Association, and the Washington Business Group on Health;

Published reports sponsored by philanthropic organizations, including the Annie E. Casey Foundation, the Kaiser Commission on the Future of Medicaid, the David and Lucile Packard Foundation, and the Robert Wood Johnson Foundation; and

Policy analyses, reports, newsletters, and news analyses by private organizations including the Alliance for Health Reform, Alpha Center, American Enterprise Institute, Bureau of National Affairs, Center for Budget and Policy Priorities, Center for Health Policy Research of George Washington University, Center for Studying Health System Change, Healthcare Leadership Council, The Heritage Foundation, National Bureau for Economic Research, National Academy for State Health Policy, National Center for Policy Analysis, National Center for Youth Law, National Health Policy Forum, and the Urban Institute; and

Reports published by the Institute of Medicine, including *The Future of Public Health* (IOM, 1988), *Access to Health Care in America* (IOM, 1993a), *Emergency Medical Services for Children* (IOM, 1993b), *Employment and Health Benefits: A Connection at Risk* (IOM, 1993c), *Telemedicine: A Guide to Assessing Telecommunications in Health Care* (IOM, 1996), *Managing Managed Care: Quality Improvement in Behavioral Health* (IOM, 1997a), *Primary Care: America's Health in a New Era* (IOM, 1997b), *Improving Health in the Community: A Role for Performance Monitoring* (IOM, 1997c), *The Computer-Based Patient Record: An Essential Technology for Health Care* (revised edition) (IOM, 1997d), and reports by the National Research Council, including *Paying Attention to Children in a Changing Health Care System* (NRC, 1996), *Including Children and Pregnant Women in Health Care Reform* (NRC, 1992), and *Assessment of Performance Measures for Public Health, Substance Abuse, and Mental Health* (NRC, 1997).

There is a real difficulty in building a consensus for a particular approach. An analyst in one state basically told me "We need a break from Medicaid." It is really hard to figure out what vehicle to choose. There is support for a number of different approaches. It is a zero sum game in states. You almost always have to take something away from somebody who has got it in order to get something new, and that is very hard.

Shelly Gehshan
National Conference of State Legislatures, Washington, DC
Public Workshop, June 2, 1997

From the perspective of employers, health care coverage was never considered an entitlement. It was always a way of paying additional compensation, and employers have had to address equity issues between employees. Say you have two employees who are performing the same job and one is single and one has a family. The one with the family would be earning more in compensation because of their family, not because they are taking on any additional responsibilities and functions. With spiraling health care costs, many employers have asked employees to contribute more towards their share of health coverage, especially toward family coverage, to address the equity issue.

Kim Monk
Washington Business Group on Health, Washington, DC
Public Workshop, June 2, 1997

It's very important to worry about safety net providers because they are doing very critical work in our communities. But I would hope that we come to some lessons about the value of insuring individuals and creating financial resources which follow the individual, as opposed to trying to set those resources into the institutions. That, it seems to me, is a policy that has failed.

Kay Johnson
George Washington University, Washington, DC
Public Workshop, June 2, 1997

The committee's goal for this report, therefore, was to draw a general set of conclusions about ways to help improve children's access to care that would apply to a variety of public and private insurance programs. The committee hopes this report will help to improve the evidence base for children's health insurance efforts and for efforts to improve the quality of children's health care. The committee's specific concerns about the need for data to evaluate the SCHIP program and its recommendations for designing a system of accountability for SCHIP are presented separately (IOM, 1998).

CONCLUSIONS

From the beginning of their deliberations, the committee members took the position that several strategies potentially could increase the number of insured children and that their task was not to recommend one particular policy option. The committee members agreed throughout their deliberations that the ultimate goal of these strategies is to provide access to coordinated, efficient, and effective health care for all American children, including children who have preventable illnesses and injuries, chronic conditions, or other special health care needs.

Based on a review of scientific evidence and analysis of current trends, the committee drew the following conclusions.

1. All children should have health insurance.

Children's access to health care depends on several financial and nonfinancial factors. Financial factors include insurance status (insured or uninsured); the nature and extent of insurance coverage, including cost-sharing requirements such as copayments and deductibles; family income; and the costs of care. Among many nonfinancial factors, the availability and proximity of providers; types of coverage accepted by providers; logistical difficulties in scheduling and transportation; racial, ethnic, and cultural backgrounds of providers and families; and parental health beliefs have been shown to influence access to care.

When compared with insured children, uninsured children are more likely to be sick as newborns, less likely to be immunized at appropriate ages, less likely to receive medical treatment when they are injured, and less likely to receive treatment for illnesses such as acute or recurrent earaches and asthma. Having analyzed the available evidence on financial and nonfinancial barriers to care, the committee concludes that children's health insurance status is the single most important influence in determining whether health care is accessible to children when they need it.

2. Public and private insurers should be encouraged to develop affordable products that address the specific needs of children, including children with chronic conditions and special health care needs.

As a matter of principle, the committee believes that all children should have appropriate access to coordinated, efficient, child-appropriate, and effective care, including generally accepted preventive services; acute care for short-term illnesses and injuries; ongoing care for children with chronic medical conditions; rehabilitative care, including allied health services, for children with disabilities; and care for children with special needs, such as speech disorders.

The committee recognizes that financial resources are not unlimited and that accountable purchasers and policymakers must set priorities in order to make reasoned and equitable decisions about spending. However, costs of treatment and coverage for children vary according to their health status and can be difficult to determine from the information available in the public domain.

There are many areas of disagreement and uncertainty about the specific services to which children should have access. Providers, parents, and insurers often have different attitudes and positions about which services are "essential" and what expenditures and sources of payment are reasonable. The limited scientific evidence and professional consensus do not clearly indicate which specific diagnostic tests, treatments, procedures, drugs, specialists, and other services should be available to children, any more than is the case for adults.

There is tremendous variability in the structure and scope of health care benefits for children according to the source and the type of insurance coverage. In the current health care system, employers, states, parents, and others who purchase coverage on behalf of children bear the responsibility for ensuring that their purchasing decisions reflect the specific needs of children as much as possible within the existing resources. In the committee's view, purchasers should take the initiative to request new child-appropriate products.

3. Nonfinancial barriers to care should be reduced through the provision of assistance with child care and transportation, through the provision of culturally appropriate services, and through the use of information technology.

Health insurance alone does not guarantee utilization of appropriate care. Studies have shown that logistical difficulties for parents, such as transportation and child care, differences in the racial, ethnic and cultural backgrounds of providers and parents, and parental health beliefs can affect children's access to care. For children who live in medically underserved urban and rural areas, the availability and proximity of providers can present barriers to access. Even with insurance, it can be difficult to obtain health care.

The committee believes that information technology holds extraordinary promise to improve access for children in underserved areas, as well as to improve clinical quality and efficiency of care and to increase the availability of clinical information for research. Although it has not been systematically studied, the application of information technology continues to increase in patient care, professional education, patient education, research, and administration.

Based on the available scientific evidence and current trends in the delivery of care, the committee believes that programmatic design and delivery system issues have a vital impact on access for children. In sum, three particular areas need to be addressed: logistical barriers, cultural barriers, and advances in the use of information technology.

4. Outreach and enrollment procedures and coordination efforts should be designed so that all programs achieve the highest enrollment possible, particularly when states offer multiple programs with different eligibility requirements.

Years of experience with Medicaid indicate that there are many reasons why children who are eligible for the program may not be enrolled. For example, parents or other caretakers may not be aware of the program, may not know they or their dependents are eligible, or may not want to accept public aid. Other parents have experienced difficulties in trying to enroll in the program, including denials of applications for procedural errors or incomplete information, or because of cultural factors such as the need for translation.

States designing and implementing new SCHIP programs have learned from these experiences and are improving their procedures. With the new children's health insurance programs and other initiatives, more efforts are being made to help parents learn about the different programs and make enrollment easier, including having common application forms and streamlining the application and enrollment process.

States also will need to improve their efforts to coordinate administration and data collection among Medicaid, SCHIP, Title V maternal and child health agencies, and other state and private programs involving children and families, especially low-income working families. More specifically, states should coordinate health insurance efforts with initiatives in maternal and child health, mental health and substance abuse treatment and prevention, education, disabilities, and other areas.

5. Information generated from children's health care and insurance programs should be designed to be useful in evaluating short-term trends and making program adjustments, and should be made widely available.

For cost-conscious purchasers and public policymakers, accountability rests on a foundation of good information. There are technical problems, gaps, and inconsistencies in analyzing health insurance and health status information from Medicaid, national surveys, and other sources. These include differences in capacity to report current information; differences in definitions and data collection methods; lack of statistical breakdowns for children, or breakdowns at different ages; lag time in collecting and reporting information; and many other technical challenges. These technical problems make it difficult to measure performance, to protect children as health care consumers, and to improve the quality of care.

In the area of clinical information, relatively few performance measures have been developed for children, and their scope and quality need to be improved. Additional research is needed to develop new measures of child health status and outcomes that can be used to assess performance of health plans in meeting children's health needs, especially for children with special health care needs.

With the design and implementation of new SCHIP programs, many new opportunities will be available to study the impact of changing mechanisms for financing and providing insurance. For example, changes in sources of care (types of providers and settings) after enrollment in SCHIP would be a useful measure of the program's impact. Comparisons of utilization rates for preventive care, basic services, and visits to specialists would be extremely useful to compare the program's impact for different subgroups, such as racial and ethnic minorities, or children with disabilities.

Commercial managed care plans measure access to care in terms of utilization and penetration rates, such as the number of visits per 1,000 enrollees; length of time to follow-up appointments; provider to enrollee ratios; and other information that is readily available from most managed care information systems. For the new SCHIP programs and Medicaid managed care, additional access measures may need to be developed to reflect the array of child-specific services such as subsidized child care or transportation assistance, or expanded services such as telephone advice nurses, translators, or health education.

Monitoring and evaluation strategies require commitments of time and resources on the part of government, private foundations, health plans, providers, and others to provide timely and useful information for a variety of audiences and purposes. The committee believes that future data and information systems can be designed and implemented in ways that are efficient and easy to use and in ways that provide timely feedback for midcourse corrections as well as for longer-term applications. Incentives should be developed to encourage the use of data sources that have rapid turnaround times, are inexpensive, and that can be used to evaluate short-term trends and make program adjustments.

ORGANIZATION OF THIS REPORT

The first three chapters of this report address the contextual issues that describe the relationship between insurance status and access to care. Chapter 1, Introduction and Overview, has described the rationale for the study, the committee's approach to the study, and its conclusions. Chapter 2, Health Insurance and Children in America, reviews evidence related to the patterns of health insurance coverage for children. including trends in employer-based coverage and Medicaid enrollment. Chapter 3, Health Insurance and Access to Care, reviews the evidence about the effects of health insurance status on the care that children receive and describes different ways of defining the scope of health care services that should be accessible to children.

The second section of the report describes a variety of means for financing health care for children. Chapter 4, Safety Net Providers, describes the current safety net providers and the ways in which they are meeting the demands for expansion of health insurance coverage for children during a period of rapid change in the health care delivery system. Chapter 5, Medicaid, describes the Medicaid program in its current form as a major source of public financing for health care and how its role is changing because of market forces, welfare reform, children's health insurance legislation, and other factors. Chapter 6, State and Private Insurance Initiatives, describes a variety of programs that have been implemented to provide children's health insurance coverage. Some of these programs are likely to be expanded by states under the terms of the new legislation on children's health insurance.

Chapter 7, Children's Health Care Needs, addresses the need for health care among healthy children and among those with chronic medical conditions and special health care needs. Based on the distribution of acute and chronic medical conditions among children, the chapter discusses the importance of designing children's insurance to better address children's needs.

Two Appendixes provide a supplement to the committee's analysis of the evidence presented throughout the report. Appendix A, "A Review of Tax-Based Approaches to Insurance Reform," was written by Robert B. Helms at the request of the other committee members. It describes some of the main federal tax policy options which have been proposed but have not yet been widely implemented, including tax credits and vouchers. Appendix B, "Information for Accountability," describes the technical aspects of the existing data and information systems that are used to monitor insurance, access, utilization, and health status over time.

Appendix C includes the agenda and list of participants who attended the committee's public workshop in Washington, D.C. on June 2, 1997. Appendix D lists the members of the liaison panel, including those who submitted written statements for the committee's consideration, and Appendix E includes short biographies for the committee and IOM staff.

REFERENCES

Baxter RJ, Mechanic RE. 1997. The Status of Local Health Care Safety Nets. *Health Affairs* 16(4):7–23.

Berk ML, Schur C, Cantor JC. 1995. Ability to Obtain Health Care: Recent Estimates from the Robert Wood Johnson Foundation National Access to Care Survey. *Health Affairs* 14(3):139–146.

Center for Health Economics Research. 1993. *Access to Health Care: Key Indicators for Policy*. Princeton, NJ: Robert Wood Johnson Foundation.

Employee Benefits Research Institute. 1997. Analysis of data provided for this study, based on estimates from the March 1996 Current Population Survey, Bureau of the Census, U.S. Department of Commerce.

Fishman LE, Bentley JD. 1997. The Evolution of Support for Safety-Net Hospitals. *Health Affairs* 16(4):30–47.

GAO (U.S. General Accounting Office). 1996. *Health Insurance for Children: Private Coverage Continues to Deteriorate*. GAO/HEHS-96-129, June 17, 1996. Washington, D.C.

IOM (Institute of Medicine). 1988. *The Future of Public Health*. Washington, D.C.: National Academy Press.

IOM. 1993a. *Access to Health Care in America*. Washington, D.C.: National Academy Press.

IOM. 1993b. *Emergency Medical Services for Children*. Washington, D.C.: National Academy Press.

IOM. 1993c. *Employment and Health Benefits: A Connection at Risk*. Washington, D.C.: National Academy Press.

IOM. 1996. *Telemedicine: A Guide to Assessing Telecommunications in Health Care*. Washington, D.C.: National Academy Press.

IOM. 1997a. *Managing Managed Care: Quality Improvement in Behavioral Health*. Washington, D.C.: National Academy Press.

IOM. 1997b. *Primary Care: America's Health in a New Era*. Washington, D.C.: National Academy Press.

IOM. 1997c. *Improving Health in the Community: A Role for Performance Monitoring*. Washington, D.C.: National Academy Press.

IOM. 1997d. *The Computer-Based Patient Record: An Essential Technology for Health Care*. Rev. ed. Washington, D.C.: National Academy Press.

IOM. 1998. *Systems of Accountability: Implementing Children's Health Insurance Programs*. Washington, D.C.: National Academy Press.

Lipson DJ, Naierman N. 1996. Effects of Health System Changes on Safety Net Providers. *Health Affairs* 15(2):33–48.

NRC (National Research Council). 1992. *Including Children and Pregnant Women in Health Care Reform*. Washington, D.C.: National Academy Press.

NRC. 1996. *Paying Attention to Children in a Changing Health Care System*. Washington, D.C.: National Academy Press.

NRC. 1997. *Assessment of Performance Measures for Public Health, Substance Abuse, and Mental Health*. Washington, D.C.: National Academy Press.

Rosenbaum S, Shin P, Smith BM, Wehr E, Borzi, PC, Zakheim MH, Shaw, K, Silver K, Johnson KA. 1997. *Negotiating the New Health System: A Nationwide Study of Medicaid Managed Care Contracts*. Washington, D.C.: George Washington University Center for Health Policy Research.

Weigers ME, Weinick RM, Cohen JW. 1998. *Children's Health 1996. MEPS Chartbook No. 1*. Rockville, MD: Agency for Health Care Policy and Research, AHCPR Pub. No. 98–0008.

2

Health Insurance and Children in America

This chapter compares trends in health insurance coverage across three major coverage groups of children in the United States: those with employer-based coverage (private insurance), those enrolled in the Medicaid program (public insurance), and those who have no insurance (uninsured). Trends in insurance coverage for adults are also included for purposes of comparison. The chapter reviews evidence of patterns in children's insurance coverage by age, race, ethnicity, parental income, and parental employment. The chapter also reports evidence on the duration of uninsurance and describes regional variations in the rates of uninsurance.

For ease in identifying trends that are described in the text, the figures in this chapter present data for individuals with the main sources of coverage—employer-based (private) and Medicaid (public) coverage—and for uninsured individuals. The tables in this chapter present a complete array of all sources of health insurance coverage and also give exact percentages.

BACKGROUND

In the United States, the private sector provides health insurance for the majority of children and adults, primarily through employer-sponsored coverage (see Table 2.1 and Table 2.2). This is in contrast to other developed countries (e.g., Canada, United Kingdom, France, and Japan), which rely primarily on public-sector financing for health insurance (IOM, 1993; Schieber and Poullier, 1989).

In the United States, public-sector financing for children's health insurance is primarily through Medicaid, a program financed by the federal and state governments and administered by the states. In 1995, approximately one in four children (23 percent) were enrolled in Medicaid (see Table 2.1). Other sources of public insurance include military health care and Medicare; together, however, these other sources provide coverage for fewer than 5 percent of insured children.

As of 1994, approximately 14 percent of American children, or about 10 million children, did not have any insurance coverage (see Table 2.1 and Table 2.3). By 1996, this figure had grown to more than 11 million children (Weigers et al., 1998). As later sections of this chapter indicate, the majority of these uninsured children live in working families. These working parents do not have coverage through their employers, earn too little to be able to afford to buy health insurance on their own, and earn too much to be eligible for public health insurance such as Medicaid.

For uninsured children, access to health care is often unaffordable or otherwise out of reach. Unable

INSURANCE COVERAGE TRENDS (PERCENTAGES) FOR CHILDREN (TABLE 2.1) AND ADULTS (TABLE 2.2)

TABLE 2.1 Trends in Health Insurance Coverage Among Children, Ages 0-17, United States, 1987-1995 (percent)

Children's Health Insurance Source	Percent								
	1987	1988	1989	1990	1991	1992	1993	1994	1995
Total private	**73.2**	**73.0**	**73.1**	**70.6**	**69.2**	**68.7**	**67.4**	**65.6**	**66.1**
Employer-based	66.7	66.5	65.8	64.0	62.7	62.0	59.5	58.1	58.6
Self-pay	6.5	6.5	7.3	6.6	6.5	6.7	7.9	7.5	7.5
Total public	**19.3**	**19.5**	**19.5**	**22.2**	**24.2**	**25.2**	**26.8**	**26.3**	**26.4**
Medicaid	15.5	15.9	16.0	18.9	20.8	22.0	23.9	22.9	23.2
Military health care[a]	4.0	3.8	3.6	3.6	3.6	3.5	3.3	3.8	3.2
Medicare	0.2	0.2	0.1	0.1	0.1	0.1	0.1	0.3	0.4
Uninsured	**13.1**	**13.3**	**13.6**	**13.2**	**12.9**	**12.7**	**13.7**	**14.2**	**13.8**
Total	**105.6**	**105.8**	**106.2**	**106.0**	**106.3**	**106.6**	**107.9**	**106.1**	**106.3**

NOTES: Columns do not add to 100 percent because individuals may receive coverage from more than one source during 1 year.

[a]Military health care also includes the Civilian Health and Medical Program of the Uniformed Services and health care through the U.S. Department of Veterans Affairs.

SOURCE: EBRI, 1997. Estimates are based on data from the March 1988-1996 Current Population Survey, Bureau of the Census, U.S. Department of Commerce.

TABLE 2.2 Trends in Health Insurance Coverage among Adults, Ages 18-64, United States, 1987-1995 (percent)

Adults' Health Insurance Source	Percent								
	1987	1988	1989	1990	1991	1992	1993	1994	1995
Total private	**77.1**	**76.2**	**76.2**	**74.8**	**73.8**	**72.3**	**72.4**	**73.1**	**72.7**
Employer-based	70.4	70.1	69.8	68.3	67.8	65.9	65.4	66.1	66.1
Self-pay	6.7	6.2	6.3	6.4	5.9	6.4	7.0	7.0	6.6
Total public	**10.7**	**10.6**	**10.4**	**11.1**	**11.7**	**11.9**	**12.3**	**12.8**	**12.2**
Medicaid	5.6	5.6	5.7	6.4	7.0	7.3	7.8	7.9	7.8
Military health care[a]	4.6	4.4	4.1	4.2	4.0	3.8	3.8	4.3	3.7
Medicare	2.1	2.0	2.1	2.2	2.3	2.4	2.3	1.8	2.0
Uninsured	**15.6**	**16.4**	**16.6**	**17.4**	**17.8**	**18.9**	**18.8**	**18.5**	**19.0**
Total	**103.4**	**103.2**	**103.2**	**103.3**	**103.3**	**103.1**	**103.5**	**104.4**	**103.9**

Table 2.2 Trends in Health Insurance Coverage among Adults, Ages 18-64, United States, 1987-1995

NOTES: Columns do not add to 100 percent because individuals may receive coverage from more than one source during 1 year.

[a]Military health care also includes the Civilian Health and Medical Program of the Uniformed Services and health care through the U.S. Department of Veterans Affairs.

SOURCE: EBRI (1997). Estimates are based on data from the March 1987-1996 Current Population Survey, Bureau of the Census, U.S. Department of Commerce.

to pay for needed care, their parents may decide to delay treatment and hope that a medical problem will resolve on its own. Health problems that are minor in their early stages can escalate to serious and costly medical emergencies, and delays in access to health care can increase the burden of suffering from disease. This is especially true for children with special needs and chronic diseases.

> Things happen. Earaches happen. Toothaches happen. Not being in a position to be able to save up for that rainy day of emergency room visits or doctor visits, I have spent more than a few minutes wondering what would I do if something happened. It's a lot like driving a car with no brakes. You know there is a stop light ahead. You just pray for green, because you don't know what you'll do if you have to stop.
>
> *Maureen Ceidro*
> *Parent and Former Participant, Caring Program of Western Pennsylvania*
> *Public Workshop, June 2, 1997*

PROFILE OF HEALTH INSURANCE COVERAGE

Who Is Insured and Who Isn't

The U.S. health care system is often described as a patchwork of funding streams, often resulting in fragmentation of the delivery of care. Depending on the methods used to collect and analyze information from these funding streams, estimates of insurance coverage vary.

For example, estimates of Medicaid coverage from the Health Care Financing Administration differ substantially from those produced by the Bureau of the Census and the Agency for Health Care Policy and Research. However, because the Current Population Survey (CPS) from the Bureau of the Census is most commonly used by governmental and nongovernmental agencies in health insurance analyses, the committee relied principally on CPS data for the estimates of insurance coverage presented in this chapter.

CPS data show that the major sources of coverage for health care for the nation's 71 million children in 1995 included the following:

- 41.7 million had employer-based coverage through their parents,
- 16.5 million were enrolled in Medicaid,
- 300,000 were Medicare beneficiaries,
- 2.3 million had military health care (primarily Civilian Health and Medical Program of the Uniformed Services, or CHAMPUS), and
- 9.8 million had no coverage.

Table 2.3 indicates the array of sources of health insurance coverage for children, and for purposes of comparison Table 2.4 indicates the same array for adults.

Trends in Coverage for Children

Figure 2.1 shows the trends in coverage for children from 1987 to 1995 as a percentage of all children (refer to Table 2.1 for the exact percentages). Employer-based coverage for children decreased 8 percent between 1987 and 1995 (see Figure 2.1). The decrease in employer-based coverage for children was

INSURANCE COVERAGE TRENDS (MILLIONS) FOR CHILDREN (TABLE 2.3) AND FOR ADULTS (TABLE 2.4)

TABLE 2.3 Trends in Health Insurance Coverage by Actual Numbers Among Children, Ages 0-17 United States, 1987-1995

	Number (in millions)								
Health Insurance Source	1987	1988	1989	1990	1991	1992	1993	1994	1995
Total private	**47.3**	**47.5**	**48.1**	**46.9**	**46.6**	**47.2**	**47.0**	**46.3**	**47.0**
Employer-based	43.1	43.2	43.3	42.5	42.2	42.6	41.5	41.0	41.7
Self-pay	4.2	4.2	4.8	4.4	4.3	4.6	5.5	5.3	5.4
Total public	**12.4**	**12.6**	**12.8**	**14.8**	**16.3**	**17.3**	**18.7**	**18.6**	**18.8**
Medicaid	10.0	10.3	10.5	12.5	14.0	15.1	16.7	16.1	16.5
Military health care[a]	2.6	2.5	2.4	2.4	2.4	2.4	2.3	2.7	2.3
Medicare[b]	0.1	0.1	0.0	0.1	0.1	0.1	0.0	0.2	0.3
Uninsured	**8.5**	**8.7**	**8.9**	**8.8**	**8.7**	**8.7**	**9.6**	**10.0**	**9.8**
Total, children 0-17	**64.6**	**65.0**	**65.8**	**66.4**	**67.4**	**68.7**	**69.8**	**70.5**	**71.1**

NOTE: Columns may not add to totals because individuals may receive coverage from more than one source during 1 year.
[a]Military Health Care includes the Civilian Health and Medical Program for the Uniformed Services and health care through the U.S. Department of Veterans Affairs.
[b]For Medicare, numbers for some years round to less than 0.1 million, and are indicated by "0.0."
SOURCE: EBRI (1997) Estimates are based on data from the March 1988-1996 Current Population Survey, Bureau of the Census, U.S. Department of Commerce.

TABLE 2.4 Trends in Health Insurance Coverage Among Adults, Ages 18-64, United States, 1987-1995 (Millions)

	Number (in millions)								
Health Insurance Source	1987	1988	1989	1990	1991	1992	1993	1994	1995
Total private	**115.6**	**115.5**	**116.3**	**115.3**	**114.8**	**113.4**	**114.6**	**116.5**	**116.9**
Employer-based	105.5	106.2	106.6	105.3	105.5	103.4	103.4	105.3	106.2
Self-pay	10.1	9.3	9.7	9.9	9.3	10.0	11.1	11.2	10.6
Total public	**16.1**	**16.1**	**15.9**	**17.1**	**18.1**	**18.7**	**19.4**	**20.4**	**19.6**
Medicaid	8.4	8.6	8.7	9.9	10.8	11.4	12.3	12.6	12.5
Military health care[a]	6.9	6.6	6.3	6.4	6.2	6.0	6.0	6.9	5.9
Medicare[b]	3.1	3.1	3.2	3.4	3.5	3.8	3.7	2.9	3.2
Uninsured	**23.3**	**24.9**	**25.3**	**26.8**	**27.7**	**29.6**	**29.8**	**29.4**	**30.5**
Total, adults 18-64	**149.9**	**151.5**	**152.7**	**154.2**	**155.5**	**156.8**	**158.3**	**159.4**	**160.7**

NOTE: Columns may not add to totals because individuals may receive coverage from more than one source source during 1 year.
[a]Military Health Care includes the Civilian Health and Medical Program for the Uniformed Services and health care through the U.S. Department of Veterans Affairs.
[b]For Medicare, numbers for some years round to less than 0.1 million, and are indicated by "0.0."
SOURCE: EBRI, 1997 Estimates are based on data from the March 1988-1996 Current Population Survey, Bureau of the Census, U.S. Department of Commerce.

offset by an increase of almost 8 percent in Medicaid coverage between 1989 and 1993 (see Table 2.1 and especially Figure 2.1).

There are a variety of interpretations and substantial disagreement, however, about the relationship between the decrease in employer-based coverage and the increase in Medicaid coverage. At the heart of the issue is the concern that employers and employees might drop private health insurance to take advantage of increasing Medicaid eligibility thresholds to higher levels of income. Others maintain that shifting employment patterns, including the large scale shift from manufacturing to service sector jobs, account for the decline in employer coverage. Thus, the issue of replacement or substitution of coverage, or "crowding out," is controversial. This issue is discussed later in this chapter.

Trends in Coverage for Adults

Employer-based coverage decreased for adults as well as for children over the period from 1987 to 1995. However, the rate of decrease was faster for children, particularly in the 1990s (see Tables 2.1 and 2.2 and Figures 2.2 and 2.3).

During the same period that private coverage for adults was decreasing, the percentage of uninsured adults was increasing (Figure 2.3) and the percentage of adults with Medicaid was about the same. This suggests that adults who lose employer-based coverage are more likely to become uninsured than to enroll in Medicaid (Figure 2.3).

DEMOGRAPHICS OF COVERAGE FOR CHILDREN

Age

As indicated in Figures 2.4 and 2.5, the age distributions for children with employer-based coverage and uninsured children are similar. However, among children with Medicaid coverage, a disproportionate number (approximately 80 percent) are in the younger age groups (43.6 percent ages 0 to 5, 36.8 percent ages 6–12). This is true, in part, because families with young children are more likely to be poor and eligible for Medicaid compared with families with older children.

In addition, the Medicaid expansions enacted in the late 1980s are being phased in by age, with younger children gaining coverage before older children. Some policy analysts and health services researchers interpret the larger number of Medicaid-insured younger children as evidence that the Medicaid expansions have effectively reached the intended age group.

Race and Ethnicity

As indicated in Figures 2.6 and 2.7, the patterns of children's health insurance coverage among children by race and ethnicity are not uniform. In general, children of color are disproportionately more likely to be uninsured. These figures present national aggregated data; state and regional differences in distribution may be significantly different.

Most children with employer-based coverage (76 percent) are white; and most white children (69 percent) have employer-based coverage.

Among black children, fewer than 40 percent have employer-based coverage, close to half (45 percent) have Medicaid coverage, and about one in six (15 percent) have no insurance.

More than one in four Hispanic children (27 percent) are uninsured, whereas 35 percent have private insurance and about 37 percent have Medicaid coverage.

Among Native Americans, about one third (33 percent) have employer-based coverage, almost half (45 percent) have Medicaid, and approximately 11 percent are eligible to use the Indian Health Service.

On a national basis, Asian-American children make up approximately 4 percent of the total in each

EMPLOYER-BASED COVERAGE HAS BEEN DECLINING AMONG CHILDREN (FIGURE 2.1) AND AMONG ADULTS (FIGURE 2.2)

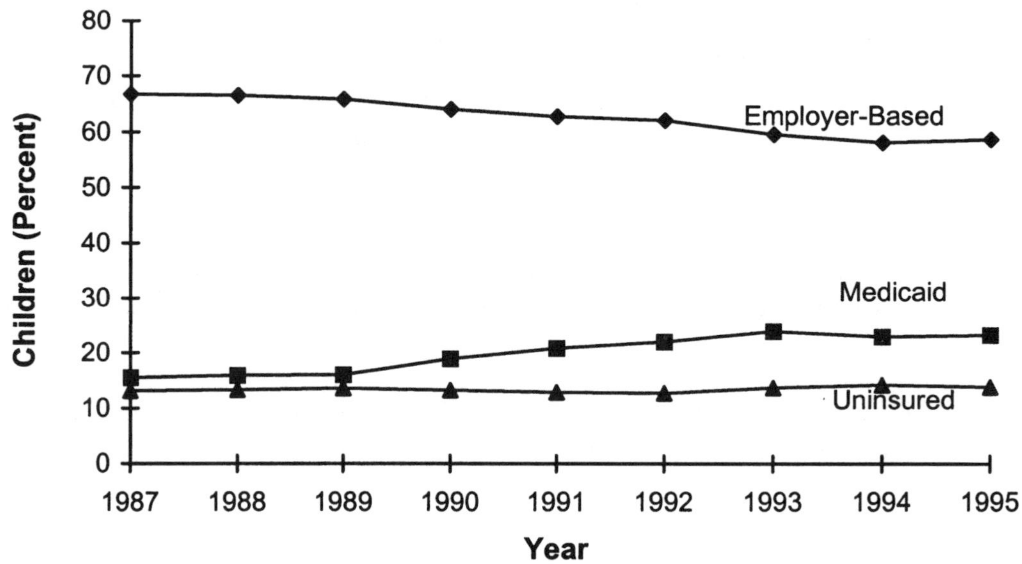

FIGURE 2.1 Trends in health insurance coverage among children, ages 0-17, United States, 1987-1995. SOURCE: EBRI (1997) Estimates are based on data from the March 1988-1996 Current Population Survey, Bureau of the Census, U.S. Department of Commerce.

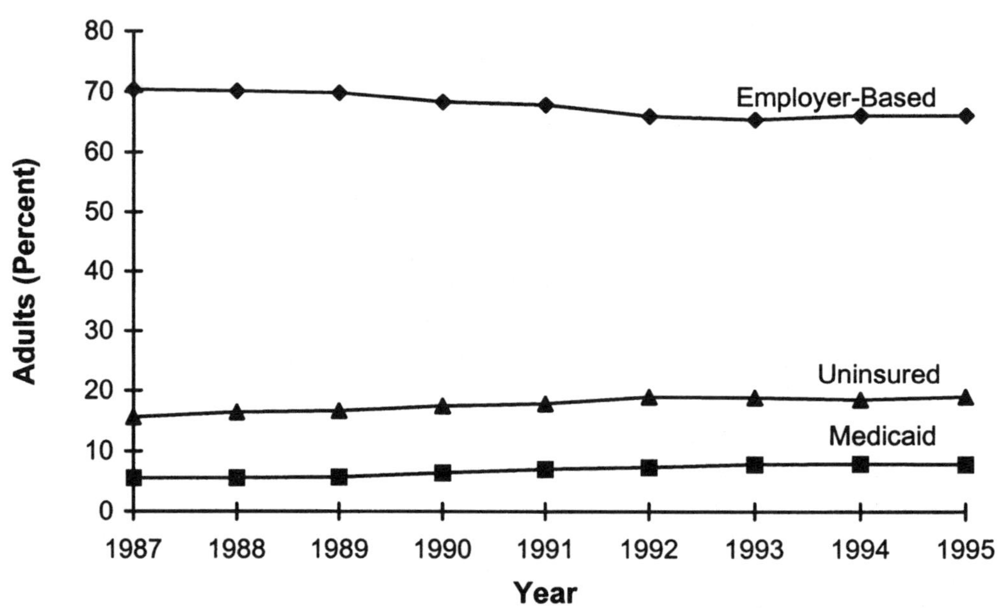

FIGURE 2.2 Trends in health insurance coverage among adults, ages 18-64, United States, 1987-1995. SOURCE: EBRI (1997) Estimates are based on data from the March 1988-1996 Current Population Survey, Bureau of the Census, U.S. Department of Commerce.

CHILDREN'S MEDICAID COVERAGE HAS INCREASED SINCE 1987

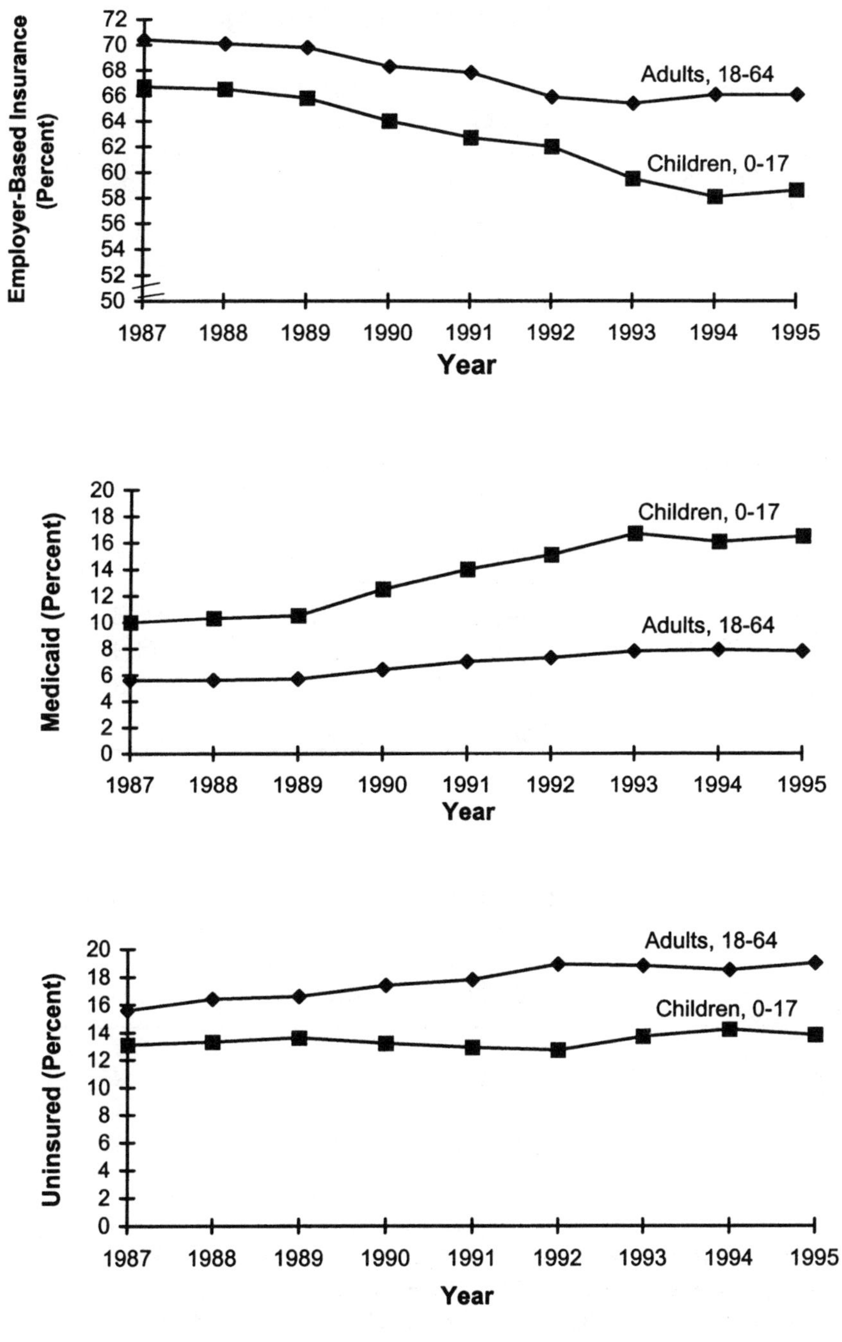

FIGURE 2.3 Comparison of trends in health insurance coverage for adults, ages 18-64, and children, ages 0-17, United States, 1987-1995. SOURCE: EBRI (1997) Estimates are based on data from the March 1988-1996 Current Population Survey, Bureau of the Census, U.S. Department of Commerce.

MEDICAID COVERS A HIGHER PROPORTION OF YOUNGER CHILDREN

Employer-Based Coverage

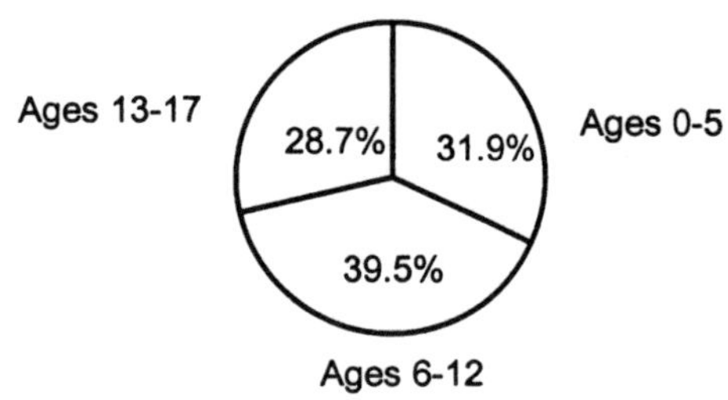

Employer-Based Coverage

Age Group	Number (in millions)	Percent
Ages 0-5	13.7	31.9
Ages 6-12	17.0	39.5
Ages 13-17	12.3	28.7
Total	43.0	100.0

Medicaid Coverage

Medicaid Coverage

Age Group	Number (in millions)	Percent
Ages 0-5	7.2	43.6
Ages 6-12	6.1	36.8
Ages 13-17	3.2	19.6
Total	16.5	100.0

Uninsured

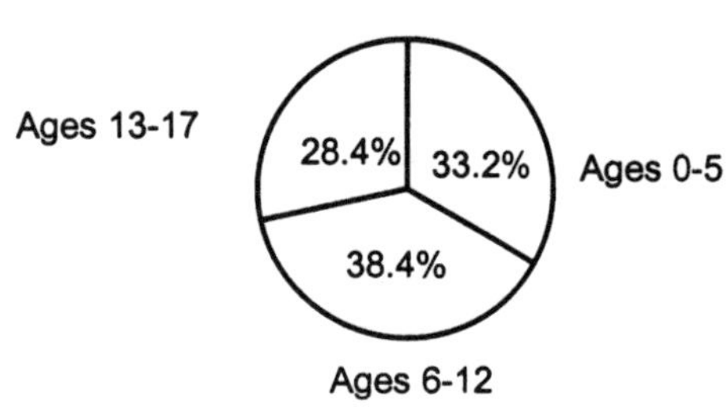

Uninsured

Age Group	Number (in millions)	Percent
Ages 0-5	3.2	33.2
Ages 6-12	3.8	38.4
Ages 13-17	2.8	28.4
Total	9.8	100.0

FIGURE 2.4 Patterns of children's health insurance coverage by age, for employer-based insurance, Medicaid, and children without coverage, United States, 1995. SOURCE: EBRI, 1997, special tabulations. Estimates are based on data from the 1996 Current Population Survey, Bureau of the Census, U.S. Department of Commerce.

SOURCES OF CHILDREN'S HEALTH INSURANCE COVERAGE VARY WITHIN AGE GROUPS

Ages 0-5

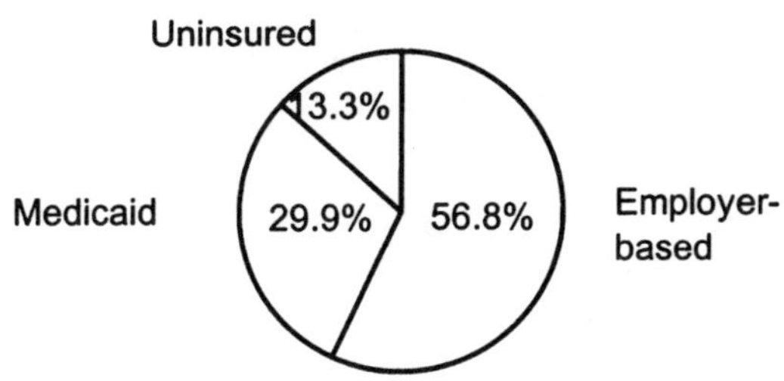

Ages 0-5

Insurance Status	Number (in millions)	Percent
Employer-based	13.7	56.8
Medicaid	7.2	29.9
Uninsured	3.2	13.3
Total	24.1	100.0

Ages 6-12

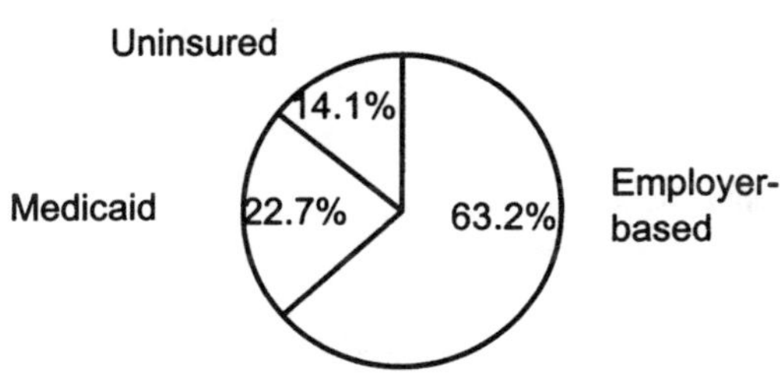

Ages 6-12

Insurance Status	Number (in millions)	Percent
Employer-based	17.0	63.2
Medicaid	6.1	22.7
Uninsured	3.8	14.1
Total	26.9	100.0

Ages 13-17

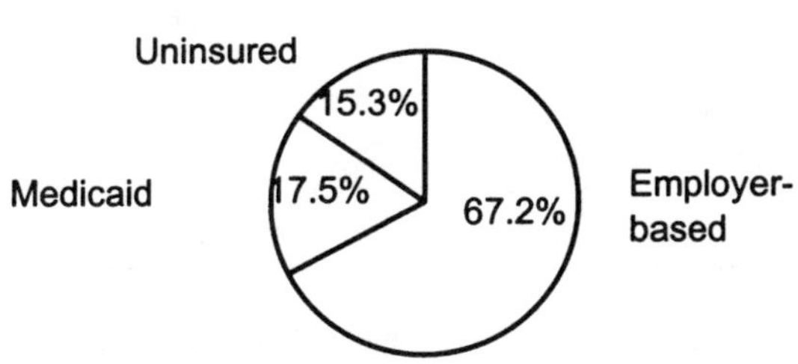

Ages 13-17

Insurance Status	Number (in millions)	Percent
Employer-based	12.3	67.2
Medicaid	3.2	17.5
Uninsured	2.8	15.3
Total	18.3	100.0

FIGURE 2.5 Children's health insurance coverage within age groups, for employer-based insurance, Medicaid, and uninsured children, United States, 1995. SOURCE: EBRI (1997). Estimates are based on data from the 1996 Current Population Survey, Bureau of the Census, U.S. Department of Commerce.

CHILDREN OF COLOR ARE MORE LIKELY TO BE ON MEDICAID OR UNINSURED

Children with Employer-Based Coverage

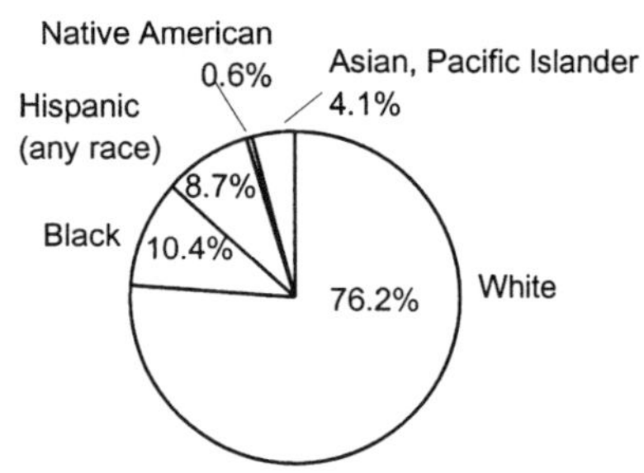

Employer-Based Coverage

Race/Ethnicity	Number (in millions)	Percent
White	31.8	76.2
Black	4.3	10.4
Hispanic (any race)	3.6	8.7
Native American, Eskimo, Aleut	0.3	0.6
Asian, Pacific Islander	1.7	4.1
Total	41.7	100.0

Children with Medicaid Coverage

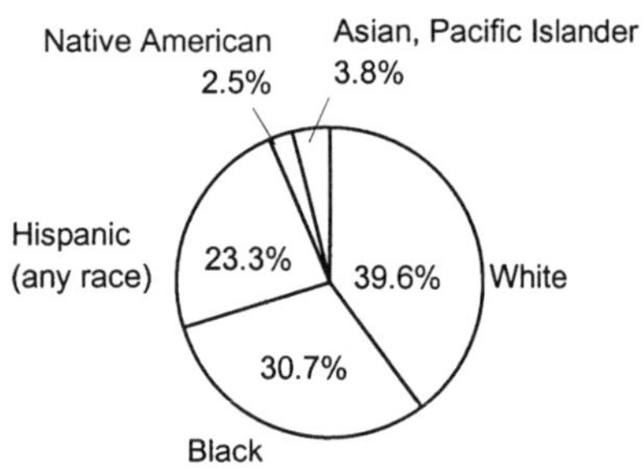

Medicaid Coverage

Race/Ethnicity	Number (in millions)	Percent
White	6.5	39.6
Black	5.1	30.7
Hispanic (any race)	3.8	23.3
Native American, Eskimo, Aleut	0.4	2.5
Asian, Pacific Islander	0.6	3.8
Total	16.5	100.0

Children with No Coverage

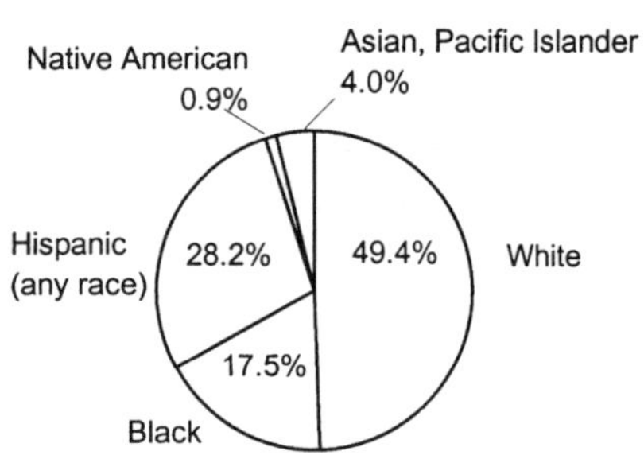

No Coverage

Race/Ethnicity	Number (in millions)	Percent
White	4.8	49.4
Black	1.7	17.5
Hispanic (any race)	2.8	28.2
Native American, Eskimo, Aleut	0.1	0.9
Asian, Pacific Islander	0.4	4.0
Total	9.8	100.0

FIGURE 2.6 Health insurance coverage among children by race and ethnicity, United States, 1995. SOURCE: EBRI (1997) Estimates are based on data from the 1996 Current Population Survey, Bureau of the Census, U.S. Department of Commerce.

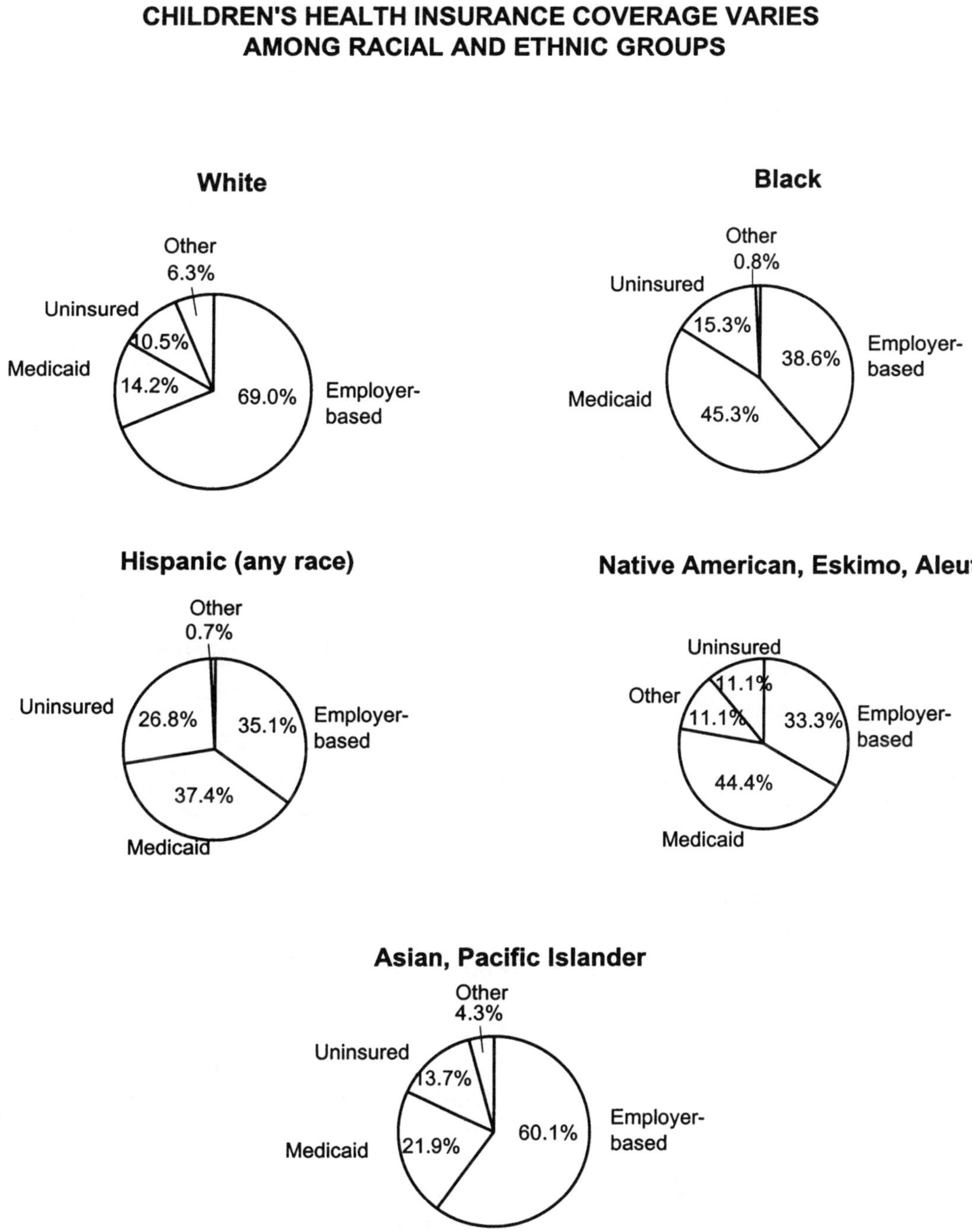

FIGURE 2.7 Patterns of health insurance coverage among children by race and ethnicity, United States, 1995. SOURCE: EBRI (1997). Data are based on estimates from the 1996 Current Population Survey, Bureau of the Census, U.S. Department of Commerce.

of the three major coverage groups: private coverage, Medicaid, and uninsured. However, in California, Asian-Americans comprise approximately 20 percent of the population and approximately 12 percent of the uninsured children (Children Now, 1997).

Many, but not all, of these differences by race and ethnicity correspond to differences in parental employment and thus relate to family income. An analysis of the data from the National Medical Expenditure Survey found that poverty, minority status, and absence of insurance each had independent effects on access to and the use of primary care, but that there was overlap among the groups: among children in at least one of these at-risk groups, 40 percent also had another risk factor. In other words, children who are uninsured are more likely to be poor and to be from a racial or ethnic minority (Newacheck et al., 1996).

Along with the growing diversity of the American population throughout all regions of the country, the availability of culturally appropriate health care services also varies. However, in designing new children's insurance expansions, it will be important to have current information on the racial and ethnic distributions of children by insurance status at the state level and local levels. Without such information, it will be more difficult to focus appropriate outreach and enrollment efforts on the communities with the highest concentrations of uninsured children.

Family Structure and Parental Employment

Figures 2.8, 2.9, and 2.10 present the breakdowns of household living arrangements, parents' employment status, family income, and parents' education status for children who have employer-based coverage and Medicaid, and for those who are uninsured, respectively.

Not surprisingly, the majority of children with employer-based coverage live in two-parent, working families (see Figure 2.8). More than half (54 percent) live in families with incomes that are 300 percent of the federal poverty level or higher. Children with Medicaid coverage are more likely to live in single-parent families (61.5 percent) in which the family income is 133 percent of the federal poverty level or less (71.8 percent) (see Figure 2.9 for Medicaid breakdowns, and see also Table 2.5 for breakdowns of federal poverty thresholds by family size).

The majority of uninsured children live in two-parent, working families (see Figure 2.10). Thus, parents of most uninsured children have been described as being among the "working poor." Almost half of uninsured children (48 percent) live in families whose incomes are below the 133 percent of the federal poverty level ($20,706.77 for a family of four in 1995).

More than half (55 percent) of the uninsured children have parents who finished high school. The majority of children who are uninsured (64 percent) live in families in which someone works full time year-round, typically in service industries, seasonal work, or other low-wage jobs in small businesses.

Evidence suggests that the majority of workers who are offered insurance coverage through their employer will enroll (Nichols et al., 1997). Small employers are less likely to offer health insurance to their workers than are large employers, and small employers tend to provide less-comprehensive benefits than do large employers (Nichols et al., 1997). However, the available evidence shows no clear relationship between firm size and the size of employees' contributions for dependent coverage (Nichols et al., 1997), suggesting that employers consider more than just the number of their employees in designing their benefits and cost-sharing requirements.

DURATION OF LACK OF COVERAGE

According to data from the Census Bureau's Survey of Income and Program Participation, millions of children spent several months without coverage between 1992 and 1994. Only 12 percent of uninsured children lacked coverage for 3 months or less. Nearly 40 percent were without coverage for 4 to 9 months, and half (50 percent) were without coverage for 10 months or more (see Figure 2.11).

MOST CHILDREN WITH PRIVATE INSURANCE LIVE IN TWO-PARENT, WORKING FAMILIES

Household Living Arrangements

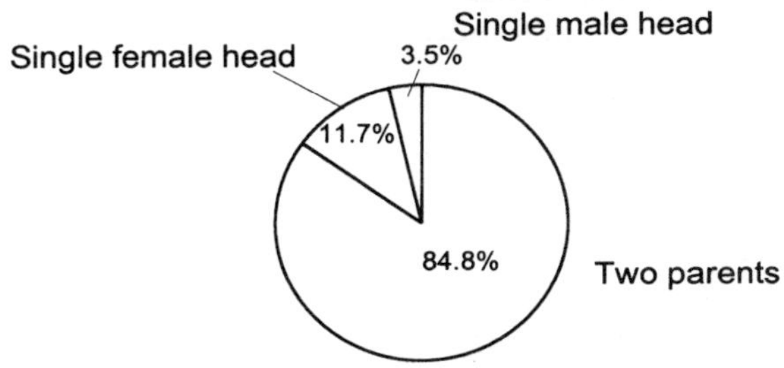

Living Arrangements	Number (in millions)	Percent
Two parents	35.3	84.8
Single female head	4.9	11.7
Single male head	1.5	3.5
Total	41.7	100.0

Parents' Employment Status

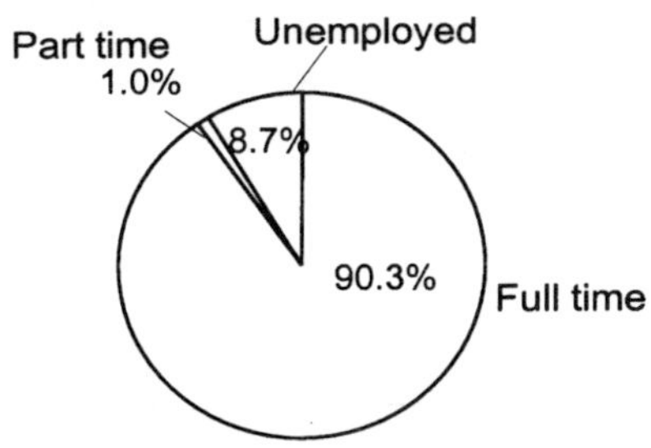

Parents' Employment Status	Number (in millions)	Percent
Full time employee	37.4	90.3
Part time employee	0.4	0.9
Unemployed	3.6	8.7
Total[a]	41.4	100.0

Family Income

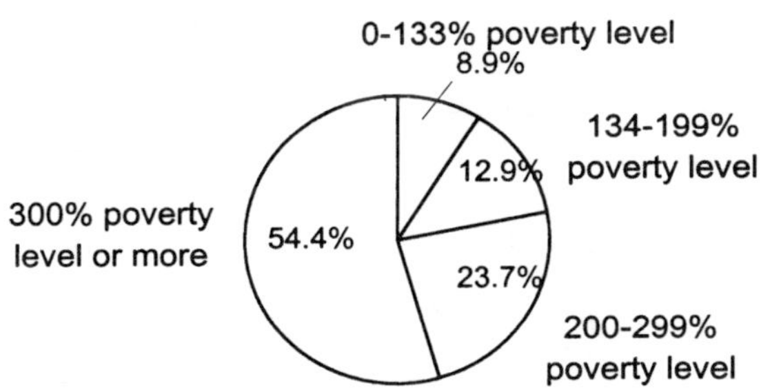

Family Income	Number (in millions)	Percent
0-133% poverty level	3.7	8.8
134-199% poverty level	5.4	12.9
200-299% poverty level	9.9	23.9
300% poverty level or more	22.7	54.4
Total	41.7	100.0

Parents' Education

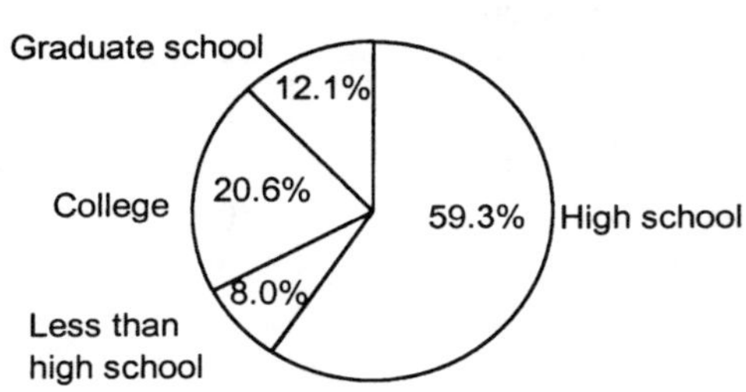

Parents' Education	Number (in millions)	Percent
High school	24.5	59.3
Less than high school	3.3	8.0
College	8.5	20.6
Graduate school	5.0	12.1
Total[b]	41.3	100.0

FIGURE 2.8 Characteristics of families of children with employer-based insurance coverage, ages 0-17, United States, 1995. SOURCE: EBRI (1997). Estimates are based on data from the 1996 Current Population Survey, Bureau of the Census, U.S. Department of Commerce. [a,b] The total number does not equal the number of children with employer-based insurance (41.7 million), because some children do not live with a parent; that is, they may live in foster care or with other relatives.

MOST CHILDREN WITH MEDICAID LIVE IN SINGLE-PARENT, WORKING FAMILIES

Household Living Arrangements

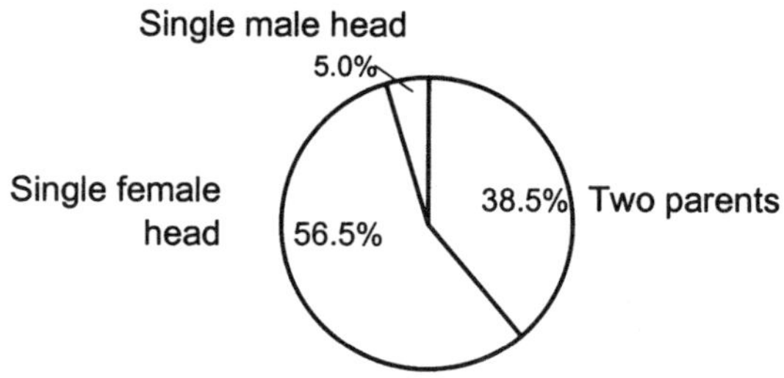

Living Arrangements	Number (in millions)	Percent
Two parents	6.4	38.5
Single female head	9.3	56.5
Single male head	0.8	5.0
Total	16.5	100.0

Parents' Employment Status

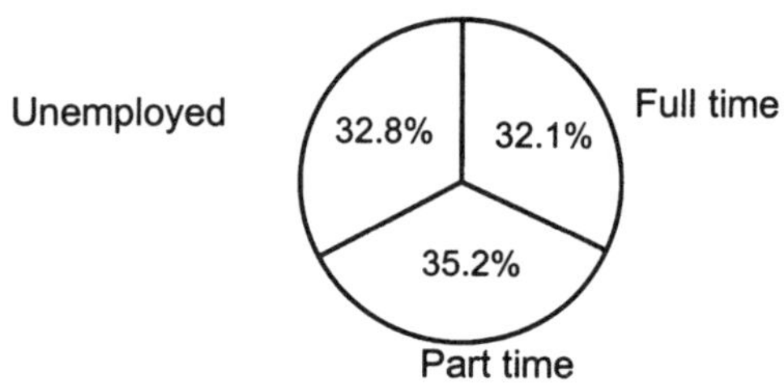

Parents' Employment Status	Number (in millions)	Percent
Full time employee	5.1	32.1
Part time employee	5.6	35.2
Unemployed	5.2	32.8
Total[a]	15.9	100.0

Family Income

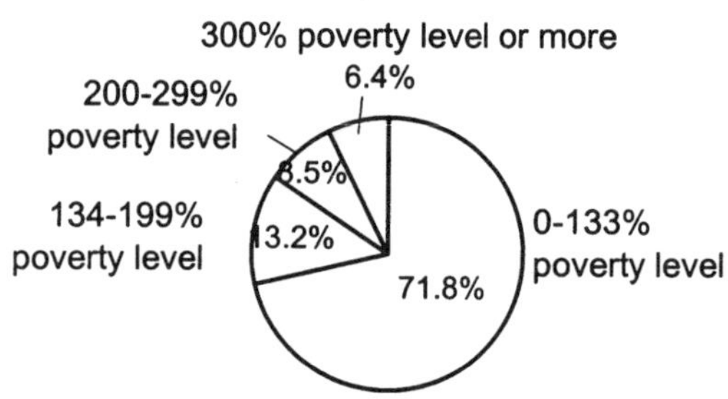

Family Income	Number (in millions)	Percent
0-133% poverty level	11.9	71.8
134-199% poverty level	2.2	13.2
200-299% poverty level	1.4	8.5
300% poverty level or more	1.2	6.4
Total	16.5	100.0

Parents' Education

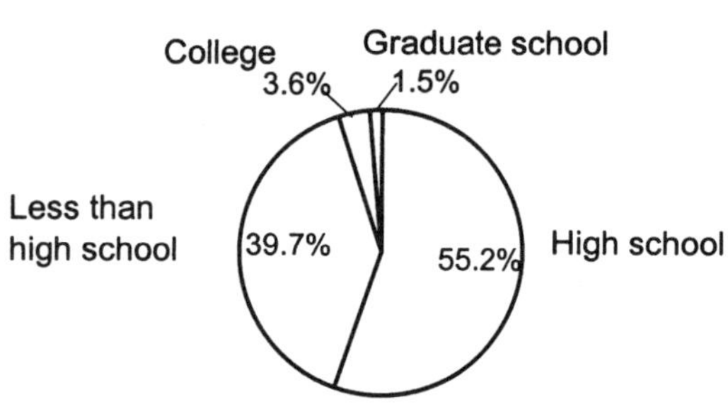

Parents' Education	Number (in millions)	Percent
High school	8.8	55.2
Less than high school	6.3	39.7
College	0.6	3.6
Graduate school	0.2	1.5
Total[b]	15.9	100.0

FIGURE 2.9 Characteristics of families of children with Medicaid coverage, ages 0-17, United States, 1995. SOURCE: EBRI (1997). Estimates are based on data from the March 1996 Current Population Survey, Bureau of the Census, U.S. Department of Commerce. [a,b] The total number does not equal the number of children with Medicaid (16.5 million), because some children do not live with a parent; that is, they may live in foster care or with other relatives.

MOST UNINSURED CHILDREN LIVE IN TWO-PARENT, WORKING FAMILIES

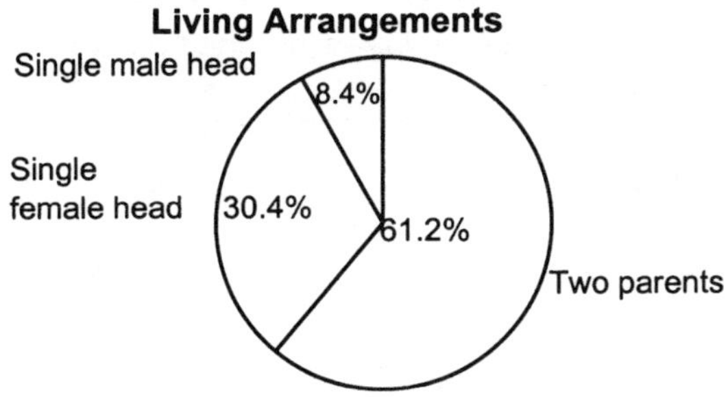

Living Arrangements	Number (in millions)	Percent
Two parents	6.0	61.2
Single female head	3.0	30.4
Single male head	0.8	8.4
Total	9.8	100.0

Parents' Employment Status	Number (in millions)	Percent
Full time employee	6.0	64.3
Part time employee	2.3	25.2
Unemployed	1.0	10.5
Total[a]	9.3	100.0

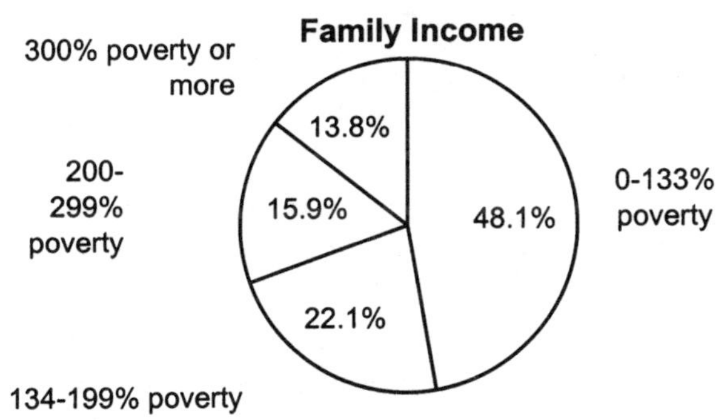

Family Income	Number (in millions)	Percent
0-133% poverty	4.7	48.1
134-199% poverty	2.2	22.1
200-299% poverty	1.6	15.9
300% poverty or more	1.43	13.8
Total	9.8	99.9

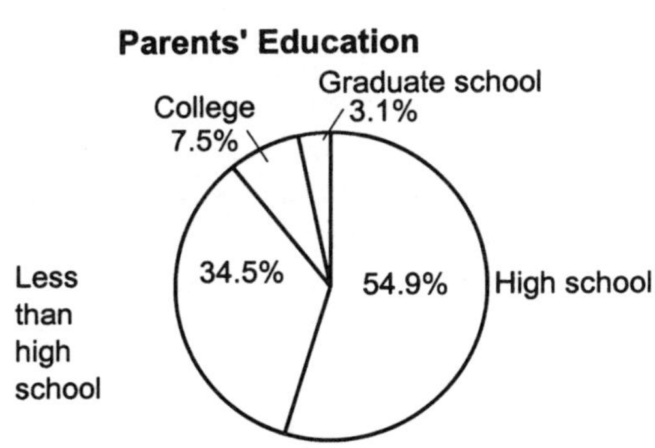

Parents' Education	Number (in millions)	Percent
High school	5.1	54.9
Less than high school	3.2	34.5
College	0.7	7.5
Graduate school	0.3	3.1
Total[b]	9.3	100.0

FIGURE 2.10 Characteristics of families of uninsured children, ages 0-17, United States, 1995. [a,b] The totals in these categories do not equal the number of uninsured (9.8 million), because some children do not live with a parent; that is, they may live in foster care or with other relatives. SOURCE: EBRI (1997). Estimates are based on data from the March 1996 Current Population Survey, Bureau of the Census, U.S. Department of Commerce.

TABLE 2.5 Federal Poverty Thresholds, by Size of Family, United States, 1995

Size of Family	Poverty Level Threshold ($)	Annual Income (in dollars) for the Following Poverty Level:		
		133%	200%	300%
One person	7,763.00	10,324.79	15,526.00	23,289.00
Under 65 years	7,929.00	10,545.57	15,858.00	23,787.00
65 years and over	7,309.00	9,720.97	14,618.00	21,927.00
Two persons	9,933.00	13,210.89	19,866.00	29,799.00
Householders under 65 years	10,529.00	14,003.57	21,058.00	31,587.00
Householders 65 years and over	9,219.00	12,261.27	18,438.00	27,657.00
Three persons	12,158.00	16,170.14	24,316.00	36,474.00
Four persons	15,569.00	20,706.77	31,138.00	46,707.00
Five persons	18,408.00	24,482.64	36,816.00	55,224.00
Six persons	20,804.00	27,669.32	41,608.00	62,412.00
Seven persons	23,552.00	31,324.16	47,104.00	70,656.00
Eight persons	26,237.00	34,895.21	52,474.00	78,711.00
Nine persons or more	31,280.00	41,602.40	62,560.00	93,840.00

SOURCE: Bureau of the Census (1995), Current Population Survey [www document]. (http://www.census.gov/hhes/poverty/threshld/thresh95.html)

Taken as a whole, these data suggest that spells without coverage can be substantial and widespread and can involve millions of children. Indeed, some 20 million children experienced at least one spell when they were uninsured during the 1992–1994 period (Table 2.6).

If children's episodes without coverage coincide with any major illnesses or injuries, their families face large out-of-pocket expenses for medical treatment. If families choose to forego treatment initially because of the cost, untreated illnesses and injuries can escalate in severity and can become much more costly to treat later on.

Much of the care provided to uninsured families becomes bad debt and is thus described by providers as "uncompensated care." As discussed in Chapter 4 of this report, uncompensated care provided by hospitals has historically been offset in part by Disproportionate Share Hospital (DSH) payments made under Medicaid and Medicare. The Balanced Budget Act of 1997 significantly reduced the amount of DSH funding and also eliminated cost-based reimbursement for community health centers. For these and other reasons discussed in Chapter 4, safety net providers need to change the structure of their services and to identify other financial resources to pay for or to offset the costs of uncompensated care.

REGIONAL VARIATIONS IN LACK OF COVERAGE

Figure 2.12 shows the state-by-state variations in the rates of uninsured children. The highest rates (greater than 20 percent) are in central southeastern, south-central, and southwestern states (Mississippi, Louisiana, Oklahoma, Texas, New Mexico, Arizona, and Nevada). The lowest rates (less than 10 percent) are in the northern tier. Moving from east to west, the rates of uninsured children are lowest in Pennsylvania, West Virginia, Ohio, Michigan, Illinois, Wisconsin, Minnesota, North Dakota, South Dakota, Nebraska, Montana, and Washington.

There are tremendous state-to-state variations in the availability of employer-sponsored health

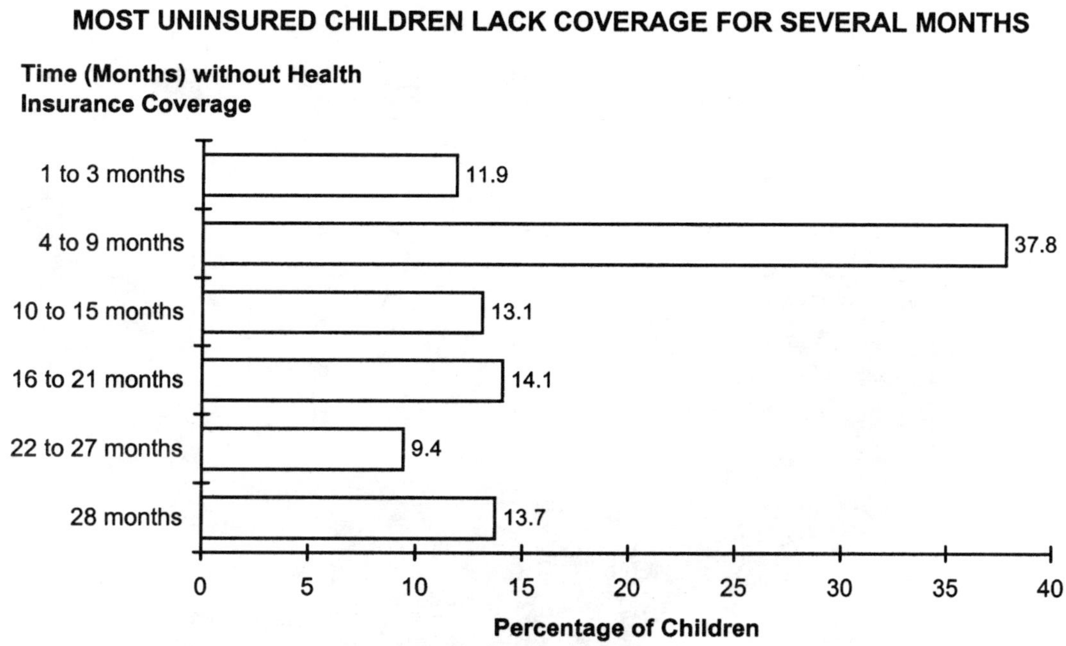

FIGURE 2.11 Percentage of children without health insurance coverage, ages 0-17, by number of consecutive months without coverage, United States, 1992-1994. SOURCE: Bennefield (1996).

TABLE 2.6 Number and Percentage of Children Without Health Insurance Coverage, Ages 0-17, by Number of Consecutive Months Without Coverage, United States, 1992-1994

Time (months) with No Coverage	Percentage of Total	Number (in millions)
None (covered full period)	**70.0**	**47.7**
1 to 28 months (uninsured)	**30.0**	**20.4**
1 to 3 months	11.9	2.4
4 to 9 months	37.8	7.7
10 to 15 months	13.1	2.7
16 to 21 months	14.1	2.9
22 to 27 months	9.4	7.9
28 months	13.7	2.8
Total	**100.0**	**68.1**

SOURCE: Bennefield (1996).

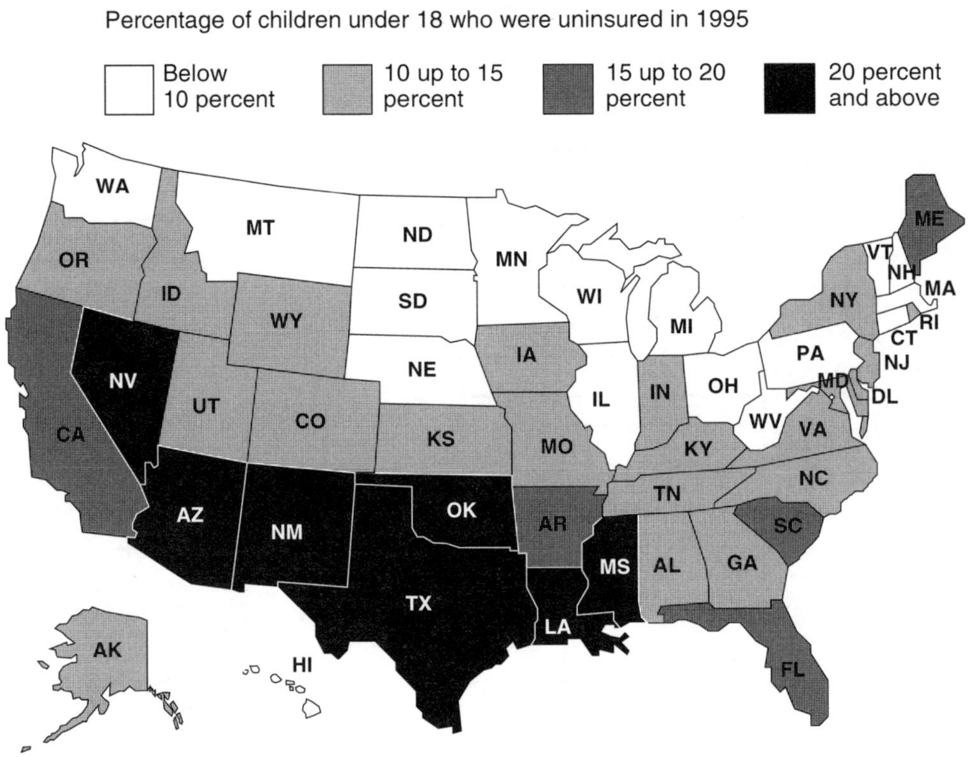

FIGURE 2.12 Distribution of uninsured children by state, 1995.

insurance (NCHS, 1998). Variability occurs because of state and regional differences in the industry and employment base, such as the distribution of large versus small employers, and in the coverage and cost-sharing options they customarily offer (Holahan, 1997). For example, children and adults in the South traditionally have had lower rates of employer-based coverage and correspondingly higher rates of uninsurance.

Another reason for state and regional differences in rates of uninsured children is because of the variability of state experiments with health insurance for children and state participation in Medicaid options. Some states—notably Massachusetts, Minnesota, and Florida—have undertaken successful expansions of children's health insurance coverage. Some private insurance initiatives (e.g., Caring Programs) operate in several states (see discussion in Chapter 6). In other states, however, there has been little or no previous activity in the children's health insurance coverage arena.

The State Children's Health Insurance Program (SCHIP) created under the Balanced Budget Act of 1997 recognized this tremendous variability among the states and built on the variety of approaches already being taken in several states. SCHIP was designed to give states flexibility and choice, and the flexibility appeals to most states. The national patterns of coverage are likely to change as a result of SCHIP, but it is too early to tell whether the states with the highest rates of uninsured children will develop programs that are most successful in expanding insurance coverage.

SUMMARY AND DISCUSSION

Trends in Children's Health Insurance Coverage

Employer-based coverage is decreasing more rapidly for children than for adults. Although the *percentage* of children without coverage remained relatively stable between 1987 and 1995, the *absolute number* of uninsured children increased, from 8.5 million in 1987 to 9.8 million in 1995. The percentage of uninsured children remained stable over that period primarily because increases in Medicaid enrollments offset declines in employer-based coverage.

Among Medicaid enrollees, young children (ages 0 to 5) are the largest age group (43.6 percent). This suggests that Medicaid expansions to younger children have been effective in reaching them.

Patterns of coverage differ for racial and ethnic minorities. Black and Hispanic children are more likely than white children to lack coverage. Nationally, one of every six black children and one of every four Hispanic children is uninsured. Among white children, 1 of every 10 is uninsured.

Racial and ethnic variations in coverage have important implications for outreach and enrollment strategies for new insurance programs. These strategies should be designed to reach the groups with highest rates of uninsurance, and should be culturally sensitive and culturally appropriate in order to increase the likelihood of participation.

Some Concerns About Substitution of Coverage

Evidence is fairly clear that rates of employer-based health insurance coverage for children declined from 1987 to 1995 and that rates of Medicaid enrollment increased for children over the same time period. It is less clear whether the relationship is causal—that is, whether the availability of Medicaid actually caused employers and employees to drop dependent coverage. The available evidence comes from aggregated data reported in national surveys. Because data on specific employer and employee decision making about these issues are not readily available, the survey data are subject to different interpretations.

Many policymakers are concerned that the availability of public insurance through Medicaid or SCHIP will encourage employers and employees to drop their private coverage, also called *substitution* or *crowding-out* of coverage (Chollet et al., 1997; Cutler and Gruber 1996, 1997; Dubay and Kenney, 1997). Substitution can take place in one of two ways: (1) An employer that currently provides coverage for children may stop covering dependents or may continue to offer coverage but increase the amount that employees must pay to receive dependent coverage, making it more likely that they will drop the coverage and try to replace it with public insurance; or (2) employees who are already paying a share of the cost of employer-based insurance might stop participating if, for example, they became eligible for new publicly funded programs.

Some researchers suggest that the decline in employer-based coverage is due primarily to the increases in health care costs, making employers less willing to offer coverage or more likely to shift the costs to employees, who in turn are less likely to accept the cost-sharing arrangements because of national declines in average real family incomes (Holahan et al., 1995). Others have suggested that the reductions in employer coverage may be largely attributable to the shift in jobs from the manufacturing sector to the service sector, where insurance is less likely to be offered as a benefit (Newacheck et al., 1995).

These employer trends thus may be occurring independently of expansions in Medicaid or other public programs like it. There does not appear to be any evidence that most employers are familiar with Medicaid program requirements in their states. Nor is there evidence that most people are aware of the Medicaid requirements in their states: in fact, the widespread underenrollment of eligible children in Medicaid would suggest the opposite.

There is evidence, however, that cost-sharing affects consumer health care purchasing decisions. For example, in a recent study of premium levels and participation in state-subsidized health insurance programs, Urban Institute researchers found that when families were charged 1 percent of their income, 57 percent joined a subsidized program; when the charge was 3 percent of income, 35 percent joined; and when the charge was 5 percent of income, only 18 percent joined (Ku and Coughlin, 1997).

Methodological differences across surveys have made it difficult to derive an exact estimate of the extent of crowd-out or coverage replacement (Chollet et al., 1997; Cutler and Gruber, 1996, 1997; Dubay and Kenney, 1997). Among poor children, those up to 200 percent of poverty, there tends to be relatively little substitution of coverage because few are likely to have private coverage in the first place (Dubay and Kenney, 1997). As income levels increase, families are increasingly likely to have private coverage through their employers, and so there is a greater risk of substitution.

States that have already expanded coverage to medium-income families (i.e., up to 400 percent of poverty) have taken several steps, sometimes referred to as *firewalls*, to reduce incentives to obtain replacement coverage. California and Minnesota use waiting periods to discourage people from moving from a private program to a public one: a child must be uninsured for at least 4 months before an application can be submitted for the new program. Several states have cost-sharing requirements, usually monthly fees charged on a sliding scale starting at 200 percent of the federal poverty level (Children Now, 1997; Chollet et al., 1997). Most state officials believe that these types of measures are effective in deterring crowd-out without preventing eligible individuals from enrolling (Chollet et al., 1997).

Concern about crowd-out was reflected in the structure of the SCHIP legislation. In general, the program was designed to target uninsured children in families with incomes up to 200 percent of poverty. Eligible children are those who are not eligible for Medicaid (whether enrolled or not) and who are not covered by private insurance. Although states are free to design their own enrollment procedures and eligibility criteria, they are required to describe the procedures they will use to prevent substitution of coverage in the state SCHIP plans they submit to the Department of Health and Human Services for approval.

A recent study by the Urban Institute estimates that only about 2.9 million uninsured children will meet the income eligibility criteria set by SCHIP, and that the available funds could insure a total of nearly 6 million children (Ullman et al., 1998). In other words, there may be enough money in the SCHIP program to insure almost twice as many children as are eligible under the current program rules, and states may have difficulty finding enough eligible children to draw down their full federal allotments. For this and other reasons, the committee urges states to develop systems of accountability that will help to enroll as many eligible children as possible, track changes in enrollment and utilization patterns, and collect and analyze other information that will help to assess the impact of SCHIP over time (IOM, 1998).

REFERENCES

Bennefield RL. 1996. *Who Loses Coverage and for How Long? Current Population Reports P70–54*. Washington, DC: Bureau of the Census, U.S. Department of Commerce.

Bureau of the Census. 1995. *Current Population Survey 1995*. Washington, DC: U.S. Department of Commerce.

Children Now. 1997. *California's Working Families and Their Uninsured Children: A Big Problem With an Affordable Solution*. Oakland, CA: Children Now.

Chollet DJ, Birnbaum ML, Sherman MJ. 1997. *Deterring Crowd-Out in Public Insurance Programs: State Policies and Experience*. Washington, DC: Alpha Center. [http://www.ac.org/]

Cutler D, Gruber J. 1997. Medicaid and Private Insurance: Evidence and Implications. *Health Affairs* 16(1):194–200.

Cutler D, Gruber J. 1996. Does Public Insurance Crowd out Private Insurance? *Quarterly Journal of Economics* 111:391–430.

Dubay L, Kenney G. 1997. Lessons from the Medicaid Expansions for Children and Pregnant Women: Implications for Current Policy. Statement for Hearing on Children's Access to Health Coverage, Subcommittee on Health, U.S. House Committee on Ways and Means, April 8, 1997. [http://www.urban.org/TESTIMON/dubay.html]

EBRI (Employee Benefit Research Institute). 1997. Special tabulations from the Bureau of the Census Current Population Survey prepared for the Institute of Medicine Committee on Children, Health Insurance, and Access to Care. Washington, DC: EBRI.

Holahan J. 1997. *Expanding Insurance Coverage for Children*. Washington, DC: Urban Institute.

IOM (Institute of Medicine). 1993. *Employment and Health Benefits: A Connection at Risk*. Washington, DC: National Academy Press.

IOM. 1998. *Systems of Accountability: Implementing Children's Health Insurance Programs*. Washington, DC: National Academy Press.

Ku L, Coughlin TA. 1997. *The Use of Sliding Scale Premiums in Subsidized Insurance Programs*. Washington, DC: Urban Institute. [http://www.urban.org/entitlements/premium.htm]

NCHS (National Center for Health Statistics). 1998. *Employer-Sponsored Health Insurance: State and National Estimates*. Rockville, MD: Centers for Disease Control and Prevention. [http://www.cdc.gov.nchswww/]

Newacheck PW, Hughes DC, Cisternas M. 1995. Children and Health Insurance: An Overview of Recent Trends. *Health Affairs* 14(1):244–254.

Newacheck PW, Hughes DC, Stoddard JJ. 1996. Children's Access to Care: Differences by Race, Income, and Insurance Status. *Pediatrics* 97(1):26–32.

Nichols LM, Blumberg LJ, Acs GP, Uccello CE, Marsteller JA. 1997. *Small Employers: Their Diversity and Health Insurance*. Washington, DC: Urban Institute. [http://www.urban.org/health/smemployers.htm]

Schieber GJ, Poullier JP. 1989. Overview of International Comparisons of Health Care Expenditures. Pp. 1–7 in *Health Care Financing Review Annual Supplement 1989*.

Ullman F, Bruen B, Holahan J. *1998. The State Children's Health Insurance Program: A Look at the Numbers*. Washington, DC: Urban Institute. [http://www.urban.org]

Weigers ME, Weinick RM, Cohen JW. 1998. *Children's Health, 1996. MEPS Chartbook No. 1*. Rockville, MD: Agency for Health Care Policy and Research.

3

Health Insurance and Access to Care

WHY ACCESS MATTERS

Children's access to health care is important to children themselves, to their families, as well as to society at large. Health care can influence children's physical and emotional health, growth, and development and their capacity to reach their full potential as adults. All children are at increased risk of developing preventable conditions if appropriate care is not provided when they are sick or injured. When children fail to receive necessary health care, their lives and the lives of their families can be affected for many years.

The Institute of Medicine (IOM) has defined access as "the timely use of personal health services to achieve the best possible health outcomes" (IOM, 1993, p. 4). The most common way to measure access is by comparing the health care utilization rates for different age groups, different racial and ethnic groups, and so on.

This chapter begins with a general discussion of the evidence that health insurance affects children's access to health care, emphasizing differences in health care utilization rates for insured and uninsured children. Next, other financial and nonfinancial barriers to care are discussed, including family income; family structure; and racial, ethnic, and cultural factors. The chapter also presents three approaches to defining what kinds of health care services should be provided for children, and then describes the services allowed under the State Children's Health Insurance Program (SCHIP).

Figure 3.1 was developed by the committee and revised several times throughout the course of the study. It presents the overall framework used by the committee to approach its analysis of a variety of influences on access to health care. This chapter reviews scientific and empirical evidence on the financial and nonfinancial influences represented in the first column of the figure.

FINANCIAL BARRIERS TO ACCESS

According to data released in July 1997 by the National Center for Health Statistics (NCHS), more than 7.3 million children—about 1 out of every 10 children—had at least one unmet medical need in 1993. These included dental care, prescription medication, eyeglasses, and mental health care. For 2.7 million children, care was reportedly delayed because of its cost (NCHS, 1997a). Children without health insurance were six times more likely to go without medical care than children with employer-

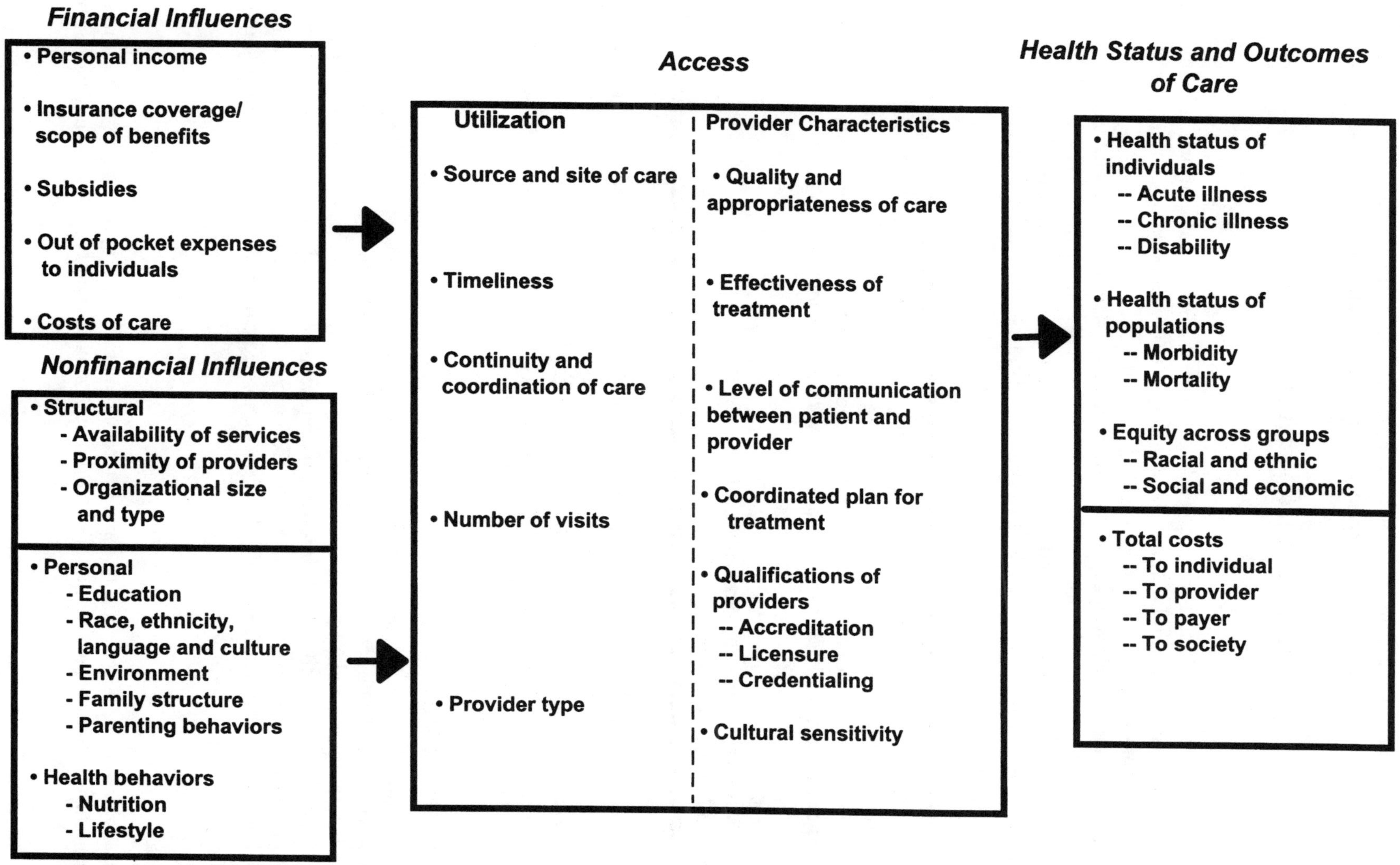

FIGURE 3.1 A framework for approaching financial and nonfinancial influences on access.

based (private) insurance. They were four times more likely than children with private insurance or Medicaid to experience a delay seeking care because their parents were concerned about payment.

Health Insurance and Access to Care

Contacts with Physicians

The prevalence of both acute and chronic conditions among insured and uninsured children—and thus their needs for care—are similar (Holl et al., 1995). However, the amount of contact with physicians differs significantly.

Children without insurance coverage are more than twice as likely as insured children *not* to visit a physician over a 12-month period (Holl et al., 1995). A study based on the 1987 National Medical Expenditures Survey found that uninsured children received care for acute earaches, recurrent ear infections, pharyngitis, and asthma only half as often as children who had either public or private coverage (Stoddard et al., 1994).

We don't know very much about the transition to managed care, either in the public or private sectors. But in the fee-for-service world we have very good evidence that children who have Medicaid as a source of coverage have utilization patterns and sources of care that look like those for children with private insurance.

Kay Johnson
George Washington University, Washington, DC
Public Workshop, June 2, 1997

Uninsured children with chronic medical conditions also have been found to have insufficient access to routine medical care. According to a national survey sponsored by the Robert Wood Johnson Foundation, nearly one in five uninsured children (17 percent) did not receive medical treatment needed for a chronic illness such as asthma, diabetes, or other conditions (32 percent) serious enough to keep a child from functioning at school (Wood et al., 1990).

Medical Attention for Injuries

Uninsured children are less likely than those with insurance to receive medical care for injuries, even for serious injuries. Among children who are uninsured, one study found that as many as 30 percent of all children with injuries and 40 percent of all children with serious injuries may not receive medical attention (Overpeck and Kotch, 1995). Injured children with Medicaid coverage and children with private insurance were found to have comparable access to medical attention (Overpeck and Kotch, 1995), which is consistent with the findings about access to medical services in other studies (Butler et al., 1985; St. Peter et al., 1992).

Hospital Services

Insured children have been found to have better outcomes from hospitalizations than uninsured children. Among children hospitalized in New York City for similar problems, one study found an in-hospital death rate that was almost one and one-half (1.46) times higher for uninsured children than for those who were insured (Carr et al., 1992). The uninsured children were more likely to be admitted to the hospital in a critical condition, and their needs for care were more urgent on admission. The study also found that hospitalization and mortality rates were highest in the poorest neighborhoods included in the study and in neighborhoods with the highest percentage of black and Hispanic residents. While each of these factors independently predicted the hospitalization rates, they were also significantly interrelated.

A California study found that newborns who were uninsured were more likely to be sick but received fewer services in the hospital than newborns who had insurance coverage (Braveman et al., 1989). The increased levels of risk for newborns were thought likely to be due in part to the lack of access to prenatal care for the uninsured mothers, who were also more likely to be black and Hispanic.

Figure 3.2 and Table 3.1 present the rates of hospitalizations for children whose conditions could have been treated on an outpatient basis (also known as "ambulatory care-sensitive conditions" or "preventable hospitalizations"). The rates are based on data from 10 states with a total population of 95 million analyzed by the Ambulatory Care Access Project of the United Hospital Fund of New York (Center for Health Economics Research, 1993, p. 57).

Children living in low-income areas have two to four times as many preventable hospitalizations as children living in high-income areas. These rates are likely to be due to poorer general health status, poorer access to preventive and routine care when needed, as well as to lack of insurance among low-income families (Newacheck and Halfon, 1988; Newacheck et al., 1996).

If you don't think coverage is important not only to remove barriers, but to restore dignity, go watch a family walk a child into an emergency room and have to ask for services that they can't pay for. They don't enjoy it, and you wouldn't enjoy it either.

James Bentley
American Hospital Association, Washington, DC
Public Workshop, June 2, 1997

Preventive Care

Insured children are much more likely to have a usual provider for routine preventive services and to receive recommended and age-appropriate services (Holl et al., 1995; Kogan et al., 1995). Preschoolers who lack insurance are less likely to be fully immunized than insured preschoolers (Wood et al., 1990), and so are children in families with incomes below poverty level (see Figure 3.3). During the course of a year, fewer than half (44.8 percent) of uninsured preschool-age children have any well-child visits, and fewer than one-third receive the recommended schedule of visits for their age (Short and Lefkowitz, 1992).

Racial comparisons of immunization rates show that white children are more likely to be immunized than are black children (see Figure 3.4). These rates are consistent with findings from other studies that have found poverty, minority status, and absence of insurance to be significant predictors of access to adequate primary care (Newacheck et al., 1996). Members of racial and ethnic minorities are disproportionately more likely to be uninsured and poor. While each of these characteristics independently is related to poor health status and lower health care utilization, these characteristics can not be viewed separately when outreach and community-based interventions are designed to increase the use of preventive services.

MOST PREVENTABLE HOSPITALIZATIONS OCCUR AMONG POOR CHILDREN

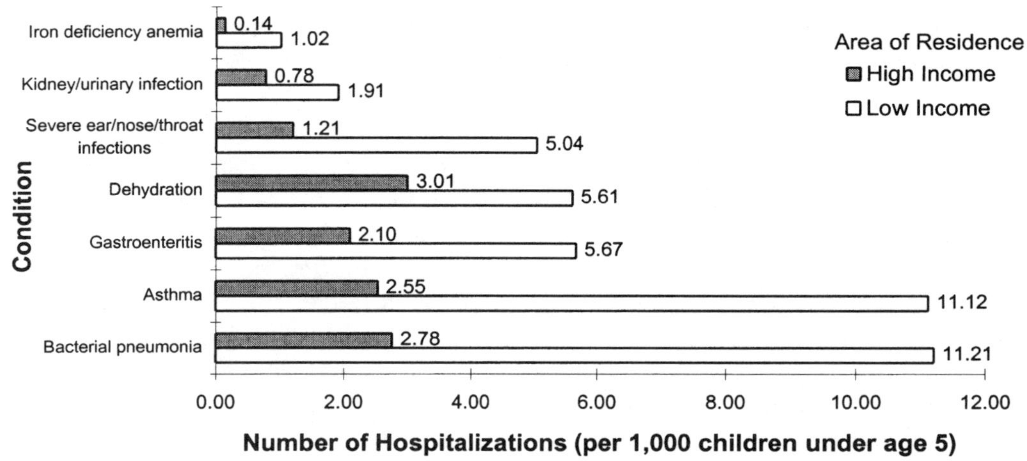

FIGURE 3.2 Hospitalizations for ambulatory care-sensitive conditions per 1,000 children under age 5, United States, 1989. Data are from 10 states having a total population of 95 million. High-income areas are zip codes in which fewer than 15 percent of households have annual incomes below $15,000; low-income areas are zip codes in which 50 percent or more of households have annual incomes below $15,000. SOURCE: Adapted from Center for Health Economics Research (1993, p. 57).

TABLE 3.1 Hospitalizations for Ambulatory Care-Sensitive Conditions per 1,000 Children Under Age 5, by Area of Residence, United States, 1989

	Number of Hospitalizations (per 1,000 children)	
Condition	Low-Income Areas	High-Income Areas
Bacterial pneumonia	11.21	2.78
Asthma	11.12	2.55
Gastroenteritis	5.67	2.10
Dehydration	5.61	3.01
Severe ear/nose/throat infections	5.04	1.21
Kidney/urinary infection	1.91	0.78
Iron deficiency anemia	1.02	0.14

NOTE: Data are from 10 states having a total population of 95 million. High-income areas are zip codes in which fewer than 15 percent of households have annual incomes below $15,000; low-income areas are zip codes in which 50 percent or more of households have annual incomes below $15,000. SOURCE: Adapted from Center for Health Economics Research (1993, p. 57).

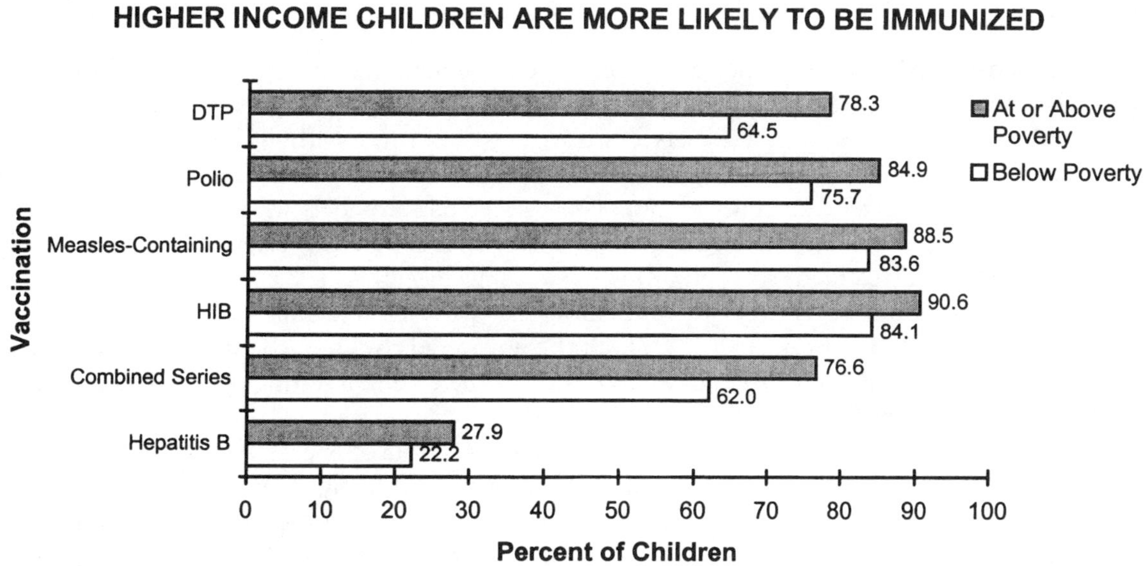

FIGURE 3.3 Vaccinations against selected diseases for children ages 19-35 months by poverty status, United States, 1994. Data are from the National Health Interview Survey, supplemented by information collected from vaccination providers in the National Immunization Provider Record Check study. NOTES: Poverty status is based on family income and family size using Bureau of the Census poverty thresholds (see Chapter 2, Table 2.5 in this report). DTP=diphtheria, tetanus toxoids, and pertussis vaccine (four doses or more); polio vaccine is three doses or more; HIB=*Haemophilus influenzae* type b vaccine (three doses or more); combined series (4:3:1) consists of four doses of DTP, three doses of polio vaccine, and one dose of measles-containing vaccine; and hepatitis B vaccine is three doses or more. SOURCE: NCHS (1997c, pp. 171-172).

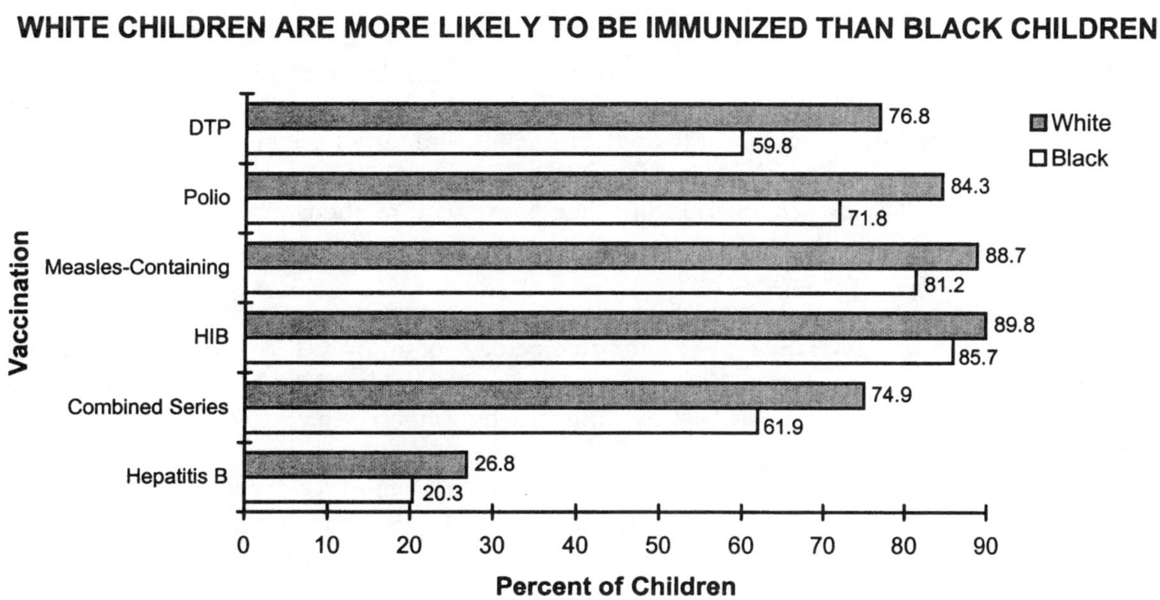

FIGURE 3.4 Vaccinations of children ages 19-35 months for selected diseases, by race, United States, 1994. Data are from the National Health Interview Survey, supplemented by information collected from vaccination providers in the National Immunization Provider Record Check study. DTP=diphtheria, tetanus toxoids, and pertussis vaccine (four doses or more); polio vaccine is three doses or more; HIB= *Haemophilus influenzae* type b vaccine (three doses or more); combined series (4:3:1) consists of four doses of DTP, three doses of polio vaccine, and one dose of measles-containing vaccine; and hepatitis B vaccine is three doses or more. SOURCE: NCHS (1997c, pp. 171-172).

Continuity of Care

One frequently used indicator of access to care is the presence of a usual source of care. Children and families who have a regular source of care are better able to obtain access to health care services when they are needed, and their utilization of services is higher than those without a regular source of care (Aday et al., 1984; Monheit and Cunningham, 1992; Newacheck et al., 1995). Having a regular source of care can also increase the continuity of care, because regular providers who know the children are more familiar with children's and families' medical histories and may be better able or more likely to monitor the progress of treatment through follow-up visits (Aday et al., 1984).

Uninsured children are seven to eight times more likely to lack a regular source for routine health care (Holl et al., 1995; Newacheck et al., 1997). Of the uninsured children who do receive routine care, 24 percent overall and 52 percent of poor children receive the care in a setting other than a physician's office (St. Peter et al., 1992).

Children who do not have a physician's office as their usual source of care are less likely to be taken to a physician when care is needed (Kasper, 1987) and are more likely than insured children to use higher-cost hospital emergency rooms or clinics (Newacheck et al., 1996; Wood et al., 1990). As indicated in Figure 3.5 and Table 3.2, a higher proportion of the total number of visits to emergency rooms are for "nonurgent" reasons than for emergencies. Children without insurance are five times more likely than children with Medicaid or employer-based coverage to use the emergency room as a regular source of care (NCHS, 1997b).

Compared with children who receive routine care at physicians' offices, children who receive routine care at community clinics have less continuity in their care. These children are 10 times more likely to go to a different provider or facility when they are sick and 10 times more likely to be taken to an emergency room (St. Peter et al., 1992).

Dental Visits

Although medical and dental services traditionally have been delivered separately, dental care is increasingly recognized as an important aspect of general health care for children (Lewit and Kerrebrock, in press). Oral diseases affect not only the teeth, gums, and rest of the mouth, but they also can lead to serious general health problems and significant pain, interference with eating, overuse of emergency rooms, as well as lost school and work time. Preventive methods such as the use of fluoride and dental sealant are comparable in effectiveness to immunizations against infectious disease, but these services are not always readily available.

Among parents who feel that their children have unmet health care needs, 57 percent report that the need is for dental care (NCHS, 1997a). Fifty-five percent of all 6- to 8-year-olds have untreated tooth decay, and these rates are even higher among minority populations (NCHS, 1996). The National Institute for Dental Research estimates that 51 million school hours per year are lost due to dental-related illness (Brunelle, 1989).

Uninsured children are 2.5 times less likely than insured children to receive dental care (Bloom et al., 1992; Monheit and Cunningham, 1992; Newacheck et al., 1997). Among children enrolled in Medicaid's Early and Periodic Screening, Diagnosis, and Treatment (EPSDT) program, only about twenty percent actually receive the required dental services (DHHS, 1996).

In the mid-1980s, the RAND Health Insurance Experiment found that reduced cost-sharing for dental services led to increased use of preventive dental services as well as significantly fewer decayed teeth (Isman, 1997; Newhouse et al., 1993). It is well established that individuals who have private dental insurance are more likely to use dental services, including preventive services, than those who are uninsured (Bloom et al., 1992; Newacheck et al., 1997). Yet copayments for dental services are still considerably higher than those for other health services (Lewit and Monheit, 1992).

BOYS VISIT EMERGENCY ROOMS MORE THAN GIRLS; WHITES VISIT MORE THAN BLACKS

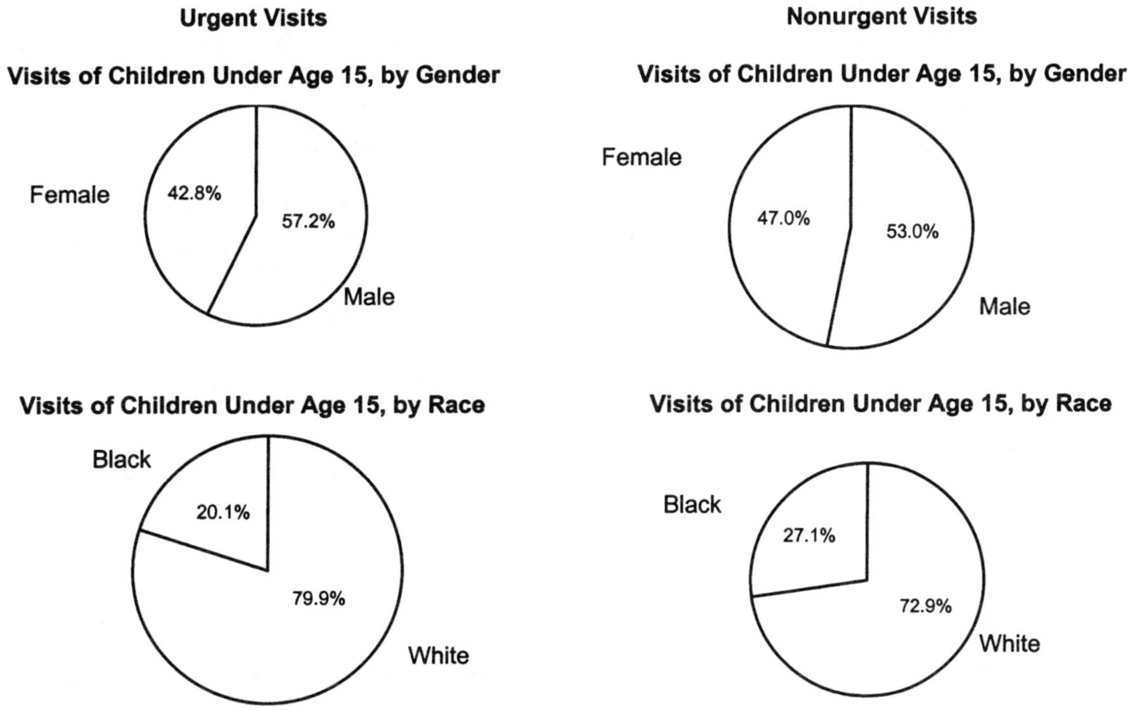

FIGURE 3.5 Urgent and nonurgent emergency room visits for children under age 15, United States, 1995. SOURCE: NCHS (1997b, pp. 4, 6). Data are from the 1995 National Hospital Ambulatory Medical Care Survey, Emergency Department Summary.

TABLE 3.2 Urgent and Nonurgent Emergency Room Visits for Children Under Age 15, United States, 1995

	Urgent Visits		Nonurgent Visits	
Group	Number (in thousands)	Percent	Number (in thousands)	Percent
Gender				
Male	4,861	57.2	7,531	53.0
Female	3,638	42.8	6,679	47.0
Race				
White	6,547	79.9	9,976	72.9
Black	1,644	20.1	3,710	27.1

SOURCE: NCHS (1997b, pp. 4, 6). Data are from the 1995 National Hospital Ambulatory Medical Care Survey, Emergency Department Summary.

Other Financial Barriers to Access

Even when they have insurance coverage, children from low-income families have fewer contacts with physicians than other insured children (Rosenbach, 1989). Low-income, privately insured families bear a greater burden of the direct costs of health care for their children than families who have higher incomes or coverage through Medicaid, because out-of-pocket expenses such as copayments and deductibles represent a higher relative proportion of family income (Newacheck, 1989; Newacheck et al., 1996). Studies have shown that when cost-sharing increases (i.e., when out-of-pocket expenses are higher), the use of outpatient services for a variety of illnesses decreases (Rosenbach, 1989; Valdez et al., 1985).

Out-of-pocket expenses can be particularly burdensome for children with chronic conditions. A recent study sponsored by the Agency for Health Care Policy and Research found that more than 60 percent of insured families with a child with insulin-dependent diabetes mellitus had to pay a deductible for either insulin, syringes, or blood testing strips and that more than 85 percent had a copayment for these items. The annual out-of-pocket expenses were 56 percent higher than those for families with comparable coverage without an insulin-dependent diabetic child ($1,125 compared to $625) (Songer et al., 1997).

Faced with additional expenses from either seeing a provider or paying for medical supplies, many insured families choose to treat a condition at home or to wait and see whether the health condition resolves on its own. According to testimony from several presenters in the committee's public workshop (Appendix C), insured families with large medical expenses may be forced to choose between paying medical bills and other bills and eventually may end up in poverty.

NONFINANCIAL BARRIERS TO ACCESS

As summarized in Figure 3.1, several other factors have been found to influence utilization, including educational background and other characteristics of parents and families; racial, ethnic, and cultural factors; and the presence of special health care needs. Public health risks as well as structural and organizational characteristics of the health care system also can reduce access to care.

> If you step back and take an overview of this issue of worrying about coverage, the debate over Medicaid versus tax credits and incentives for people to buy their own insurance is curious. For thirty or forty years, we have known that if you really want to change health status, the surefire way to do it is to increase personal disposable income, improve education, improve nutrition, and make sure people have safe and affordable housing. From a public health perspective, direct access to health care services would come in fifth.
>
> *Carl Schramm*
> *Greenspring Advisors, Inc., Towson, MD*
> *Public Workshop, June 2, 1997*

Parental and Family Characteristics

Children depend on their parents, family members, and other caretakers to determine when they need care and to seek care on their behalf. Studies have shown that several characteristics of parents and families can reduce children's access to care. These include low levels of parental education (Newacheck,

1992; Short and Lefkowitz, 1992; Woodward et al., 1988), an inability to read outreach and other health-related materials (Riportella-Muller et al., 1996), and a lack of skills related to caretaking, including a lack of knowledge about prevention and health care needs (Margolis et al., 1995; Newacheck, 1989; Riportella-Muller et al., 1996). Routine preventive services are sometimes neglected for children with chronic health problems and special health care needs (Riportella-Muller et al., 1996).

Low-income parents may be more likely to experience logistical difficulties in arranging care, such as a lack of transportation and lack of a telephone to arrange appointments (Fossett et al., 1992). Regardless of income, parents may have trouble arranging health care appointments because of a lack of child care for siblings or other family members (Riportella-Muller et al., 1996) and difficulty in taking time off from work (Riportella-Muller et al., 1996; Wolfe, 1980).

Family structure also relates to health care access. With the exception of children of young teenage mothers who live with their own mothers (Short and Lefkowitz, 1992), first-born children, only children, and younger children tend to have more outpatient visits (Cafferata and Kasper, 1985; Horwitz et al., 1985; Newacheck, 1992).

Parental health problems or other personal problems and family crises also can compete with children's health care needs as priorities for parental attention (Riportella-Muller et al., 1996). Families who have health and social problems may be less likely to seek health care for a child when it is needed.

Race, Ethnicity, and Cultural Factors

In the increasingly diverse U.S. society, the influences of racial, ethnic, and cultural factors on access to care are gaining a greater degree of recognition. Several studies have shown that nonwhite children have fewer physician visits than white children (Cornelius, 1993; Newacheck, 1992; Wolfe, 1980), independent of the need for care (Horwitz et al., 1985; Riley et al., 1993). Even with insurance coverage, minority adolescents have fewer visits to physicians, are less likely to have a usual source of care, and lack continuity of care in comparison with non-Hispanic white adolescents (Lieu et al., 1993).

Black and Hispanic children are more likely to live in poverty (46.4 percent of black and 39.7 percent of Hispanic children) than white children (12.2 percent). They are also more likely than white children to be uninsured (15.3 percent of black children and 26.8 percent of Hispanic children compared with 10.5 percent of white children in 1995 (see Figure 2.5).

Compared with the distribution of racial and ethnic groups in the U.S. population, there is a shortage of African-American, Hispanic, and Asian-American physicians and other health professionals (Lewin-Epstein, 1991). Health care services are often located outside of a racial or ethnic neighborhood. In areas where there is segregation or racial tension, this may increase an individual's reluctance to seek care outside of the neighborhood (Fossett et al., 1992).

Children with asthma are more likely to require hospitalization (an indicator of ineffective outpatient care) if they are poor, black, or Hispanic, and the outcomes of treatment are often worse (Carr et al., 1992; Perrin et al., 1989; Wissow et al., 1988). For example, a study in New York City found that poor black and Hispanic children who were hospitalized for asthma were three to six times more likely than white children to die from the episode, and also tended to come from lower-income families than the white children (Carr et al., 1992).

Cultural factors also influence care-seeking behaviors. A study of African Americans, Mexican Americans, Puerto Ricans, and non-Hispanic whites in poor areas of Chicago found that African Americans tended to use hospital-based facilities, while Mexican Americans were the least likely of all the groups to have a regular source of care, in large part because of social and cultural barriers such as language and immigration status (Lewin-Epstein, 1991). Hispanics with traditional health beliefs and health care practices may not perceive a need for health care, especially for preventive interventions (Andersen et al., 1986). Southeast Asians who believe in the inevitability of suffering and the acceptance of a predetermined time of death are less likely to seek care (Hoang and Erickson, 1985; Uba, 1992).

Language and other communication difficulties between families and providers can increase dissatisfaction with care and decrease the likelihood that the family will seek care again (Malach and Segal, 1990; Uba, 1992). Spanish-speaking asthmatics whose clinicians did not speak Spanish were found to be less likely to come to follow-up appointments, less likely to take medications appropriately, and more likely to use an emergency department (Manson, 1988).

Changes in the health care system can reduce the racial, ethnic, and cultural differences in the patterns of care. For example, after barriers to care were reduced through 24-hour availability of care and limiting the waiting time for appointments, a Baltimore study found that the use of health care became more comparable for black and white children (Orr et al., 1984, 1988). Similarly, when language and income barriers were minimized, urban Mexican American and white elementary-school children no longer differed in their use of health care services (Gilman and Bruhn, 1981).

There is growing recognition of the importance of including culturally competent health care as a measure of health care quality (IOM, 1997; Lavizzo-Mourey and Mackenzie, 1996). HEDIS 3.0 (Health-plan Employer Data and Information Set), the most widely used set of performance measures for managed care organizations, includes "availability of language and interpretation services" as a measure of access to care. Many professional organizations are developing training programs to increase providers' ability to meet the needs of patients from diverse backgrounds (AAPCHO, 1994; AMA, 1994; Tirado, 1995).

Organizational and Systems Barriers to Access

Many aspects of the health care system also can decrease children's access to care. Waiting time for available appointments, lack of 24-hour availability of physicians, travel time, waiting room time, and actual processing time for patients can present significant barriers to seeking and receiving care (Fossett et al., 1992; Riportella-Muller et al., 1996).

For families living in underserved urban or rural areas, access to qualified providers can be even more difficult because provider shortages limit the number of available appointments (Fossett et al., 1992; St. Peter et al., 1992). For example, a study in Chicago found that pediatricians in inner-city residential areas cared for almost twice as many children as pediatricians located in the most prosperous areas (Fossett et al., 1992).

> We tend to look at this health insurance or access issue as the end product. It really isn't. The end product is really better outcomes for kids. So health insurance becomes one piece of a broader social and public health safety net that we ought to be thinking about for kids.
>
> *Patrick Chaulk*
> *Annie E. Casey Foundation, Baltimore, MD*
> *Public Workshop, June 2, 1997*

As discussed throughout this report, managed care is changing the delivery of American health care. There are relatively few studies of the impact of managed care on children's access to care, and the results are decidedly mixed. For example, there is some evidence that children are more likely to receive preventive services when they are enrolled in managed care plans than when they have traditional indemnity insurance (Carey et al., 1990; Szilagyi et al., 1990). However, studies in the early 1990s showed that children with special health care needs had difficulties obtaining access to inpatient hospitalization and to specialty pediatric providers in managed care organizations (Cartland and Yudkowsky, 1992; Halfon et al., 1995; Hughes et al., 1995; Newacheck et al., 1994). In recent years, health plans have begun to implement programs specifically for children with special health care needs, often in partnership with public health clinics (AAHP, 1997). It will be important to evaluate the impact of these newer disease management programs in improving access to care.

ACCESS TO WHAT? DEFINING NECESSARY HEALTH SERVICES

As a matter of principle, the committee believes that all children should have appropriate access to coordinated, effective, and child-appropriate care, including the following health care services:

- generally accepted preventive services for health promotion and disease prevention (anticipatory guidance, health supervision, or maintenance);
- acute care for immediate short-term illnesses and injuries;
- ongoing care for children with chronic medical conditions (e.g., diabetes mellitus, cerebral palsy, and muscular dystrophy);
- rehabilitative care, including allied health services, for children with disabilities; and
- care for children with special needs (e.g., speech disorders).

As shown in Figure 3.6 and Table 3.3, the cost of preventive or "wellcare" visits is a small proportion of all money spent on health care. The committee believes that a comprehensive scope of benefits with an increased emphasis on prevention is especially important for children because of their developmental needs.

However, scientific evidence and professional consensus do not give clear indications for specific diagnostic tests, treatments, procedures, drugs, specialists, and other services to which children should have access. This is true for all of medical care, but especially for children, in the committee's view. Professional organizations, parents, and purchasers of care have different attitudes and positions about which services are essential for children, and there are many areas of disagreement and uncertainty. Parents, insurers, and policymakers also may have different views on whether a given expenditure is reasonable, but some priorities must be set if payers and policymakers are to be able to make reasoned and equitable decisions in the face of limited resources (Klein et al., 1996).

A complete analysis or comparison of benefit structures for comprehensive care for children would be beyond the scope of this study. However, Boxes 3.1 to 3.3 summarize three approaches to defining recommended services for children. These are the recommendations of a previous Institute of Medicine committee, the National Forum on the Future of Children and Families; the U.S. Preventive Services Task Force guidelines; and the health care services recommendations of the American Academy of Pediatrics. Box 3.4 summarizes the health care benefits allowed under SCHIP.

Preventive care is important. Immunizations are important. The health of our children is just as important as the education of our children. It is something we value.

Charles LaVallee
Western Pennsylvania Caring Foundation for Children, Pittsburgh, PA
Public Workshop, June 2, 1997

IMPLICATIONS

Evidence is clear that uninsured children receive fewer health care services than children who have insurance coverage. Compared with children who have insurance coverage, uninsured children have fewer visits to physicians, are less likely to be seen by physicians when they are sick or injured, and are less likely to receive adequate preventive services, including immunizations.

Untreated illnesses and injuries can have long-term—even lifelong—consequences. For example, untreated ear infections can lead to hearing loss or deafness. Children who are unable to hear well can have trouble performing well in school and trouble interacting normally with their families and friends. Language or other developmental delays due to untreated neurological problems also can frustrate normal development and social interactions.

Although children who are uninsured have less access to care, it is important to recognize that the presence of insurance alone will not eliminate all of the barriers to accessing appropriate health care services. Children are dependent on their parents to identify problems and seek treatment, and even insured and responsible parents may delay seeking care because of the cost of the out-of-pocket expenses or because it is difficult or inconvenient to schedule appointments. Delays in ambulatory care because of cost may result in diagnosis or treatment later in the course of illness or disease, when treatment may be more complex and more expensive.

Some aspects of the health care system also can create barriers to access, particularly the shortages of providers to serve low-income groups, lack of cultural sensitivity, and inconvenient scheduling. With an increasing emphasis on the quality of care, it is likely that some of these aspects will begin to change over time.

In the meantime, health insurance expansions for children should emphasize benefits that include preventive services and age-appropriate interventions. With health insurance, children are more likely to experience healthy physical and emotional growth, development, and overall health and well-being. Without insurance, their health care needs are far more likely to go unmet.

If we get all kids covered, that is not going to solve all of their health problems, but it is going to make solving them a lot easier.

John McDonough
Massachusetts Legislature, Boston, MA
Public Workshop, June 2, 1997

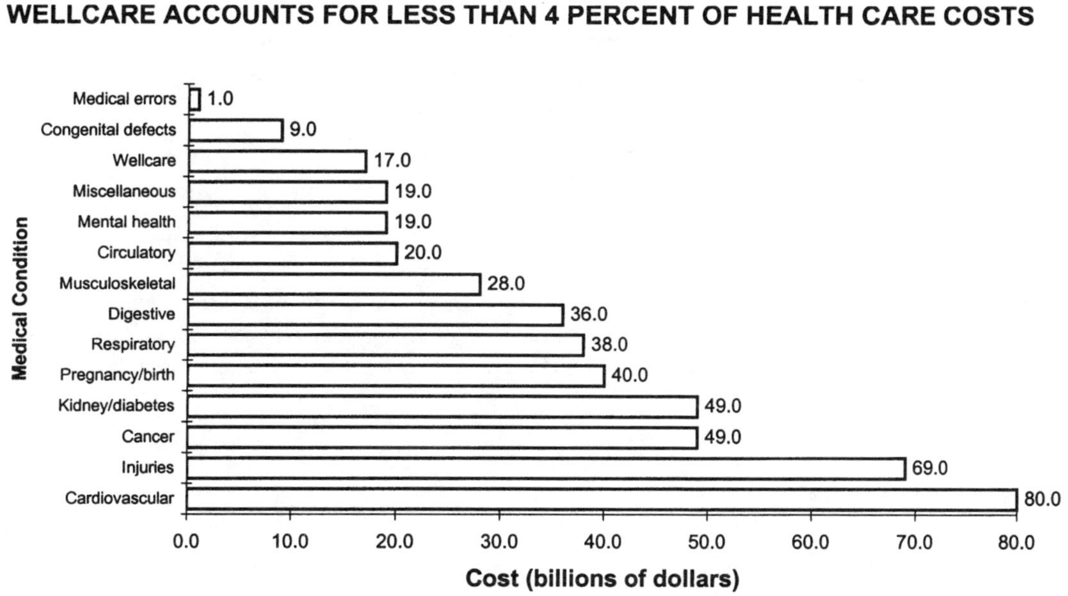

FIGURE 3.6 Drivers of health care dollars, United States, 1993. Miscellaneous includes anemia, unconsciousness, headache, and hormonal disorder other than diabetes. Data from the National Health Interview Survey. Source: Adapted from HIAA (1997, p. 86).

TABLE 3.3 Drivers of Health Care Dollars, United States, 1993.

Medical Condition	Cost (in billions of dollars)
Medical errors	1.0
Congenital defects	9.0
Wellcare	**17.0**
Mental health	19.0
Miscellaneous	19.0
Circulatory	20.0
Musculoskeletal	28.0
Digestive	36.0
Respiratory	38.0
Pregnancy/birth	40.0
Cancer	49.0
Kidney/diabetes	49.0
Injuries	69.0
Cardiovascular	80.0
TOTAL	**474.0**

NOTE: Miscellaneous includes anemia, unconsciousness, headache, and hormonal disorders other than diabetes. SOURCE: Data are from the National Health Interview Survey, NCHS, 1997. Adapted from HIAA (1997, p. 86).

BOX 3.1
Benefits Recommended by the National Forum on the Future of Children and Families

1. Preventive health services

- comprehensive prenatal, delivery, and postpartum care, emphasizing continuous risk assessment in pregnancy, education and intervention when problems are detected;
- regular, routine preventive health care from birth through adolescence, including immunizations, anticipatory guidance and health education, and health screening (beginning with screening of newborns);
- family planning services and supplies; postpartum care and counseling; and other related reproductive health services; and
- preventive dental care.

2. Major medical services

- services in hospitals and other licensed health facilities, including inpatient care for acute and chronic illnesses, emergency room care, surgery (including ambulatory surgery), and anesthesia;
- services of physicians and of other licensed providers, such as certified nurse-midwives, obstetric-gynecologic, and pediatric nurse practitioners, and physicians' assistants;
- diagnostic services, including laboratory and radiology services;
- mental health and substance (alcohol and drug) abuse treatment services; and
- acute dental care and noncosmetic orthodontia.

3. Special services and supplies for persons with extensive or complex health care needs

- durable medical equipment;
- extended mental health and substance abuse services;
- home health care and nursing in specialized day care for mentally fragile children;
- nutritional services;
- recuperative stays in long-term care facilities
- hospice care;
- home visiting;
- respite care;
- coordination of care for chronically ill or high-risk individuals with special health care needs; and
- occupational, physical, and speech therapy and rehabilitation.

SOURCE: Adapted from NRC and IOM, 1996, p. 13.

BOX 3.2
U.S. Preventive Services Task Force Recommended Routine Preventive Services for Children (0–10 years)

Screening
- Height and weight
- Blood pressure
- Vision screen (ages 3–4 years)
- Hemoglobinopathy screen (birth)
- Phenylalanine level (birth)
- T4 and/or TSH (birth)

Counseling
- Injury prevention
- Diet and exercise
- Substance use
- Dental health

Chemoprophylaxis
- Ocular prophylaxis (birth)

Immunizations
- Diphtheria-tetanus-pertussis
- Oral poliovirus
- Measles-mumps-rubella
- *Haemophilus influenzae* type b conjugate
- Hepatitis B virus
- Varicella

Interventions for Children with Special Risk Factors
- Hemoglobin/hematocrit
- Human immunodeficient virus testing
- Blood lead level
- Hepatitis A vaccine
- Pneumococcal vaccine
- Influenza vaccine
- Fluoride supplements

SOURCE: Adapted from U.S. Preventive Services Task Force, 1996.

BOX 3.3
American Academy of Pediatrics Recommended Health Care Services for Children and Adolescents

1. Medical care, including:
   (a) health supervision with preventive care and immunizations,
   (b) diagnosis and treatment of acute and chronic illness, developmental disabilities, learning disorders, and behavioral problems.
2. Surgical care.
3. Mental health services.
4. Emergency and trauma care services.
5. Inpatient hospital services.
6. Specialty and pediatric subspecialty consultations.
7. Family planning services.
8. Pregnancy services.
9. Care of all newborns and infants:
   (a) attendance and management at high-risk deliveries,
   (b) health supervision, and
   (c) treatment of congenital anomalies and other illnesses.
10. Laboratory and pathology services.
11. Diagnostic and therapeutic radiology services.
12. Anesthesia services.
13. Rehabilitation and early intervention services (e.g., physical, speech, and occupational therapy).
14. Home health care, private-duty nursing.
15. Hospice care.
16. Respite care.
17. Long-term care at home or skilled nursing facility.
18. Case management and care coordination.
19. Medical and social services for suspected physical or sexual abuse or neglect.
20. Transfer/transport to hospital or health care facility.
21. Dental care and oral surgery.
22. Nutritional counseling.
23. Prescription drugs, medical and surgical supplies, corrective eyeglasses or lenses, hearing aids, and special nutritional supplements.
24. Durable medical equipment and prostheses/braces.

SOURCE: Adapted from American Academy of Pediatrics Committee on Child Health Financing, 1993.

BOX 3.4
Services Allowed Under SCHIP

States can choose to expand Medicaid or offer one of the following: (1) one of three "benchmark" packages mentioned identified in the SCHIP legislation; (2) a package actuarially equivalent to one of the benchmark packages; (3) a comprehensive benefits package under an existing child health insurance program [available only to Florida, New York, and Pennsylvania.]; or (4) another benefit package approved by DHHS.

Actuarially equivalent packages must include four minimum benefits:

- inpatient and outpatient hospital services,
- physicians' surgical and medical services,
- laboratory and X-ray services, and
- well-baby and well-child care that includes age-appropriate immunizations.

Equivalent coverage must have an actuarial value that is 75% of the costs of the following categories:

- prescription medications,
- mental health services,
- vision services, and
- hearing services.

The following are optional services:

- clinic services;
- over-the-counter medications;
- prenatal care and family planning supplies;
- inpatient mental health services;
- durable medical equipment and other medical devices;
- disposable medical supplies;
- home- and community-based services;
- nursing-care services;
- dental services;
- inpatient and outpatient substance abuse treatment and services;
- case management services;
- care coordination;
- physical, occupational, and speech therapy;
- hospice care;
- medical transportation;
- enabling services (e.g., transportation and translation services); and
- any other services specified by DHHS or recognized by state law and prescribed by a licensed physician or practitioner.

SOURCE: Johnson and McDonough, 1998.

REFERENCES

Aday LA, Fleming GV, Anderson R. 1984. *Access to Medical Care in the U.S.: Who Has It, Who Doesn't.* Chicago: Pluribus Press for the University of Chicago.

AAHP (American Association of Health Plans). 1997. *AAHP Fact Sheets: Chronic Care.* Washington, D.C.: AAHP Medical Affairs Department.

AAPCHO (Association of Asian Pacific Community Health Organizations). 1994. *Culturally Competent Health Service Delivery Under Managed Care for Asians and Pacific Islanders.* Oakland, CA: AAPCHO.

AMA (American Medical Association). 1994. *Culturally Competent Health Care for Adolescents: A Guide for Primary Care Providers.* Chicago: AMA.

American Academy of Pediatrics Committee on Child Health Financing. 1993. Scope of Health Care Benefits for Infants, Children, and Adolescents Through Age 21 Years. *Pediatrics* 91:508.

Andersen RM, Giachello AL, Aday LA. 1986. Access of Hispanics to Health Care and Cuts in Services: A State-of-the-Art Overview. *Public Health Reports* 101:238–252.

Bloom B, Gift HC, Jack SS. 1992. Dental Services and Oral Health, United States, 1989. *Vital and Health Statistics* 10:183.

Braveman P, Oliva G, Miller MG, Reiter R, Egerter S. 1989. Adverse Outcomes and Lack of Health Insurance Among Newborns in an Eight-County Area of California, 1982–86. *The New England Journal of Medicine* 330:1421–1425.

Brunelle JA. 1989. *Oral Health of United States Children: The National Survey of Dental Caries in U.S. School Children, 1986–87.* Bethesda, MD: National Institute of Dental Research. NIH Pub. No. 89–2247.

Butler JA, Winter WD, Singer JD, Wenger M. 1985. Medical Care Use and Expenditure Among Children and Youth in the United States: Analysis of a Probability Sample. *Pediatrics* 76:495–507.

Cafferata GL, Kasper JD. 1985. Family Structure and Children's Use of Ambulatory Physician Services. *Medical Care* 23:350–360.

Carey T et al. 1990. Prepaid versus Fee-for-Service Medicaid Plans: Effects on Preventive Health Care. *Journal of Clinical Epidemiology* 43:1213–1220.

Carr W, Zeitel L, Weiss K. 1992. Variations in Asthma Hospitalizations and Deaths in New York City. *American Journal of Public Health* 82:59–65.

Cartland JDC, Yudkowsky BK. 1992. Barriers to Pediatric Referral in Managed Care Systems. *Pediatrics* 89:183–192.

Center for Health Economics Research. 1993. *Access to Health Care, Key Indicators for Policy.* Princeton, NJ: Robert Wood Johnson Foundation.

Cornelius LJ. 1993. Barriers to Medical Care for White, Black, and Hispanic American Children. *Journal of the National Medical Association* 85:281–288.

DHHS (U.S. Department of Health and Human Services). 1996. *Children's Dental Services Under Medicaid: Access and Utilization. Report of the Office of the Inspector General, OEI–09–93–00240.* San Francisco: DHHS.

Fossett JD, Perloff JD, Kletke PR, Peterson JA. 1992. Medicaid and Access to Child Health Care in Chicago. *Journal of Health Politics, Policy and Law* 17:273–298.

Gilman SC, Bruhn, JG. 1981. A Comparison of Utilization of Community Primary Health Care and School Health Services by Urban Mexican-American and Anglo Elementary School Children. *Medical Care* 19:223–232.

Halfon N, Inkeles M, Wood D. 1995. Nonfinancial Barriers to Care for Children and Youth. *Annual Review of Public Health* 16:447–472.

HIAA (Health Insurance Association of America). 1997. *Source Book of Health Insurance Data.* Washington, D.C.: HIAA.

Hoang GN, Erickson RV. 1985. Cultural Barriers to Effective Medical Care Among Indochinese Patients. *Annual Review of Medicine* 36:229–239.

Holl JL, Szilagyi PG, Rodewald LE, Byrd RS, Weitzman MD. 1995. Profile of Uninsured Children in the United States. *Archives of Pediatric and Adolescent Medicine* 149:398–406.

Horwitz SM, Morgenstern H, Berkman LF. 1985. The Impact of Social Stressors and Social Networks on Pediatric Medical Care Use. *Medical Care* 23:946–959.

Hughes DC, Newacheck PW, Stoddard JJ, Halfon N. 1995. Medicaid Managed Care: Can It Work for Children? *Pediatrics* 95(4):591–594.

IOM (Institute of Medicine). 1993. *Access to Health Care in America.* Washington D.C.: National Academy Press.

IOM. 1997. *Managing Managed Care: Quality Improvement in Behavioral Health.* Washington, D.C.: National Academy Press.

Isman R. 1997. *Dental Services in Healthy Families: Issue Paper 1.* Sacramento, CA: California Department of Health Services.

Johnson K, McDonough JE. 1998. *Expanding Health Coverage for Children: Matching Federal Policies and State Strategies.* New York: Milbank Memorial Fund.

Kasper JD. 1987. The Importance of Type of Usual Source of Care for Children's Physician Access and Expenditures. *Medical Care* 25:386–398.

Klein R, Day P, Redmayne S. 1996. *Managing Scarcity.* Buckingham, England: Open University Press.

Kogan MD, Alexander GR, Teitelbaum MA, et al. 1995. The Effect of Gaps in Health Insurance on Continuity of a Regular

Source of Care Among Preschool-Aged Children in the United States. *Journal of the American Medical Association* 274(18):1429–1435.

Lavizzo-Mourey, Mackenzie ER. 1996. Cultural Competence: Essential Measurements of Quality for Managed Care Organizations. *Annals of Internal Medicine* 124(10):919–921.

Lewin-Epstein N. 1991. Determinants of Regular Source of Health Care in Black, Mexican, Puerto Rican, and Non-Hispanic White Populations. *Medical Care* 29(6):543–557.

Lewit EM, Monheit AC. 1992. Expenditures on Health Care for Children and Pregnant Women. *The Future of Children* 2(2):95–114.

Lewit EM, Kerrebrock N. In press. Dental Indicators: *The Future of Children*.

Lieu TA, Newacheck PW, McManus MA. 1993. Race, Ethnicity, and Access to Ambulatory Care Among U.S. Adolescents. *American Journal of Public Health* 83(7):960–965.

Malach RS, Segal N. 1990. Perspectives on Health Care Delivery for American Indian Families. *Children's Health Care* 19:219–228.

Manson A. 1988. Language Concordance as a Determinant of Patient Compliance and Emergency Room Use in Patients with Asthma. *Medical Care* 26:1119–1128.

Margolis PA, Carey T, Lannon CM, Earp JL, Leininger L. 1995. The Rest of the Access-to-Care Puzzle: Addressing Structural and Personal Barriers to Health Care for Socially Disadvantaged Children. *Archives of Pediatric and Adolescent Medicine* 149:541–545.

Monheit AC, Cunningham PJ. 1992. Children Without Health Insurance. *The Future of Children* 2(2):154–170.

NCHS. 1996. *Healthy People 2000 Review 1995–96*. Hyattsville, MD: Public Health Service. DHHS Pub. No. PHS 96–1256.

NCHS. 1997a. Access to Health Care Part I: Children. *Vital and Health Statistics*, Series 10, No. 196. Hyattsville, MD: NCHS.

NCHS. 1997b. National Hospital Ambulatory Medical Care Survey: 1995, Emergency Department Summary. Prepared by Stussman BJ. *Advance Data from Vital and Health Statistics*, No. 285. Hyattsville, MD: NCHS.

NCHS. 1997c. *Health, United States 1996–1997 and Injury Chartbook*. Washington, D.C.: U.S. Government Printing Office.

Newhouse JP and the Insurance Experiment Group. 1993. *Free for All? Lessons from the RAND Health Insurance Experiment*. Los Angeles: RAND.

NRC and IOM (National Research Council and Institute of Medicine). 1996. Including Children and Pregnant Women in Health Care Reform, pp. 1–32. *Paying Attention to Children in a Changing Health Care System: Summaries of Workshops*. Washington, D.C.: National Academy Press.

Newacheck PW. 1989. Improving Access to Health Services for Adolescents from Economically Disadvantaged Families. *Pediatrics* 84(6):1056–1063.

Newacheck PW. 1992. Characteristics of Children with High and Low Usage of Physician Services. *Medical Care* 30(1):30–41.

Newacheck PW, Halfon NH. 1988. Preventive Care Use by School-Aged Children: Differences by Socioeconomic Status. *Pediatrics* 82:462–468.

Newacheck PW, Hughes DC, Stoddard JJ. 1996. Children's Access to Care: Differences by Race, Income, and Insurance Status. *Pediatrics* 97(1):26–32.

Newacheck PW, Hughes DC, Cisternas M. 1995. Children and Health Insurance: An Overview of Recent Trends. *Health Affairs* 14(1):244–254.

Newacheck PW, Hughes DC, Stoddard, JJ, Halfon N. Children With Chronic Illness and Medicaid Managed Care. 1994. *Pediatrics* 93:497–500.

Newacheck PW, Stoddard JJ, Hughes DC, Pearl M. 1997. Children's Access to Health Care: The Role of Social and Economic Factors. In Stein REK, ed. *Health Care for Children: What's Right, What's Wrong, What's Next.* New York: United Hospital Fund.

Orr ST, Charney E, Straus J. 1988. Use of Health Services by Black Children According to Payment Mechanism. *Medical Care* 26:939–947.

Orr ST, Miller CA, James SA. 1984. Differences in Use of Health Services by Children According to Race. *Medical Care* 22: 848–853.

Overpeck MD, Kotch JB. 1995. The Effect of U.S. Children's Access to Care on Medical Attention for Injuries. *American Journal of Public Health* 85:402–404.

Perrin JM, Horner CJ, Berwick DM, Woolf AD, Freeman JL, Wennberg JE. 1989. Variations in Rates of Hospitalizations of Children in Three Urban Communities. *The New England Journal of Medicine* 320:1183–1187.

Riley AW, Finney JW, Mellits ED, et al. 1993. Determinants of Children's Health Care Use: An Investigation of Psychosocial Factors. *Medical Care* 31:767–783.

Riportella-Muller R, Selby-Harrington ML, Richardson LA et al. 1996. Barriers to the Use of Preventive Health Care Services for Children. *Public Health Reports* 111:71–77.

Rosenbach ML. 1989. The Impact of Medicaid on Physician Use by Low-Income Children. *American Journal of Public Health* 79:1220–1226.

St. Peter RF, Newacheck PW, Halfon N. 1992. Access to Care for Poor Children: Separate and Unequal? *Journal of the American Medical Association* 267:2760–2764.

Short P, Lefkowitz D. 1992. Encouraging Preventive Services for Low-Income Children: The Effect of Expanding Medicaid. *Medical Care* 30:766–780.

Songer TJ, LaPorte RE, Lave JR, et al. 1997. Health Insurance and the Financial Impact of IDDM in Families with a Child with IDDM. *Diabetes Care* 20:577–584.

Stoddard JJ, St. Peter R, Newacheck P. 1994. Health Insurance Status and Ambulatory Care for Children. *The New England Journal of Medicine* 330:1421–1425.

Szilagyi PG et al. 1990. The Effect of Independent Practice Association Plans on Use of Pediatric Ambulatory Medical Care in One Group Practice. *Journal of the American Medical Association* 263(16):2198–2203.

Tirado MD. 1995. *Tools for Monitoring Cultural Competence in Health Care*. San Francisco: Latino Coalition for a Healthy California.

Uba L. 1992. Cultural Barriers to Health Care for Southeast Asian Refugees. *Public Health Reports* 197:544–548.

United States Preventive Services Task Force. 1996. *Guide to Clinical Preventive Services* (2nd ed.). Baltimore: Williams & Wilkins.

Valdez RB, Brook RH, Rogers W et al. 1985. Consequences of Cost-Sharing for Children's Health. *Pediatrics* 75:952–961.

Wissow L, Gittelshon AM, Szklo M, Starfield B, Mussman M. 1988. Poverty, race, and hospitalization for childhood asthma. *American Journal of Public Health* 78:777–782.

Wolfe BL. 1980. Children's Utilization of Medical Care. *Medical Care* 18:1196–1207.

Wood D, Hayward R, Corey C, et al. 1990. Access to Medical Care for Children and Adolescents in the United States. *Pediatrics* 86:666–673.

Woodward CA, Boyle MH, Offord DR, et al. 1988. Ontario Child Health Study: Patterns of Ambulatory Medical Care and Their Correlates. *Pediatrics* 82:425–434.

Part II

Financing Health Care for Children

4

Safety Net Providers

DEFINITION OF SAFETY NET

For the purposes of this report, safety net providers can be described by any of the following:

- A substantial proportion of the care they provide is for individuals who lack insurance coverage and who cannot afford to pay for care themselves.
- They rely primarily on Medicaid and Medicare revenues and charitable sources of funds.
- They offer specialized or essential health services not generally offered by other providers, including intensive medical services for indigent individuals (e.g., people with HIV and AIDS); public health services, such as health education; and support services, such as transportation, translation services, child care, and other services.

In general, the safety net includes the following groups of providers:

- hospitals (public, children's, teaching, and community hospitals serving low-income individuals),
- community and migrant-worker health centers,
- health services programs for homeless children and adults,
- local public health departments providing clinical services,
- school-based clinics,
- some home health agencies, and
- some individual primary care practitioners in private practice.

The safety net is not an organized national entity, but rather a composite of different agencies, organizations, and individuals in each community across the country (Baxter and Mechanic, 1997). The mix of financing, concentration of organizational responsibility for care for low-income and uninsured groups, and the demand for uncompensated care are different in every community. The mix of services also differs depending on the community's provider base, its commitment to serving low-income and uninsured groups, and individual providers' ability to participate.

This chapter of the report describes the sources and amounts of financing for safety net providers and then describes the general utilization rates and patterns for four types of safety net providers: community health centers, children's hospitals, health departments, and school-based health centers. The chapter also describes some of the most significant budgetary and other challenges to safety net providers in the late 1990s, including changes in the structure and delivery of Medicaid.

SOURCES OF FUNDING FOR SAFETY NET PROVIDERS

For several decades, safety net providers have helped to increase access to primary and preventive health care for underserved and vulnerable people who experience financial, geographic, or cultural barriers to care. Groups served by safety net providers include uninsured children and adults, homeless families and individuals, migrant farmworkers, adolescents, people who live in rural and frontier areas, residents of public housing, and others (HRSA, 1997a).

Over the past 30 years, the federal government and several states have taken legislative and other steps to build the health care infrastructure supporting safety net providers in underserved areas. Typically, funding for these providers comes from a blend of public and private funding streams that subsidize free or low-cost care. Public sources of funding may include the Medicaid program, federal and state service delivery and research grants, local tax dollars, and state uncompensated care pools. Private sources may include foundations and philanthropic organizations, charities (e.g., hospitals whose missions include serving patients regardless of health insurance coverage or ability to pay), and other sources that are not part of an organized philanthropic funding program (e.g., individual donations).

> I worry about the whole collapse of any sort of safety net for families and kids. We have hospitals being converted from not-for-profit to for-profit, which eliminates emergency room obligations. Community health centers are under an enormous squeeze in trying to deal with increasing numbers of uninsured families. Federal and state dollars flowing to local health departments and local providers have decreased, and managed care is taking some Medicaid dollars out of health departments and moving people into different systems. These are complex changes which need to be addressed because they affect people in very real terms on a daily basis.
>
> *Patrick Chaulk*
> *Annie E. Casey Foundation, Baltimore, MD*
> *Public Workshop, June 2, 1997*

Until recently, cost-shifting allowed many mainstream providers serving the general population to offset the costs of uncompensated care. As purchasers have turned to managed care for cost savings, the cross-subsidies and excess revenue sources that could support uncompensated care are disappearing. Purchasers have been negotiating deep discounts in contracts with mainstream hospitals and group practices, forcing those who formerly provided care for uninsured individuals to refer these patients to safety net providers. Uncompensated care costs are becoming more concentrated among fewer hospitals and other traditional safety net providers, and there also is a significant increase in the amount of uncompensated care provided by individual physicians (Cunningham and Ha, 1997).

Table 4.1 presents the main sources of public funding for safety net providers up to 1996. These figures represent total federal funding amounts; matching funds from the states and age-specific breakdowns were not available.

After Medicaid, discussed in Chapter 5, the largest source of funding in the past has been Disproportionate Share Hospital (DSH) payments. Because of concerns that DSH funds were not all being used to provide care for uninsured and low-income individuals, these payments were significantly reduced by the Balanced Budget Act of 1997.

TABLE 4.1 Sources and Amounts of Funding for Selected Safety Net Programs in Health Services, United States, 1992-1995

Program	Source of Funding			Total Funding (in millions of dollars)			
	Federal	State	Local	1992	1993	1994	1995
Medicaid[1]	✓	✓	NA	115,200	127,400	137,100	151,300
Medicaid DSH[2]	✓	✓		17,526	17,016	16,890	18,990
Medicare DSH[3]				2,200	2,700	3,400	3,800
Supplemental Nutrition Program for Women Infants, and Children[4]	✓	NA	NA	2,566	2,820	3,160	3,451
Bureau of Primary Health Care Programs[5] Community health centers, migrant health centers, health care for the homeless, public housing primary care	✓	✓	✓	1,698	1,798	1,995	2,507
Title V Maternal and Child Health Care Services block grant[a,6]	✓	✓	✓	547	552	575	572
Vaccines for Children[7]	✓	NA	NA	*b*	*b*	*b*	280

NOTE: All programs are administered by the U.S. Department of Health and Human Services.

NA = not applicable. [a]Federal grants only; state matches not available. [b]Program not in existence

SOURCES: [1] Kaiser Commission on the Future of Medicaid (1997); [2] The Urban Institute (1997) (calculations based on data from Health Care Financing Administration Form 64); [3] ProPAC (1997); [4] U.S. House of Representatives, Committee on Ways and Means (1996); [5]HRSA/BPHC (1997a); [6]HRSA/MHCB (1997b); [7]CDC (1997).

DISPROPORTIONATE SHARE HOSPITAL PAYMENTS

When DSH payment provisions were enacted, they were intended to offset the costs of uncompensated care provided by community hospitals and other hospitals caring for a disproportionate share of low-income individuals, including uninsured patients and patients covered by Medicaid. Because Medicaid's reimbursement levels were low and because these hospitals also tended to serve few privately insured individuals, they were unable to shift or otherwise subsidize the costs of uncompensated care.

From the late 1980s to the mid-1990s, the number of uninsured individuals increased and the total costs of uncompensated care climbed steadily (see Figure 4.1, Table 4.2). After passage of OBRA (Omnibus Budget Reconciliation Act) 1987 DSH provisions, DSH payments grew from approximately $400 million in 1988 to $19 billion in 1995, with the federal government's share of these payments in 1995 approaching $11 billion (Holahan et al., 1997).

The DSH funds, however, have not always been targeted to hospitals serving low-income individuals. Rather than helping safety net hospitals solve their financial problems, some states used the DSH funding to substitute for other state expenditures through intergovernmental transfers and other methods (Holahan et al., 1997). Only about two-thirds of the funding reached safety net hospitals (Coughlin and Liska, 1997; Ku and Coughlin, 1995).

Congress capped DSH payments at 12 percent of Medicaid program expenditures in 1991. In the Balanced Budget Act of 1997, future federal funding for DSH was reduced by a projected $10 billion. The savings helped Congress to finance part of the $24 billion in allocations set aside over five years for states to implement children's insurance programs (the State Children's Health Insurance Program, or SCHIP). A limited amount of SCHIP funding (up to 10 percent) may be spent on administrative costs, outreach, provider subsidies (including safety net), and direct services. Although safety net providers believe that efforts to increase the number of insured Americans are essential, these efforts are unlikely to eliminate the need for subsidies for the uninsured. Even if SCHIP is fully implemented, millions of children will remain uninsured, and the numbers of uninsured adults are likely to continue to increase.

For example, the Congressional Budget Office has estimated that states' efforts under SCHIP could result in fewer than 2 million newly-insured children by 1999, far below the 11 million children who were estimated to be uninsured in 1996. Moreover, at current rates, more than 2 million currently insured individuals will lose coverage between now and 1999. As commercial payers continue to negotiate severely discounted payment rates, mainstream providers may be forced to reduce or eliminate charity care. Thus, the availability of care for the increasing numbers of uninsured children and adults will be further concentrated among safety net providers.

COMMUNITY HEALTH CENTERS

Under Section 330 of the Public Health Service Act, community health centers (CHCs) have a congressional mandate to serve uninsured and underinsured individuals and families. More than 2,200 health center service sites deliver preventive and primary health care to more than 9 million people in underserved urban and rural communities. They adjust their charges according to a patient's ability to pay (Hawkins and Rosenbaum, 1997).

CHCs are governed by community boards and tailor their services to meet the specific needs of the communities and the special populations that they serve, including migrant and seasonal workers, homeless individuals, and people living with AIDS. Most CHCs are private, not-for-profit corporations. In addition to primary care and preventive services, they offer a comprehensive array of expanded services such as outreach, translation services, home visits, care management, and other support services (HRSA, 1997a).

In addition to the federal funds administered by the Bureau of Primary Health Care of the Health Resources and Services Administration, CHCs are supported by Medicaid, Medicare, federal grants,

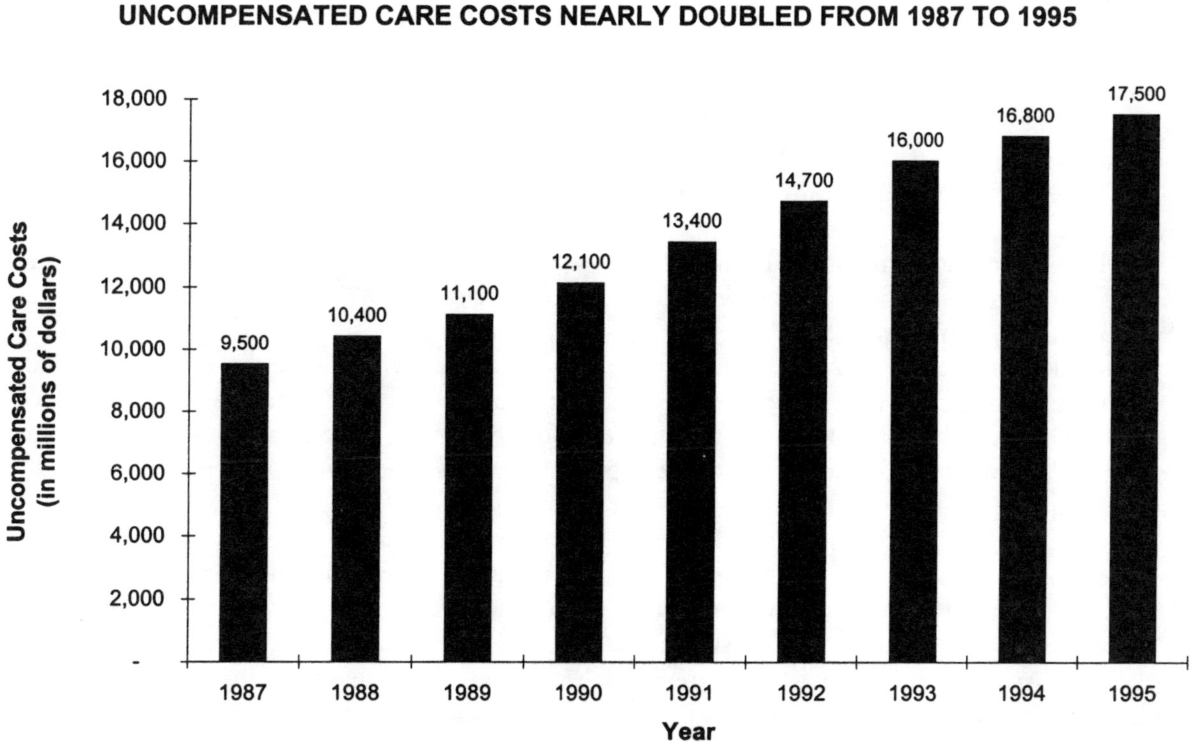

FIGURE 4.1 National cost of uncompensated care in registered community hospitals, United States, 1987-1995. SOURCE: AHA (1995).

TABLE 4.2 National Cost of Uncompensated Care for Registered Community Hospitals, United States, 1987-1995

Year	Uncompensated Care Cost (in millions of dollars)	Number of Hospitals
1987	9,500	5,597
1988	10,400	5,499
1989	11,100	5,448
1990	12,100	5,370
1991	13,400	5,329
1992	14,700	5,287
1993	16,000	5,252
1994	16,800	5,206
1995	17,500	5,166

SOURCE: AHA (1995).

state and local sources, private insurance payments, and patient payments (see Figure 4.2 and Table 4.3). In 1995, 3.8 million individuals—more than 40 percent of all patients served by CHCs—were uninsured. Medicaid patients accounted for more than one third (38 percent) of the patient visits to CHCs in 1995.

The number of patients served by CHCs almost doubled between 1980 and 1995 (5 million to 9.3 million) (NACHC, 1997). During the same time, the funding required to support increases in staffing levels did not keep pace, often resulting in long waits for appointments. Medicaid reimbursements for CHCs have been increasing, but the amount of grant funding provided to support innovative programs and offset the costs of uncompensated care has fallen off since 1990 (see Figure 4.3 and Table 4.4) (Hawkins and Rosenbaum, 1997).

The Balanced Budget Act of 1997 introduced provisions that will change the structure of Medicaid and make a significant impact on community health centers. Cost-based reimbursement was important to CHCs because CHC patients tend to have multiple problems and their treatment tends to be more expensive, and also because CHCs offer more expanded services than most commercial plans, including translation, case management, and other support services.

Originally, Medicaid had to reimburse 100 percent of the cost of serving Medicaid patients, although many Medicaid waivers changing the amount and structure of reimbursement were already in effect by the time the Balanced Budget Act was enacted. In 1997, Congress changed the cost-based reimbursement provisions for Federally Qualified Health Centers, including CHCs. It eliminated the minimum payment standards that states previously were required to meet in setting reimbursement rates for community health centers, as well as for hospitals and nursing homes (Schneider, 1997). By 2002, Medicaid agencies will be required to reimburse only 70 percent of CHC patient costs, and by 2003, this requirement will be completely phased out (Schneider, 1997).

In environments in which Medicaid is shifting to managed care, CHCs are seeking to be included in provider panels and networks that serve low-income individuals. Medicaid managed care is having other effects on CHCs as well. Through default enrollment mechanisms in state mandatory Medicaid managed care programs, individuals who do not go through a process of choosing a primary care provider are assigned providers automatically. If these individuals are unaware that their assigned provider is not the CHC and seek care there, Medicaid will not provide reimbursement for services provided by the center.

With such a competitive health care marketplace, it remains to be seen whether CHCs can be sustained by capturing an expanding share of Medicaid patients. The changes in Medicaid reimbursement, particularly the loss of cost-based reimbursement, reductions in federal grant support, and increases in the number of uninsured families seeking care will combine to produce significant and ongoing financial challenges.

CHILDREN'S HOSPITALS

Because they are philosophically committed to taking care of all children regardless of their parents' ability to pay for care, many children's hospitals are described as safety net providers. There are three primary types of children's hospitals:

- freestanding children's acute-care hospitals;
- nonfreestanding units such as a pediatrics department in a larger community hospital, a distinct children's center within an academic health center, or some other model; and
- freestanding children's specialty and rehabilitation hospitals.

The United States has approximately 45 freestanding acute care children's hospitals, 222 pediatrics programs at teaching hospitals, and about 20 freestanding specialty and rehabilitation hospitals for

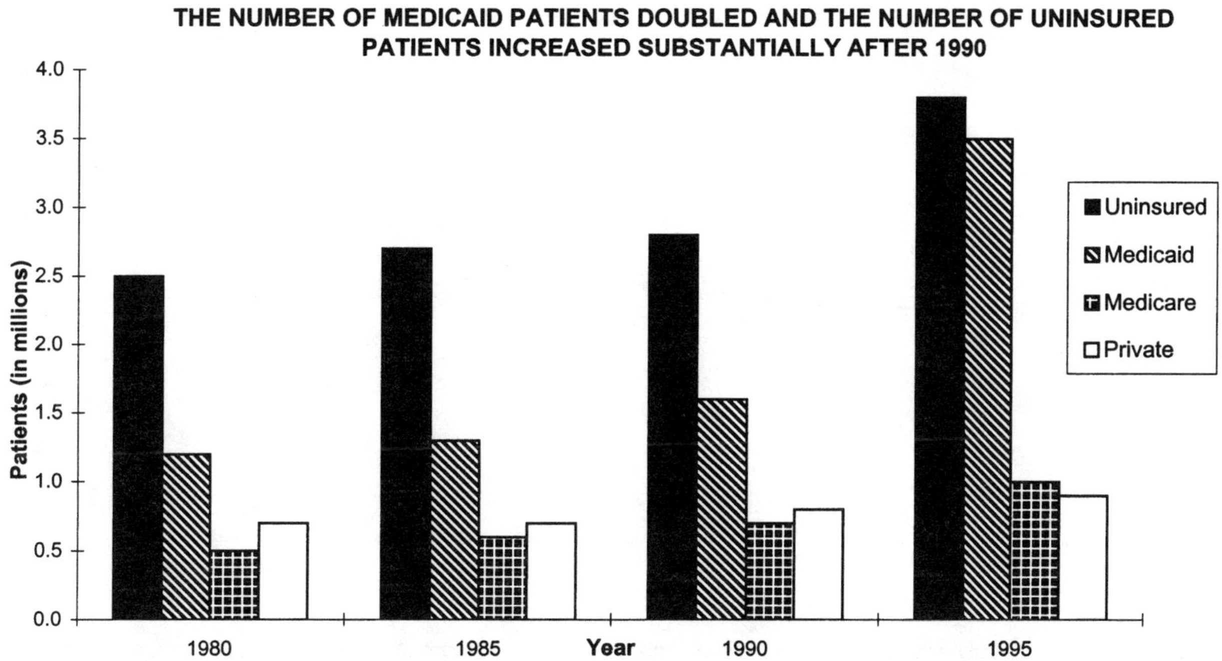

FIGURE 4.2 CHC patients by payer source, United States, selected years, 1980-1995. SOURCE: NACHC (1997).

TABLE 4.3 Insurance Status of CHC Patients, United States, Selected Years, 1980-1985

	Numbers of Patients (in millions)			
Insurance Status	1980	1985	1990	1995
Uninsured	2.5	2.7	2.8	3.8
Medicaid	1.2	1.3	1.6	3.5
Medicare	0.5	0.6	0.7	1.0
Private	0.7	0.7	0.8	0.9
Total	4,900,000	5,300,000	5,900,000	9,200,000

SOURCE: NACHC (1997).

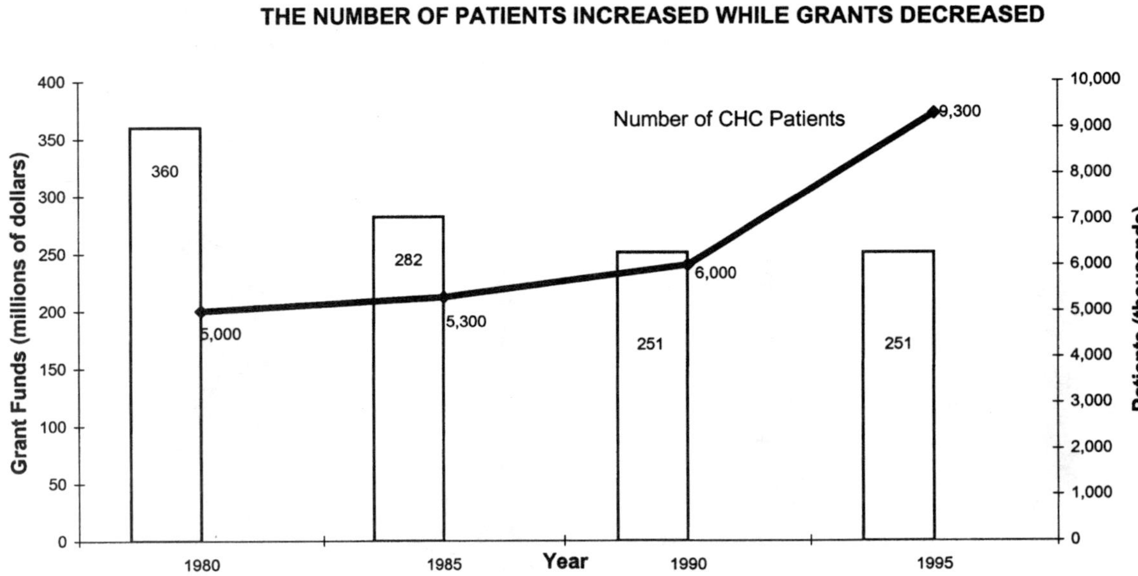

FIGURE 4.3 Community health center (CHC) federal grant funds and number of patients, United States, selected years, 1980-1995. SOURCE: NACHC (1997).

TABLE 4.4 Community Health Center (CHC) Federal Grant Funds and Number of Patients, United States, Selected Years, 1980-1995

Year	Grant Funds (in millions of dollars)	Patients (in thousands)
1980	360	5,000
1985	282	5,300
1990	251	6,000
1995	251	9,300

SOURCE: NACHC (1997).

children. Public financing, primarily through the Medicaid program, provides a higher proportion of revenues for the specialty and rehabilitation hospitals than for hospitals that provide acute care (Figure 4.4).

Most of the data in this section were collected by the National Association of Children's Hospitals and Related Institutions (NACHRI) and come from freestanding children's hospitals, which have their own administrative and financial reporting systems. (Data for pediatric patients from nonfreestanding units are not readily available.) Freestanding acute care children's hospitals make up only 1 percent of all hospitals in the United States, but they deliver 18 percent of inpatient days of care for children who need to be hospitalized. In 1993, they provided 3.2 million days of inpatient care at a cost of more than $7 billion, along with more than 8.3 million visits to outpatient clinics (Gage et al., 1995).

Because the developmental needs of children are better served by fewer overnight visits, outpatient and ambulatory visits are increasing as alternatives to inpatient care (Table 4.5). The increases in revenue for inpatient and outpatient care are comparable (Figure 4.5). The data also indicate that as the proportion of Medicaid patients is increasing, the proportion of uninsured patients is decreasing (Table 4.5).

Another trend for children's hospitals is the growth in regionalized pediatric medical specialty centers, or centers of excellence. Patients from a large metropolitan area, from a multi-state region, or from all over the country may be referred to these centers. A high percentage of the hospitalized children are those with chronic health problems and special health care needs such as cystic fibrosis, cerebral palsy, HIV infection, or other conditions. According to data from NACHRI, 70 to 80 percent of the hospitalizations for complex children's health conditions take place in children's hospitals or general hospitals with pediatric residency programs, which together make up only 5 percent of the total hospitals nationwide (Neff and Anderson, 1995).

PUBLIC HEALTH DEPARTMENTS

In 1989, in its report entitled *The Future of Public Health*, the Institute of Medicine (IOM) defined the mission of public health as "fulfilling society's interest in assuring conditions in which people can be healthy" (IOM, 1989, p. 7). The IOM report described the core responsibilities of public agencies as protecting the nation's health through the application of scientific and technical knowledge to prevent disease and to promote health. Public health agencies thus have responsibilities for the assessment, monitoring, and surveillance of health problems; for collecting information that can be used to direct resources to areas of need; and for designing and implementing programs that will improve the health of the public (IOM, 1989, 1997).

Title V of the Social Security Act, the maternal and child health block grant, ensures that in every state there is a unit that focuses on the health of women, children, and adolescents. Depending on your state or community, public health programs for children may be called maternal and child health, family health, or community health, but they are all involved in ensuring access to care. The dollars flow through local health departments, health centers, visiting nurses associations, school-based clinics, and other groups—whoever is out there in a community, we'll work with them.

Catherine Hess
National Association of Maternal and Child Health Programs, Washington, DC
Public Workshop, June 2, 1997

REHABILITATION HOSPITALS HAVE A HIGHER PROPORTION OF PUBLIC FUNDING

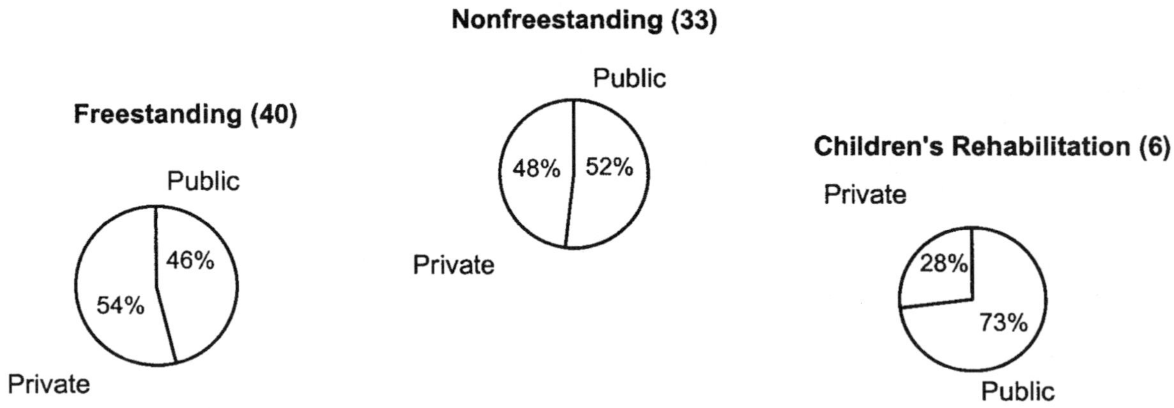

FIGURE 4.4 Percentage of revenues from public and private sources for children's hospitals, United States, 1995. Public sources include Medicaid and other state and local sources. Private includes insured and self-paying individuals. Data are based on survey responses from children's hospitals. SOURCE: NACHRI (1997).

HOSPITAL REVENUES HAVE INCREASED STEADILY SINCE 1991

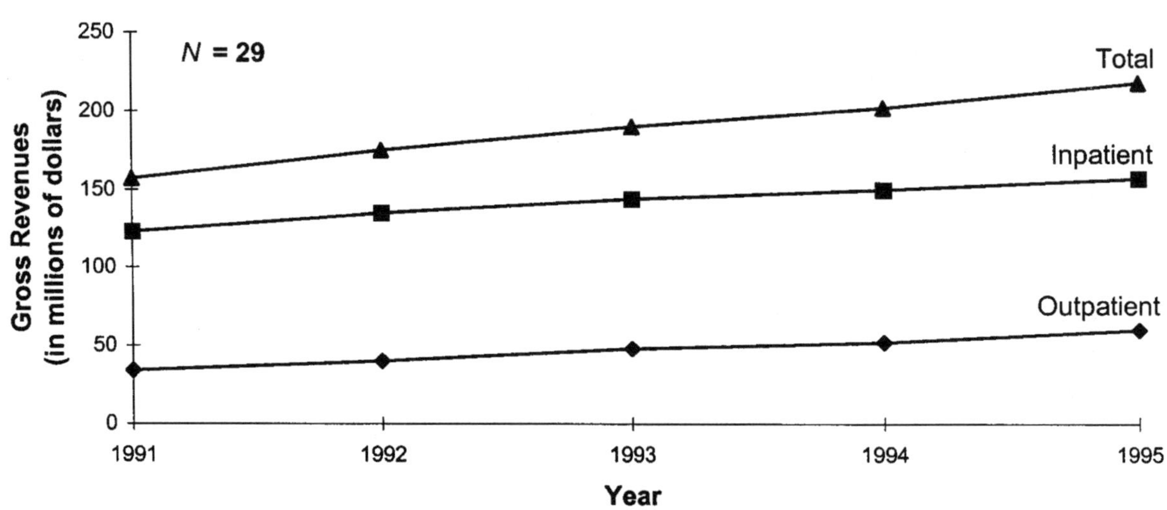

FIGURE 4.5 Average gross revenue per freestanding acute-care children's hospital, United States, 1991-1995. SOURCE: NACHRI (1997).

TABLE 4.5 Trends in Hospital Admissions, Length of Stay, and Percentage of Care Devoted to Low-Income Patients, Freestanding Children's Hospitals, United States, Selected Fiscal Years. 1990-1995

	Fiscal Year		
	1990	1993	1995
Total number of hospitals	50	50	50
Average length of stay (days)	6.6	6.4	5.5
Admissions			
Total no. of admissions	422,039	455,015	458,308
Average no. of admissions per hospital	8,441	9,100	9,166
Outpatient visits [a]			
Total no. of outpatient visits	5,769,724	7,424,988	7,841,756
Average no. of outpatient visits per hospital	115,394	148,500	156,835
Emergency room visits			
Total no. of emergency room visits	1,967,837	2,140,735	2,163,084
Average no. of emergency room visits per hospital	39,357	42,815	43,262
Low-income patient care			
Average percentage of care devoted to low-income[b] patients	40.3	46.7	47.2
Average percentage of care devoted to Medicaid patients	34.2	41.4	44.6
Average percentage of care devoted to uninsured patients	7.2	5.3	4.9

NOTE: Averages are based on data from 40 hospitals for all 3 years; totals are extrapolated to the industry.
[a]Outpatient visits include emergency room visits.
[b]Low-income patients include those with Medicaid, those who self-pay, and those who do not pay (bad debt).
SOURCE: NACHRI (1997). Data are from the NACHRI annual survey of the nation's 50 freestanding children's hospitals.

State and local health departments also form an integral part of the safety net. Using funding from a variety of sources, they provide a variety of services relevant for children's health: immunizations, well-child clinics, nutrition programs, Medicaid's Early and Periodic Screening, Diagnosis, and Treatment Program (EPSDT), school-based health clinics, and other services (see Figure 4.6 and Table 4.6).

There are health departments that do classic public health functions, but in many areas of the country they also deliver health services, some of which are funded by Medicaid, some by state dollars, some by Title V or grant dollars or Title XX. We don't have a system in this country: we have a series of funding streams with a lot of cracks.

Shelly Gehshan
National Conference of State Legislatures, Washington, D.C.
Public Workshop, June 2, 1997

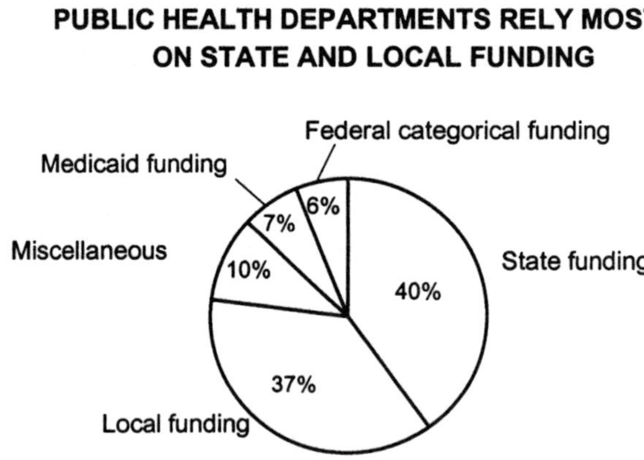

FIGURE 4.6 Sources and percentages of funding for local health departments, United States, 1992-1993. SOURCE: NACCHO, 1995.

TABLE 4.6 Percentage of City and County Health Departments Offering Selected Health Care Programs (*N* = 2,092), United States, 1992-1993

Program	Percentage of Health Departments with Specified Program
Immunizations	96
Well-child clinic services	79
Supplemental Nutrition Program for Women, Infants, and Children	78
EPSDT	72
Testing and counseling for sexually transmitted diseases	71
Family planning services	68
School-based health clinics	25

SOURCE: NACCHO (1995).

Efforts to analyze changes in the rates of utilization, in the characteristics of the populations served by health departments, and in the sources of financing are hampered by a lack of data. State and local health departments often have inadequate computer systems, and activities to develop reporting systems or performance measures are generally underfunded (IOM, 1989, 1997). Thus, health departments often cannot track patients within their own systems; for example, they may not be able to identify whether a patient has already been seen at a clinic in another location in the city or county.

Moreover, as for all safety net providers, continuity of care is often difficult to maintain because of the geographic mobility of these patients. It is not uncommon for low-income patients to move frequently and to have no telephone, so it may not be possible to send appointment reminders or to schedule follow-up visits.

Health departments face many challenges in their role as safety net providers. Although they play a large role in meeting the national health goals set out in *Healthy People 2000*, health departments continue to face cuts in funding. Many are shifting from the provision of direct services to contracting with managed care organizations in the hope of achieving cost savings (Lipson and Naierman, 1996). Other health departments are seeking to form networks with CHCs, public hospitals, and other traditional safety net providers so that they can continue to serve their traditional patient populations.

SCHOOL-BASED HEALTH CENTERS

During the 1995–1996 school year, more than 900 school-based health centers provided care to children and adolescents. According to a national survey, 65 percent of the centers delivered both primary and mental health care, with the remaining 35 percent providing primary care only (Making the Grade, 1997). Most centers have multidisciplinary teams of nurse practitioners, clinical social workers, physicians, and other health professionals working cooperatively with school nurses, athletic coaches, counselors, teachers, and school administrators to help the health center become an integral part of the school's activities.

School-based health centers operate in 43 states and the District of Columbia. Nationally, the majority (43 percent) are in the northeastern and mid-Atlantic states. The 10 states with the largest number of centers are New York, Florida, Texas, Connecticut, Pennsylvania, Maryland, California, Massachusetts, Michigan, and Arizona.

State governments are a primary source of financial support for these centers. In 1995–1996, 34 states allocated $41.9 million in state and federal block grant funds, which was an increase of 8 percent from 1994. The primary sources of these funds included Maternal and Child Health Block Grants and state categorical sources. Other sources of federal support are the Preventive Health Block Grant and funds provided through the Drug-Free Schools and Communities Act. Support also is provided through Medicaid, although that amount has not been tracked.

The centers are located in all types of schools. High schools are the primary sites, housing 41 percent of all centers; 32 percent are in elementary schools, and 17 percent are in middle schools. Studies have shown that the students who use school-based health centers are similar in gender, ethnicity, and age to the rest of the school population (McCord et al., 1993) although they are more likely to be uninsured (Kisker and Brown, 1996).

IMPLICATIONS

In a market-driven health care system, the impact of providing unreimbursed or partially reimbursed care is profound. No managed care organization will compete to care for uninsured individuals, and government subsidies to care for low-income and uninsured individuals are generally being reduced.

Uncompensated care costs are not generally broken down by age group, but the number of uninsured children has been increasing steadily for several years. With the new children's health insurance programs initiated through the Balanced Budget Act of 1997, states that increase their Medicaid eligibility thresholds and otherwise subsidize coverage for previously uninsured children can raise the rates of insurance coverage and thus reduce the burden of providing uncompensated care among safety net providers. However, in order for SCHIP funds to make significant reductions in the numbers of uninsured children, states must draw down all of the available funds, actively pursue effective outreach and enrollment strategies, and also minimize the risk of replacing existing private coverage.

Over the next several years, it will be important to measure the extent to which the new children's health insurance programs alleviate the pressure on other sources of funding for uncompensated care. Unless better data systems are developed, with more consistent age breakdowns, this will be extremely difficult to measure. Thus, the advent of the SCHIP program offers a unique opportunity to track and measure changes in the number of uninsured children and to assess the program's effectiveness from its onset. Lessons learned from the evaluation of the program will have important implications for the likelihood and nature of future insurance expansions.

The lack of consistent data also could limit the evaluation of changes in SCHIP funding in terms of their impact on safety net providers. Not all safety net providers will be able to make a successful transition to the competitive health care marketplace. Success may be based on the degree to which providers can offer and market strong primary care services, can compete for Medicaid managed care contracts, and can negotiate payment arrangements that not only cover their costs but also contribute to their financial health.

REFERENCES

AHA (American Hospital Association). 1995. *Annual Survey Data, 1980–1995*. Chicago: AHA.

Baxter RJ, Mechanic RE. 1997. The Status of Local Health Care Safety Nets. *Health Affairs* 16(4):7–23.

CDC (Centers for Disease Control and Prevention). 1997. *National Immunization Program*. Atlanta: CDC.

Coughlin TA, Liska D. 1997. *The Medicaid Disproportionate Share Hospital Payment Program: Background and Issues*. Washington, D.C.: Urban Institute. [http://newfederalism.urban.org/html/anf14.html]

Cunningham PJ, Ha TT. 1997. A Changing Picture of Uncompensated Care. *Health Affairs* 16(4):167–175.

Gage LS, Hawkins D, Willson PD, Finerfrock B. 1995. *America's Essential Providers: The Foundation of Our Nation's Health Systems*. Alexandria, VA: National Association of Children's Hospitals and Related Institutions.

Hawkins DR, Jr., Rosenbaum S. 1997. The Challenges Facing Health Centers in a Changing Healthcare System. In *The Future U.S. Healthcare System: Who Will Care for the Poor and Uninsured?* Edited by S. Altman, U. Reinhardt, and A. Shields. Chicago, IL: Health Administration Press.

Holahan J, Wiener JM, Liska D. 1997. *The Medicaid Reform Debate in 1997* Washington, D.C.: The Urban Institute. HRSA (Health Resources and Services Administration). [http://newfederalism.urban.org]

HRSA (Health Resources and Services Administration). 1997a. *Bureau of Primary Health Care in 1997*. [http://www.bphc.hrsa.dhhs.gov/bphc.map?112,190]

HRSA. 1997b. Data provided to the Institute of Medicine by the office of Larry Dickson, Maternal and Child Health Bureau. Personal Communication.

Institute of Medicine (IOM). 1989. *The Future of Public Health*. Washington D.C.: National Academy Press.

IOM. 1997. *Improving Health in the Community: A Role for Performance Monitoring*. Washington, D.C.: National Academy Press.

Kaiser Commission on the Future of Medicaid. 1997. *The Medicaid Program at a Glance*. Washington, D.C.: Kaiser Commission on the Future of Medicaid.

Kisker EE, Brown RS. 1996. Do School-Based Health Centers Improve Adolescents' Access to Health Care, Health Status, and Risk-taking Behavior? *Journal of Adolescent Health* 18:335–343.

Ku L, Coughlin TA. 1995. Medicaid Disproportionate Share and Other Special Financing Programs. *Health Care Financing Review* 16(3):27–54.

Lipson DJ, Naierman N. 1996. Effects of Health System Changes on Safety Net Providers. *Health Affairs* 15(2):33–48.

Making the Grade. 1997. *National Survey of State SBHC Initiatives, School Year 1995–96*. Washington, D.C.: The George Washington University.

McCord MT, Klein JD, Joy JM, Fothergill K. 1993. School-Based Clinic Use and School Performance. *Journal of Adolescent Health* 14:91–98.

NACHRI (National Association of Children's Hospitals and Related Institutions). 1997. *Annual Report on Utilization and Financial Indicators of Children's Hospitals*. Alexandria, VA: NACHRI.

NACHC (National Association of Community Health Centers). 1997. Data provided to the Institute of Medicine by the office of Dan Hawkins, NACHC, Washington, D.C.: NACHC.

NACCHO (National Association of County and City Health Officials). 1995. *1992–1993 National Profile of Local Health Departments*. Washington, D.C.: NACCHO.

Neff JM, Anderson G. 1995. Protecting Children with Chronic Illness in a Competitive Marketplace. *Journal of the American Medical Association* 274:1866–1869.

Prospective Payment Assessment Commission (ProPAC). 1997. *Report and Recommendations to the Congress, March 1, 1997*. Figure 1–5, p. 30. Washington, D.C.: ProPAC.

Schneider A. 1997. *Overview of Medicaid Provisions in the Balanced Budget Act of 1997, P. L. 105–33*. Washington, D.C.: Center for Budget and Policy Priorities [http://www.cbpp.org/908mcaid.htm]

Urban Institute. 1997. *The Medicaid Disproportionate Share Hospital Program: Background and Issues (no. 14)*. By Teresa A. Coughlin and David Liska. Washington, D.C.: Urban Institute.

U.S. House of Representatives, Committee on Ways and Means. 1996. *1996 Green Book*. Washington, D.C.: U.S. Government Printing Office.

5

Medicaid

Medicaid is the largest single health insurance program for American children. In 1997, more than 22 million children—one of every four children—were covered by Medicaid.

Although children in low-income families make up nearly half of all Medicaid beneficiaries, expenditures for children are less than 20 percent of total Medicaid spending (see Figure 5.1). In 1995, Medicaid spent an average of $1,175 per child, which is the lowest amount per person for any of the groups enrolled in the program (Kaiser Commission on the Future of Medicaid, 1997).

This chapter describes the Medicaid program in the context of its role in financing health care for low-income children. After a brief description of the history and scope of the program, recent trends in Medicaid spending and enrollment are described. Next, the chapter describes the program's impact on access to care. In summary, the chapter describes trends in the program as a result of managed care and recent federal legislation.

HISTORY AND OVERVIEW OF THE MEDICAID PROGRAM

The Medicaid program was created in 1965 as Title XIX of the Social Security Act. It was designed as a federal-state partnership to provide public funding for health care for low-income children and adults.

Specific Medicaid benefits for children were established in 1967, when Congress created the Early and Periodic Screening, Diagnostic, and Treatment (EPSDT) Program. The EPSDT program is a comprehensive package of children's medical, ancillary, and support services with an emphasis on regular screenings and preventive services. As discussed later in this chapter, the scope of EPSDT benefits is quite comprehensive compared to the scope of most commercial benefit packages.

In the mid-1980s, the Congress took several incremental legislative steps to expand Medicaid eligibility, first as state options and then as state mandates (see Box 5.1). The number of children enrolled in Medicaid nearly doubled in 10 years, rising from 10 million in 1987 to 18 million in 1995 (see Figure 5.2). The increase was substantial after 1989, when coverage was mandated for all children under age 5 years whose families had incomes up to 133 percent of the federal poverty level, and 1990, when all children under poverty up to age 19 began to be phased in.

In 1989, Congress also began to require states to provide any medically necessary treatment that was indicated through an EPSDT screen, whether or not that service is included in the state's Medicaid plan. Combined with the increase in Medicaid enrollment, this offset the simultaneous decreases in children's

CHILDREN MAKE UP HALF OF THE MEDICAID BENEFICIARIES AND ONE FIFTH OF THE COSTS

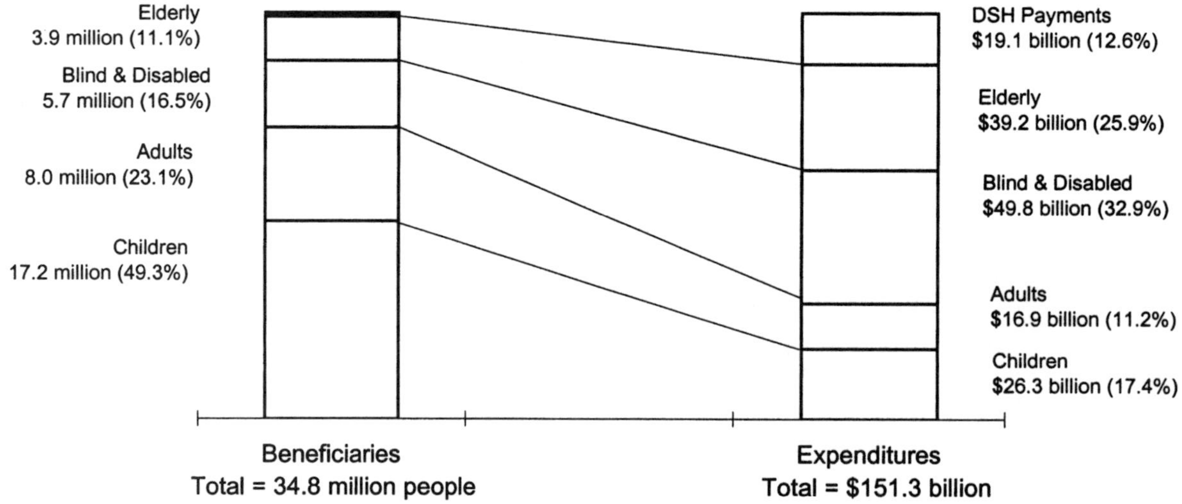

FIGURE 5.1 Medicaid beneficiaries and expenditures, by enrollment group, United States, 1995. Total expenditures exclude administrative expenses. Children are dependent children ages 0-21 years. SOURCE: Kaiser Commission on the Future of Medicaid, 1997. Data are from the Urban Institute analysis of the HCFA 2082 and 64 Statistical Reports.

CHILDREN'S MEDICAID EXPANSIONS RESULTED IN INCREASED ENROLLMENT

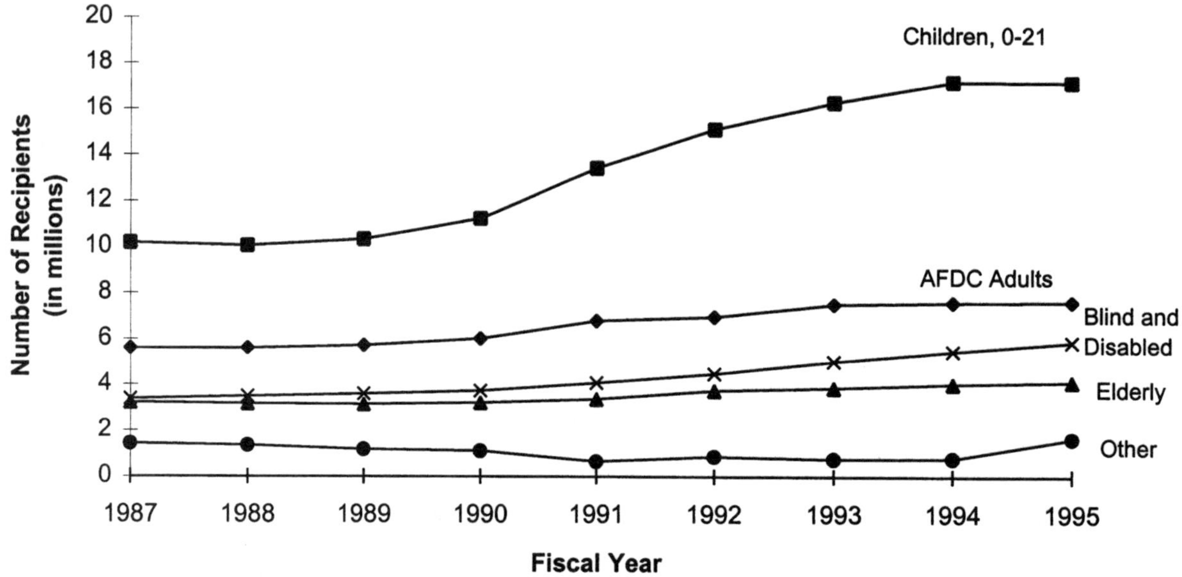

FIGURE 5.2 Trends in the number of Medicaid recipients, by enrollment group, United States, 1987-1995. AFDC = Aid to Families with Dependent Children. SOURCE: HCFA (1997b). Data were provided by the Division of Information Distribution and were derived from the HCFA 2082 Statistical Report on Medical Care: Eligibles, Recipients, Payments, and Services.

coverage through private sources, lowered the number of children without insurance, and significantly reduced the disparities in access to health care for poor children.

However, the increase in enrollment began to alarm governors and state legislatures, who were concerned about the rate of Medicaid cost increases as a proportion of state budgets (see Figure 5.3). In the late 1980s, the number of children enrolled in Medicaid was increasing at the same time that health care costs were rising across the country (see Figures 5.4 and 5.5). Because of the growth in Medicaid as a percentage of state expenditures, most states turned to some form of managed care to control Medicaid costs.

Medicaid represents an average of 20 percent of state budgets, and state officials and policymakers are continuing to experiment with ways to achieve cost savings. Some state policymakers are concerned about the costs of expanding the eligibility for entitlement to Medicaid, whereas 26 other states have expanded their Medicaid programs beyond the minimum federal requirements with a goal of improving access to care for low-income individuals (Gauthier and Schrodel, 1997).

By 1997, Medicaid cost increases seemed to have leveled off, in part because of the shift to Medicaid managed care, and also because of declining welfare enrollment due to welfare reform and the growth in the nation's economy. However, children's enrollment in Medicaid is expected to continue to increase through 2002, when phased-in coverage for older children is complete, and as some states choose to use Medicaid to cover groups of previously uninsured children under the State Children's Health Insurance Program (SCHIP) of the Balanced Budget Act of 1997.

Currently, the Medicaid program comprises 13 percent of all health care spending in this country. Medicaid expenditures totaled $157 billion in 1995: $90 billion from federal funds and $67 billion from state matching funds (GAO, 1997a). During fiscal year 1998, states will spend about $27 billion to purchase health care coverage for children through their Medicaid programs (Mann, 1997). As large-scale purchasers of managed care, states have an increasing ability to negotiate reasonable rates and control costs while increasing access to care.

When we think of Medicaid, we should not be thinking about the Medicaid program of 15 years ago. We should be thinking about the new emphasis in the program on managed care, on primary care, on prevention, and on predictable capitated costs for care. States have been increasingly willing to use their Medicaid programs for children's coverage because the move to managed care gives them more predictable costs per child. So they are putting children into systems of care where preventive and primary care are available.

Diane Rowland
The Kaiser Commission on the Future of Medicaid, Washington, DC
Public Workshop, June 2, 1997

ELIGIBILITY

The Medicaid program is a federal-state partnership with funding and administrative responsibilities shared by the federal government and state governments. It has both mandatory and optional categories of eligibility and services. Mandatory eligibility and service requirements apply in every state, whereas the states have the flexibility of choosing among optional categories at their own programmatic and financial discretion. In essence, the Medicaid program is different in every state.

Eligibility for Medicaid is mandatory for the following groups:

BOX 5.1
A Brief History of Medicaid Legislation Concerning Children

1965	The Social Security Act of 1965, Title XIX, authorizes Medicaid, a federal-state matching entitlement program, to provide medical assistance for low-income families with dependent children and low-income aged, blind, or disabled individuals.
1967	Congress creates the Early and Periodic Screening, Diagnosis, and Treatment (EPSDT) Program to ensure that all Medicaid-eligible children under age 21 receive appropriate comprehensive, periodic health assessments and follow-up treatments for detected illnesses.
1981	The Omnibus Budget Reconciliation Act (OBRA) of 1981 removes limits on the number of state waivers granted under Medicaid.
1986	OBRA of 1986 gives states the option of covering pregnant women and children with incomes up to the federal poverty level, regardless of the state's Aid to Families with Dependent Children (AFDC) eligibility guidelines. Thus, Medicaid is delinked from AFDC, and more pregnant women and children become eligible for Medicaid, particularly in southern and western states.
1987	OBRA of 1987 gives states the option of covering children through age 7 who live in families with incomes below 100 percent of the federal poverty level.
1988	The Medicare Catastrophic Coverage Act of 1988 mandates a phased-in Medicaid eligibility for pregnant women and infants in families with incomes below 100 percent of the federal poverty level.
1989	OBRA of 1989 mandates Medicaid eligibility for all pregnant women and children ages 0 to 5, in families with incomes up to 133 percent of the federal poverty level.
	The law requires that states provide any medically necessary treatment called for through an EPSDT program screening, whether or not that treatment service is included in the state's Medicaid plan. Most governors are opposed to this new provision because of its budgetary implications.
	The EPSDT program is strengthened: states must establish separate schedules for health, vision, and dental screenings, and states are required to increase participation in screening and diagnosis to 80 percent for children enrolled in the Medicaid program.

- Children under the age of 6 years whose families have incomes up to 133 percent of the federal poverty level.
- Older children up to 19 years of age who were born after September 30, 1983, and who live in families with incomes at or below the federal poverty level.
- Children who receive adoption assistance or foster care.
- Pregnant women whose incomes are up to 133 percent of the federal poverty level.
- Infants born to Medicaid-eligible pregnant women.
- Children who receive federal Supplemental Security Income (SSI).
- Children in families that meet the AFDC criteria in place prior to welfare reform.

1990 OBRA of 1990 requires states to cover all children under age 19, who were born after September 30, 1983, and who live in families with incomes below 100 percent of the federal poverty level.

1991 Medicaid Voluntary Contribution and Provider-Specific Tax Amendments of 1991 cap the federal Medicaid payments to states for spending from provider-related donations or health care taxes (the greater of 25 percent or the total amount collected in taxes for the next year).

Disproportionate Share Hospital (DSH) payments are capped at 12 percent for the national total.

1993 OBRA of 1993 allows children who are covered by Medicaid to also be covered by private insurance carried by a noncustodial parent. The law mandates that states have laws in place to require the cooperation of employers and insurers in obtaining parental coverage.

States may not designate a hospital as a DSH unless the hospital shows that Medicaid beneficiaries account for 1 percent or greater of its inpatient hospital days. Also, DSH payments may not exceed the hospital's Medicaid and uninsured patient costs combined.

1996 The Personal Responsibility and Work Opportunity Reconciliation Act of 1996 replaces AFDC with Temporary Assistance for Needy Families (TANF), and at the same time delinks Medicaid enrollment from the cash assistance program. States are now permitted to use more liberal income and resource standards to determine Medicaid eligibility.

1997 The Balanced Budget Act of 1997 (BBA) includes the largest reductions in federal Medicaid spending since 1981. The largest source of cost savings is new limitations on federal matching payments to states for reimbursements to DSH hospitals. State-specific allotment limits are also reduced.

BBA also allocates about $20 billion in federal matching grants over 5 years for states to expand health insurance coverage to uninsured children who are not eligible for Medicaid, along with about $4 billion for Medicaid improvements. Amendments to Title XXI of the Social Security Act create the State Children's Health Insurance Program (see Box 1.1 for details).

SOURCES: U.S. House of Representatives (1996); NIHCM (1996); HCFA (1996, 1997b); Balanced Budget Act of 1997 (P.L. 105-33); Schnieder (1997).

States have the option of expanding Medicaid coverage to pregnant women and children beyond the minimum federal requirements. In 1997, 26 states had expanded Medicaid eligibility for children by increasing the age criteria, the income criteria, or both (Gauthier and Schrodel, 1997). Under SCHIP, several states will implement further expansions of eligibility.

Medicaid has had strict eligibility requirements on the basis of income, and this has been a problem for families whose income levels fluctuate. Parents who have seasonal work, parents who work in service industries where there is rapid turnover, and parents who are between jobs may not be able to predict their levels of monthly income and may move in and out of eligibility if they are close to the income limits set in their state.

Medicaid administrative systems typically lack the capacity to follow these children and families at

MEDICAID SPENDING AS A PORTION OF STATE BUDGETS NEARLY DOUBLED IN 10 YEARS

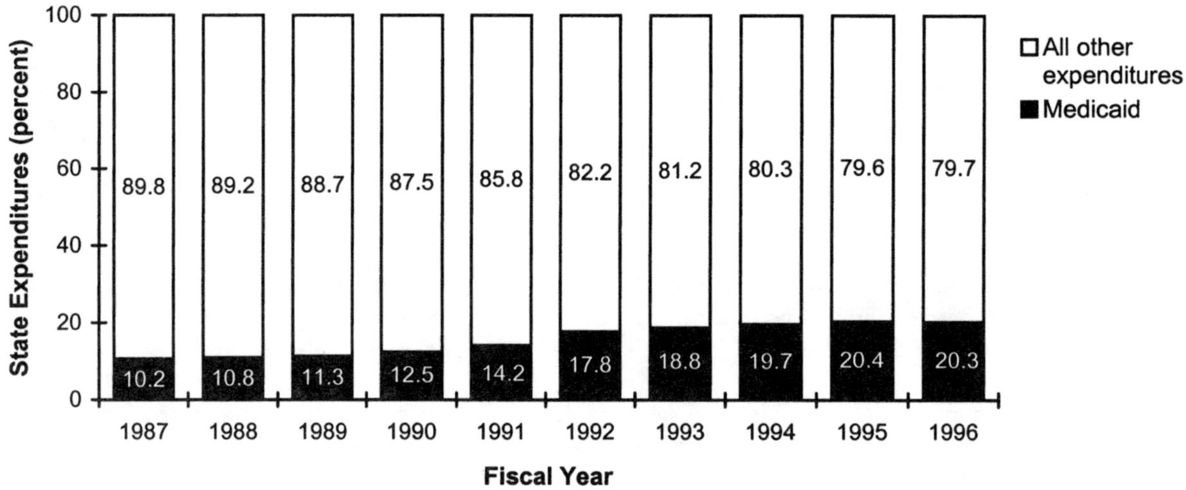

FIGURE 5.3 State Medicaid expenditures as a percentage of total state expenditures, by fiscal year, United States, 1987-1996. SOURCE: NASBO (1997). Data are from NASBO 1989-1997 State Expenditure Reports.

the margins of eligibility. Additionally, many state Medicaid directors believe that their reporting and billing systems not only impose substantial administrative burdens on states, but also fail to provide useful information on utilization and services for planning purposes.

The level of administrative complexity has varied among the states, and some states have been changing the administrative structures of their Medicaid programs. In recent years, a number of states have simplified their enrollment forms, improved their outreach efforts, improved their provider billing and payment procedures, and moved into managed care and capitated payment systems.

> Family income may fluctuate seasonally, particularly for those below 150 percent of the Federal Poverty Level. It may fluctuate on the basis of periods of employment and unemployment. If families are going to be in Medicaid this month, and they are going to get the premium subsidy next month, but they are not going to qualify for anything in the third month, are we really looking at policies that will help families get coverage for their children that is meaningful on a continuous and ongoing basis?
>
> *Kay Johnson*
> *George Washington University, Washington, DC*
> *Public Workshop, June 2, 1997*

ACCESS TO CARE

Eligibility and Enrollment

With Medicaid eligibility no longer linked to eligibility for welfare, some states are trying to improve enrollment by reducing the traditional embarrassment some people feel about being associated with

ENROLLMENT AND COSTS PER CHILD INCREASED AT THE SAME TIME

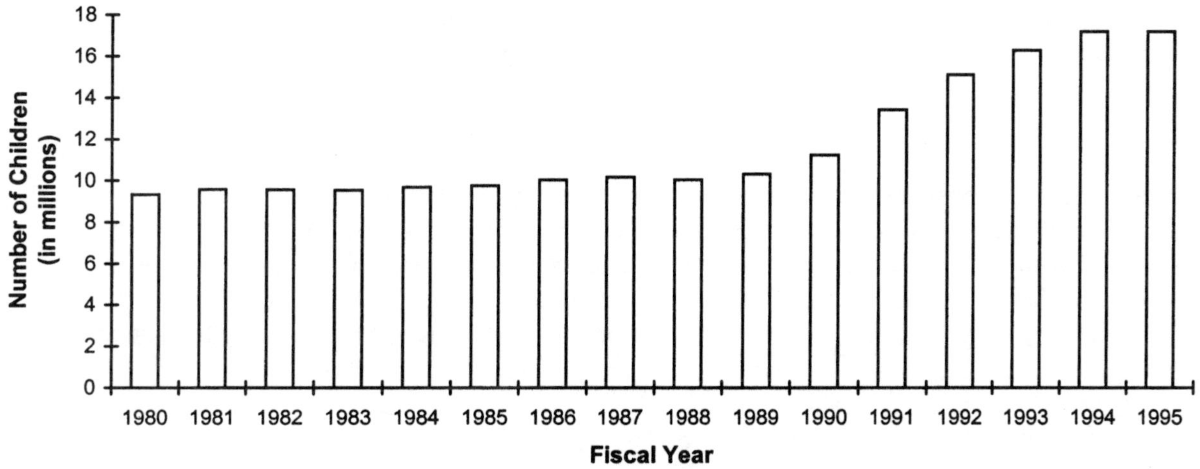

FIGURE 5.4 Trends in the number of dependent children ages 0-21 years receiving Medicaid, United States, 1980-1995. SOURCE: HCFA (1997b). Data were provided by the Division of Information Distribution and were derived from the HCFA 2082 Statistical Report on Medical Care: Eligibles, Recipients, Payments and Services.

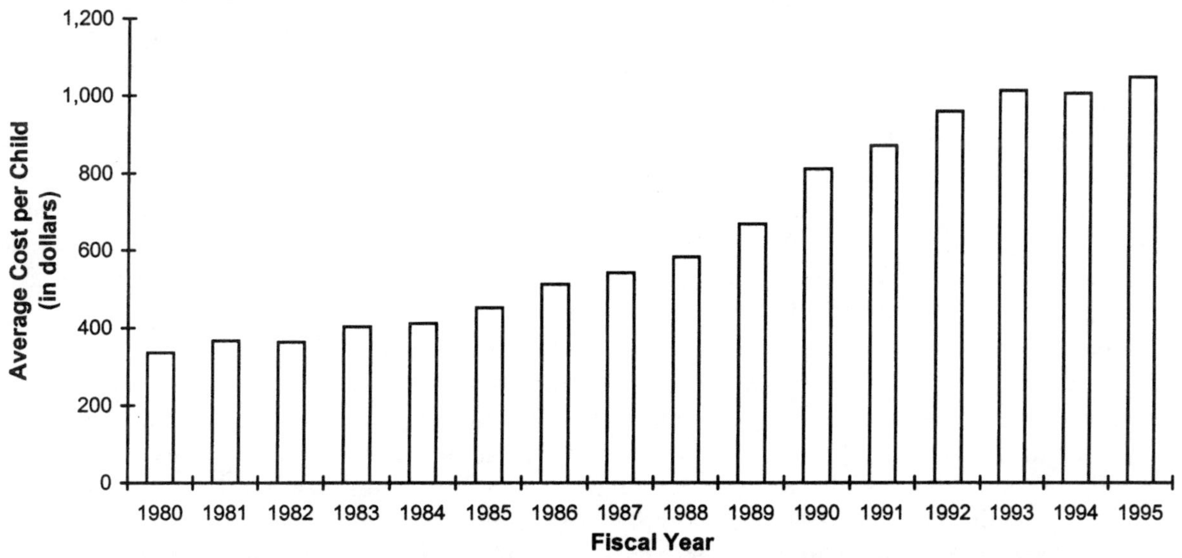

FIGURE 5.5 Trends in the average annual cost per dependent child receiving Medicaid, United States, 1980-1995. SOURCE: HCFA (1997b). Data were provided by the Division of Information Distribution and were derived from the HCFA 2082 Statistical Report on Medical Care: Eligibles, Recipients, Payments and Services.

welfare, such as by changing the name of the Medicaid program (e.g., Dr. Dynasaur in Vermont). The SCHIP program will pay a limited amount for outreach activities and also includes a "presumptive eligibility" option that will allow states to immediately enroll Medicaid-eligible children in the program, pending the results of the determination process. In the course of implementing new programs, states are adopting easier application processes, such as mail-in or telephone applications, which may help to enroll more eligible children.

In Somerville, Massachusetts, they required every child coming into the school not only to show their immunization record, but to document whether or not they had either Medicaid or private coverage. They were then able to enroll a whole host of kids who were eligible for Medicaid and who had not been enrolled, but who were legally entitled.

James Bentley
American Hospital Association, Washington, DC
Public Workshop, June 2, 1997

Historically, Medicaid eligibility was tied to eligibility for cash payments under welfare. For the Aid to Families with Dependent Children (AFDC) program, states set the financial standards for eligibility. Enrollment in the Medicaid program involved the rigorous, inconvenient, and often complex or burdensome administrative procedures of qualifying for welfare. Lengthy applications requiring documentation of income and assets, limited hours and locations for the submission of applications, and other challenges made it difficult to enroll in the program.

Although many states have been developing innovative outreach and enrollment strategies, millions of children who are eligible for Medicaid are not enrolled in the program. Estimates of the numbers of these children range from 2 million (Holahan, 1997) to 3.5 million, or 30 percent of uninsured children ages 0–11 (GAO, 1996). About 80 percent of these eligible children have a working parent, and parents who work and who are not themselves eligible for cash assistance are less likely to enroll their children in Medicaid (GAO, 1996; Summer et al., 1997).

Eligible children may not be enrolled for a variety of reasons. Some working parents are likely to be unaware of the program or unable to leave work to go through an enrollment process. Other parents do not trust the health care system for cultural, racial, ethnic, or other reasons; some find the application process difficult; and some do not want to participate in a program that has traditionally been associated with welfare. Other parents' applications have been denied for procedural reasons other than the lack of eligibility, such as the lack of written documentation of income.

Targeted outreach efforts, culturally sensitive public information campaigns, simpler enrollment procedures, and strategies that distinguish the program from welfare are a few ways for improving the rate of enrollment. Outreach and public education efforts will need to include providers, to allow them to become familiar with program changes and to recruit them to participate.

Provider Participation

Medicaid has no premiums and permits only nominal cost-sharing for its enrollees. However, even when children have Medicaid coverage, providers may not be available to see them. A disproportionate number of low-income children and children who are members of racial and ethnic minorities live in areas where there are shortages of medical providers. Even when providers are locally available, there may be few who accept Medicaid payments, and those few may be too busy to accept appointments.

On average, Medicaid payment rates have been about 40 percent lower than the rates paid by private insurers (ProPAC, 1992). A substantial number of providers have limited their participation or have not participated at all because of the lower reimbursement levels. Some safety net providers and health care systems argue that they have already absorbed as many Medicaid patients as they can without disturbing the balance of payments from other sources.

Movement of Medicaid enrollees into managed care may begin to increase provider participation and availability. As health plans begin to compete for market share by enrolling Medicaid beneficiaries into capitated programs and as more providers become part of Medicaid managed care plans or networks, more providers will be available to see Medicaid patients. However, unless managed care plans also address nonfinancial barriers, such as transportation, language translation, and child care services, access may continue to be difficult for Medicaid enrollees (Lipson, 1997).

The reduction of Disproportionate Share Hospitals (DSH) funding in the Balanced Budget Act of 1997 could have an independent impact on hospitals that serve relatively large numbers of Medicaid and uninsured patients. Congress capped DSH payments at 12 percent of Medicaid program expenditures in 1991. In the Balanced Budget Act of 1997, future federal DSH funding was reduced by a projected $10 billion.

DSH funds were intended to offset the costs to providers who served a disproportionate share of low-income and uninsured individuals. However, some states used the DSH funding to substitute for other state expenditures through intergovernmental transfers and other methods (Holahan et al., 1997). Only about two-thirds of the funding reached safety net hospitals (Coughlin and Liska, 1997).

The impact of changes in DSH are already visible as safety net providers react to Medicaid managed care and market pressures by trying to become more competitive (Baxter and Mechanic, 1997). Some health plans that are new to the Medicaid market have underestimated the need for expanded services such as case management, language translation, and outreach efforts that are traditionally handled by safety net providers. Thus, they have sought partnerships with community-based providers who know the Medicaid populations and are experienced in providing expanded services. Some community-based providers are entering into partnerships with Medicaid-contracting health plans, and others are developing their own managed care plans (Lipson, 1997).

Why do states expand their Medicaid programs? They expand them to poor kids because they know that health insurance matters. It is clear from the Medicaid experience that differentials in access to care between children with Medicaid and children who are uninsured have been markedly changed, in that private patients and Medicaid patients access the health care system in very comparable ways. The uninsured are still lagging considerably behind.

Diane Rowland
Kaiser Commission on the Future of Medicaid, Washington, DC
Public Workshop, June 2, 1997

Accountability for Access to Care

Some studies have shown that children with Medicaid coverage have access to health care comparable to that for children who are privately insured (Overpeck and Kotch, 1995; St. Peter et al., 1992). However, access to care varies significantly from community to community (Baxter and Mechanic, 1997), making it difficult to generalize from these studies. Moreover, many studies of low-income populations are not able to separate out the related effects of income, lack of insurance, generally poorer health status, and exposure to other public health risks, such as poor nutrition or unsafe neighborhoods.

At the state level, accountability for access tends to focus on adherence to eligibility criteria, allowing access only for those who are eligible to enroll in the program. After 30 years of the Medicaid program and at least 10 years of more standardized national data on enrollment and expenditures, the infrastructure of information that can be used to evaluate the impact of the program is fragmented and incomplete. Under a fee-for-service system, it was possible to track utilization through billing information. Under managed care, individual encounter data are needed to determine utilization patterns, but states either may not have access to the data from health plans or may lack the technical capacity to analyze the data (Howell, 1996; GAO, 1997b). Because of these technical problems, information on access under managed care will continue to be difficult to evaluate.

Maybe we need private health insurance reform. I'm not saying that we don't. What I'm saying is that Medicaid is a rationing program. Everybody familiar with it knows it is a rationing program. What happens with government-provided health care in all of the developed countries is that they do a very good job of providing inexpensive services, and they skimp on what is expensive. They skimp on heart surgery, the CAT scans—on all of the life-saving technology. For the future, that is exactly what is going to happen to Medicaid and to Medicare. You can see it right now in the budget. Congress wants to cut down on payments to hospitals and doctors, which means they are going to skimp on care for the expensive, sick patients. I don't see any way around that. As a matter of public policy, maybe we are going to have to create global budgets for poor people, but give those poor people an opportunity to get into a better system.

John Goodman
National Center for Policy Analysis, Dallas, TX
Public Workshop, June 2, 1997

SCOPE OF SERVICES

As a condition for receiving federal Medicaid matching funds, Medicaid coverage and services must be in effect statewide and must be comparable for everyone within a particular eligibility group. The following services must be provided for individuals who are enrolled in Medicaid (also see Box 5.2):

- inpatient and outpatient hospital services,
- physician services,
- medical and surgical dental services,
- nursing facility services for individuals ages 21 years and older,
- home health care for people eligible for nursing home services,
- family planning services and supplies,
- rural and federally qualified health clinic services,
- laboratory and X-ray services,
- pediatric and family nurse practitioner services, and
- nurse midwife services.

Although the federal law requires these services to be provided, states have had discretion and a substantial degree of control over the amount, scope, and duration of each service.

BOX 5.2
Medicaid Services

Mandatory Services

Inpatient hospital
Outpatient hospital
Rural health clinic
Laboratory and x-ray services
Nurse practitioners' services
Nursing facility services
Home health services
EPSDT program services
Family planning services and supplies
Physicians' services
Nurse-midwife services
Dental (medical/surgical)
Transportation, medical

Optional Services

Podiatrists' services
Optometrists' services
Chiropractors' services
Private duty nursing
Clinic services
Dental services
Physical therapy
Occupational therapy
Speech, hearing, and language disorders
Prescription drugs
Dentures
Prosthetic devices
Eyeglasses
Nurse anesthetist service
Psychologists' services
Medical social worker services
Telemedicine
Diagnostic services
Screening services
Preventative services
Rehabilitative services
Inpatient hospital services
Nursing facility services
ICF-MR services
Inpatient psychiatric services
Christian Science nurses
Christian Science sanitariums
Nursing facility services
Emergency hospital services
Personal care services
Transportation services
Case management services
Hospice care services
Respiratory care services
Tuberculosis-related services

SOURCE: Adapted from Figure 64 of HCFA (1996).

Scope of Benefits

Comprehensive benefits (the EPSDT program) for children enrolled in Medicaid have been in place for several years. These benefits are mandatory for all eligible children, although their provision is not always enforced and the specified benefits are not always available when they are needed.

So, although the intended scope of Medicaid benefits has been comprehensive, children have not always received treatment that was regarded as medically necessary when required by law. For example, if a child were determined by a physician to need an organ transplant, but lived in a state that does not cover the procedure under Medicaid, the parents could face a choice of foregoing the procedure, raising the funds independently, such as through charity donations, or incurring enormous financial costs.

> Obviously it would be easier if states had more flexibility. On the other hand, if we don't have any regulatory guidelines, I'm afraid we'll see no preventive care, and parents being offered packages that are cheap and that don't cover very much except catastrophic care. If we are going to look after children, we need to look after all of their health care needs. We should define a comprehensive package pretty close to the EPSDT package and include children with multiple problems and serious illness. The cost is minuscule if you spread it over the whole society.
>
> *Steve Edwards*
> *American Academy of Pediatrics, Raleigh, NC*
> *Public Workshop, June 2, 1997*

Early and Periodic Screening, Diagnosis and Treatment Program

Medicaid-eligible children up to the age of 21 are ensured participation in the EPSDT program (see Box 5.3 for a description of EPSDT program services). The EPSDT program was enacted by the U.S. Congress in 1967 and was designed to provide children with comprehensive and periodic physical and mental health assessments as well as to diagnose and treat any problems discovered in the course of routine screenings.

The EPSDT program is unique among programs that provide children's health care benefits. First, it sets a standard of comprehensive care for all enrolled children. Second, the EPSDT program emphasizes age-appropriate preventive strategies and not simply the treatment of acute illnesses and injuries. Third, the EPSDT benefit package was intended to address the needs of chronically and congenitally ill children, including those who need to improve their age-appropriate functioning as well as those who have congenital conditions, need to maintain their limited functional capacity, but who are not expected to improve. In this way, the EPSDT benefit package is significantly different from most commercial benefit packages, which typically provide treatments for illnesses and injuries and coverage for physical, occupational, and speech therapy on a limited and temporary basis to restore lost functioning for acute conditions.

Because responsibilities for the Medicaid program are split across federal, state and local boundaries, information about how many children are receiving EPSDT program services, where they receive them, and the quality of those services is largely inadequate. Another problem discussed at the committee's public workshop is that the screening and diagnostic components of the EPSDT program are provided more frequently than are the treatment components, particularly when the treatment that is considered "medically necessary" is not included among the state's list of allowable expenses (e.g., organ transplants).

BOX 5.3
EPSDT Health Services Requirements

The Early and Periodic Screening, Diagnosis and Treatment Program (EPSDT) requires states to provide or arrange for the following health services to all Medicaid-eligible children under the age of 21:

1. Comprehensive, periodic health assessments, or screenings, from birth through age 20, according to medically appropriate periodicity schedules. The medical screen must include:

- a comprehensive health and developmental history, including assessment of physical and mental health development;
- a comprehensive unclothed physical exam;
- immunizations in accordance with the Advisory Committee on Immunization Practices' schedule (AAP, 1993);
- laboratory tests, including blood lead level assessment; and
- health education, including anticipatory guidance.

2. Interperiodic screens to be provided if there is reason to suspect a health problem between regularly scheduled screenings.
3. Comprehensive preventive, restorative and emergency dental services furnished according to state-defined periodicity schedules;
4. Periodic hearing examinations, according to medically appropriate timetables, and all follow-up services, including hearing aids;
5. Periodic vision examinations, according to medically appropriate timetables, and all follow-up services, including eyeglasses; and
6. Any "medically necessary" diagnostic and treatment services for illnesses or conditions identified during screening. Covered services include all mandatory and optional services available under Medicaid, whether or not an individual state chooses to offer the service to its general Medicaid population.

SOURCE: Adapted from box on page 3, NIHCM, 1996.

If state contracts fail to specify the range of interventions and services that should be provided for Medicaid enrollees, health plans may not actually provide all of the required benefits for children covered by Medicaid (Fox and McManus, 1996; Rosenbaum et al., 1997). A 1997 study by the Inspector General of the U.S. Department of Health and Human Services found that only 28 percent of the children enrolled in Medicaid managed care received all of the EPSDT program screens called for in their state, and 60 percent of the children in the study received none of the services called for in their states' periodicity schedules (DHHS, 1997a).

There is a great deal of evidence to support the fact that over the past 30 years the children's health benefits package under Medicaid has become the richest children's health benefit package. I don't know of a private insurance package that provides the degree of comprehensive coverage that you get under EPSDT.

Kay Johnson
George Washington University, Washington, DC
Public Workshop, June 2, 1997

These figures are not much different from the findings of a 1992 Health Care Financing Administration (HCFA) study, when Medicaid was still predominantly a fee-for-service system. HCFA found that only about 36 percent of the eligible children were reportedly receiving the EPSDT program screens, although the actual numbers may have been higher because providers may not have been accurately coding encounters as EPSDT program screens (Koppelman, 1993).

In addition to covering the costs of EPSDT program services, states are required to provide outreach and education services to inform families of Medicaid-eligible children about services and to assist them in obtaining those services (NIHCM, 1996). These services are typically not provided by health care plans, and as more states move toward managed care, some groups are concerned that children may not get the comprehensive services included in the EPSDT program.

MEDICAID MANAGED CARE

The number of Medicaid beneficiaries enrolled in managed care plans increased fourfold between 1991 and 1996 (see Figure 5.6 and Table 5.1). Much of the increase was due to the granting of Medicaid waivers. The 1115 and the 1915 (b) and (c) waivers allowed states to limit Medicaid recipients to particular provider groups, thereby making it possible for them to contract with managed care plans.

As of September 1997, every state except Alaska and New Hampshire had acquired a waiver to begin managed care programs for Medicaid beneficiaries (Epstein, 1997; Zuckerman et al., 1997). More than one third of the nation's Medicaid beneficiaries were enrolled in some form of managed care program as of June 1996. The vast majority of these enrollees were children and single parents, who are generally more easily enrolled in health plans than aged, blind, or disabled Medicaid beneficiaries.

This national shift to managed care has had a tremendous impact on the nature of the program and has significantly changed the role of state Medicaid agencies. A turning point was reached in the early 1990s as states increasingly began to move their Medicaid programs into managed care in search of cost savings, but also to increase access to preventive services. Under a fee-for-service system, the traditional role of state Medicaid agencies was to provide oversight of financial performance and monitoring of providers for overutilization. In the market-driven systems of managed care, the Medicaid agencies' roles have been transformed. Billions of public dollars are being paid prospectively to managed care plans, raising issues of accountability and public trust.

As large-scale buyers of private managed health care coverage, Medicaid agencies are now challenged to use the bargaining skills of other large purchasers in order to negotiate reasonable rates while protecting enrollees. States must be able to develop specific contract language, define the scope of services within existing resources, and establish performance measures for health plans that assure access and quality of care (Landon et al., 1998; Rosenbaum et al., 1997).

There is really a shift from thinking of Medicaid as a welfare program, to thinking of it as a purchaser and a payer of services. The further along that road we get, the better we are going to do for our kids.

Shelly Gehshan
National Conference of State Legislatures, Washington, D.C.
Public Workshop, June 2, 1997

Under fee-for-service arrangements, Medicaid was a financing stream and a mechanism for reimbursing providers for services. Under Medicaid managed care, state Medicaid administrators are purchasing comprehensive, integrated delivery systems for the first time. This shift to managed care gives them

MEDICAID MANAGED CARE ENROLLMENT QUADRUPLED IN 5 YEARS

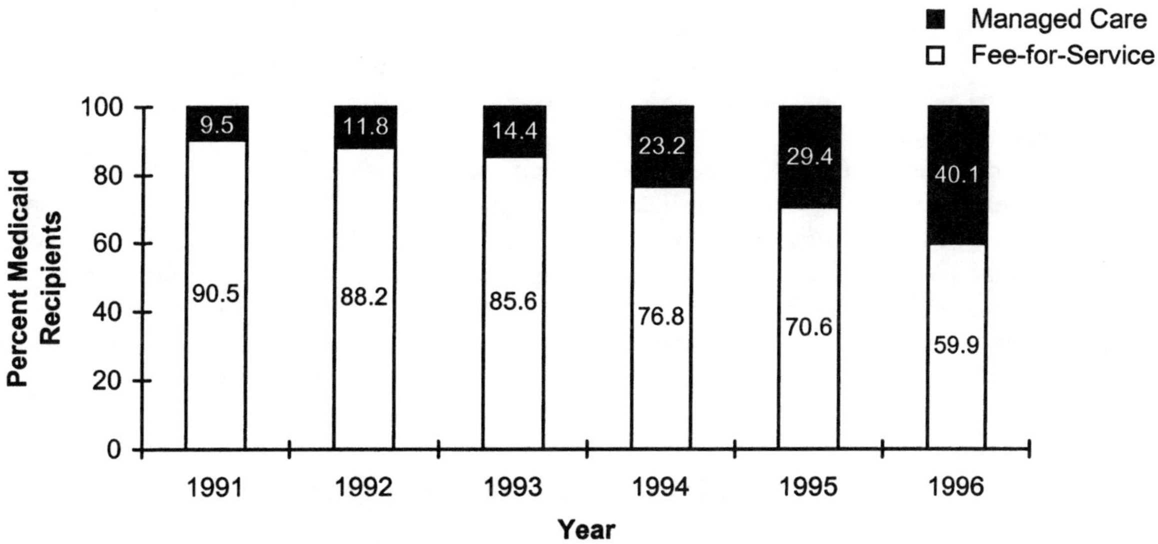

FIGURE 5.6 Percentage of Medicaid recipients enrolled in fee-for-service and managed care plans, United States, 1991-1996. SOURCE: HCFA (1997c). Data were provided by the Division of Information Distribution and were derived from the HCFA 2082 Statistical Report.

TABLE 5.1 Trends in Managed Care and Fee-for-Service Enrollment under Medicaid, United States, 1991-1996

	Year					
Type of Plan	1991	1992	1993	1994	1995	1996
	Number of Recipients (in millions)					
Total Medicaid Population	28.3	30.9	33.4	33.6	33.4	33.2
Fee-for-Service	25.6	27.3	28.6	25.8	23.6	19.9
Managed Care	2.7	3.6	4.8	7.8	9.8	13.3
	Percentage of Total Medicaid Population					
Fee-for-Service	90.5	88.2	85.6	76.8	70.6	59.9
Managed Care	9.5	11.8	14.4	23.2	29.4	40.1

SOURCE: HCFA (1997c). Data were provided by the Division of Information Distribution and were derived from the HCFA 2082 Statistical Report.

the authority to negotiate specifications for the components and services of a delivery system that must be available as a condition of awarding contracts to health plans.

In addition to controlling costs, managed care arrangements can provide the states opportunities to increase access to services, to improve coordination and quality of care, and to mainstream their beneficiaries into the general health care system. In comparison with fee-for-service Medicaid, managed care with capitation has more regular and predictable expenditures. In theory, managed care can improve access to prenatal and dental care, improve immunization rates, and increase access to preventive health services.

In practice, however, managed care does not automatically improve access to care. Many people in the children's health community are concerned about Medicaid managed care, especially for vulnerable populations such as children with special health care needs. Medicaid beneficiaries are likely to have greater health risks, poorer health status, and limited disposable cash for purchasing health care that may be needed but is beyond what is covered by Medicaid. Although managed care produces cost savings by reducing the overuse of inpatient hospitalization and emergency departments, there may also be a reduced access to pediatric specialists, which is a particular concern for children with chronic medical conditions and other special health care needs (Newacheck et al., 1996).

IMPACT OF RECENT FEDERAL LEGISLATION

Welfare Reform

From the time that Medicaid began until the welfare reform law was enacted in 1996, individuals who were eligible for the Aid to Families with Dependent Children (AFDC) program automatically qualified for Medicaid coverage. Effective July 1, 1997, as part of the Personal Responsibility and Work Opportunity Reconciliation Act of 1996 (P.L. 104-193; also referred to as "welfare reform"), the AFDC entitlement program was replaced with a new cash block grant to states known as Temporary Assistance to Needy Families (TANF) (see Table 5.2).

The welfare reform law included major changes affecting Medicaid eligibility. Eligibility for cash assistance no longer automatically guaranteed Medicaid eligibility. In addition, the law gave states flexibility to modify their Medicaid eligibility criteria in one of three ways:

- reduce eligibility by lowering the income standard to a level that was in effect no earlier than May 1, 1988;
- expand eligibility by increasing income or resource standards by a percentage that does not exceed the percentage increase in the Consumer Price Index; or
- use methods for determining income and resources that are less restrictive than those in effect on July 16, 1996.

The majority of states chose the third option, and most states are choosing whether to expand Medicaid further under the terms of the SCHIP program in the Balanced Budget Act of 1997. The welfare reform law required states to provide 1 year of transitional Medicaid coverage for those individuals who lost their eligibility as a result of beginning to receive child support payments or beginning employment. To further address the changes of welfare reform, the Balanced Budget Act of 1997 provided funding to allow states to continue to provide Medicaid coverage for these individuals for a transitional 1-year period. With federal approval, some states have extended this transitional period to two years.

The delinking of Medicaid and welfare through the law creating TANF acts two ways: (1) Medicaid enrollment is no longer dependent upon receipt of welfare; and (2) children can be eligible for Medicaid without being on welfare. Parents leaving the welfare rolls to take new jobs may not be aware that their

TABLE 5.2 Comparison of Prior Welfare Laws and the Personal Responsibility and Work Opportunity Reconciliation Act of 1996 (P.L. 104-193), United States.

	Prior Welfare Laws	P.L. 104-193 / TANF
Medicaid	• Eligibility determined by receipt of family assistance through AFDC • States also mandated to cover other specified categories of individuals, such as recipients of SSI	• Eligibility delinked from receipt of family assistance through TANF • States may employ more liberal income and resource standards for Medicaid eligibility, within specific range. [*Balanced Budget Act of 1997 restores Medicaid coverage to those SSI recipients who lost coverage because of change in definitions.]
	• Aliens who were PRUCOL were eligible for Medicaid; those not PRUCOL were eligible only for emergency Medicaid services	• Qualified aliens will be ineligible for five years for Medicaid (except emergency Medicaid); most current legal immigrants already in the U.S. may be deemed ineligible for Medicaid [*Balanced Budget Act of 1997 restores eligibility to this group.]
AFDC, JOBS, EA	• AFDC provided income support to families with children deprived of parental support • JOBS was an employment and training program for AFDC recipients • EA provided short term emergency services and benefits to needy families	• Eliminates AFDC, JOBS, and EA, forming a single program TANF
	• Open-ended funding provided for AFDC benefits and EA, while JOBS was a capped entitlement	• Block grants AFDC, EA, and JOBS into a single capped entitlement to the states
	• AFDC eligible individuals were guaranteed aid at state-established benefit levels	• No individual guarantee of benefits
	• A set percentage of non-exempt AFDC caseload was required to participate in JOBS activities for at least 20 hours per week	• States must demonstrate that they will require families to work after two years on assistance
	• States were required to provide basic and secondary education, as well as job training	• TANF individuals are required to participate in unsubsidized or subsidized job training, hours to be counted toward the work requirement
	• AFDC benefits were available to each eligible dependent child and parent, regardless of age of mother	• Unmarried minor parents are required to live in an adult-supervised setting and participate in educational activities in order to receive Federal assistance
	• Families on welfare received additional AFDC benefits whenever they had another child	• No provision, no state option
SSI	• Children who did not meet or equal the Listing of Medical Impairments were determined to be disabled if they suffered from physical or mental impairment of comparable severity to an adult	• Provides a new definition of disability for children, which removes references to maladaptive behavior as a medical criterion in SSA's listing of impairments used for evaluating mental disabilities in children
	• Aliens who were PRUCOL were eligible for SSI benefits.	• Most legal immigrants will be ineligible for SSI until citizenship, at time of recertification
Food Stamps	• Six categories of legal aliens were allowed to receive food stamp benefits if they met eligibility criteria	• Most legal immigrants will be ineligible for Food Stamps until citizenship
	• Set maximum benefit levels at 100% of the Thrifty Food Plan	• Sets maximum benefit levels at 103% of the Thrifty Food Plan and retains annual indexing
	• Able-bodied adults were expected to hold jobs or participate in the Employment and Training Program	• Able-bodied recipients between 18 and 50 with no dependents must work (at least 20 hours per week) in order to be eligible for food stamps

SOURCE: DHHS(1997b).

NOTE: AFDC = Aid to Families with Dependent Children; EA = Emergency Assistance; PRUCOL = Permanently Residing Under Color of Law; SSI = Supplemental Security Income; TANF = Temporary Assistance to Needy Families.

children are still eligible for Medicaid, and state Medicaid agencies will need to find new ways to notify parents about their children's eligibility.

Some observers believe that the changes in the welfare system may result in an increase in the number of Medicaid-eligible children who are not enrolled in the program and that outreach and public education efforts will need to be further strengthened and supported. Early in 1998, the Clinton Administration announced new initiatives to increase outreach and enrollment efforts in Medicaid.

Welfare Reform and SSI *Recipients*

In 1996, approximately 1 million children under age 18 received Medicaid on the basis of the determination of a disability and associated eligibility for cash payments under the SSI program (SSA, 1997). The 1996 welfare reform law changed the way in which childhood eligibility for SSI is determined by introducing more stringent requirements for SSI eligibility in the following ways:

- establishment of new definitions of childhood disability,
- redetermination of the eligibility status of current children receiving SSI under previous regulations and definitions, and
- continuing reviews of disability status.

With the enactment of the Balanced Budget Act of 1997, Medicaid eligibility (but not cash SSI payments) was restored to many of the SSI recipients who lost coverage under the new welfare law. However, as of August 1997, the new, more restrictive eligibility rules for children with emotional and behavioral problems resulted in the termination of cash disability benefits for more than 95,000 children (SSA, 1997). Eventually, 15 percent of the 1 million children in the program could lose their cash benefits if that rate continues (see Chapter 7, Box 7.1, for a description of the SSI program).

A new option in the Balanced Budget Act of 1997 allows states to create a Medicaid "buy-in" program for individuals whose incomes are under 250 percent of the federal poverty level and who would otherwise meet the medical eligibility criteria for SSI. The buy-in amounts will be set on a sliding scale based on family income. The new option is geared toward children with disabilities, but it is unclear how many of the children with emotional and behavioral disabilities will eventually be included because of the changes in the determination criteria and procedures.

Why not have Medicaid as a secondary insurance? If you need it and you are running out of your own insurance, pay a premium. That motivates you to work. You could still go to work and could pay your taxes into a Medicaid system, like we pay into the Medicare system. Our spend down amount is $1,100 a month. How are we supposed to pay our mortgage and eat?

Karen LaPlante
Parent, Dublin, VA
Public Workshop, June 2, 1997

The Balanced Budget Act of 1997

Increasingly, managed care has become the delivery system for both privately and publicly insured children and families. One of the most significant changes made by the Balanced Budget Act of 1997 is allowing states to move most Medicaid beneficiaries into managed care without a federally approved waiver. States that choose to enroll Medicaid beneficiaries in managed care have the potential to increase children's access to preventive health care services and to increase the comparability of quality in health care to that provided by private insurance.

However, the law specifies that some at-risk groups will still require federal waivers, including children with special needs (those who meet the definition of disability under the SSI program) and children in foster care or other out-of-home placements. These provisions were enacted in response to concerns among the children's health care community about the quality of care for special-needs children, based on clinical experiences in which managed care organizations have limited patients' access to pediatric specialists and support services.

The 1997 law allows Medicaid-only plans for the first time and also includes some general consumer protections. For example, the law requires that beneficiaries must be able to choose from among at least two plans, that the plans must have adequate provider capacity and a range and mix of appropriate providers, and that plans must have grievance procedures and quality assurance assessment and improvement mechanisms.

More than 1,000 pieces of legislation were introduced in state legislatures in 1997 to address some aspect of consumer protection under managed care. The inclusion of federal requirements in the Balanced Budget Act of 1997 for consumer protection for those who are covered by Medicaid was viewed as a landmark.

We have a Medicaid system which is providing important services to a substantial share of the population. We have the opportunity to improve that system which is in place, and to offer strategic suggestions on how it can be improved.

J. Michael McGinnis
National Research Council, Washington, DC
Public Workshop, June 2, 1997

IMPLICATIONS

Much of the resistance among states to the Medicaid program has been based on the mandated levels of benefits, which are viewed by some states as arbitrary, excessively expensive, and as limiting the ability of states to choose covered services based on the basis of their own preferences and perceived needs. Many providers and children's health advocates, however, view mandatory benefits as the only way of setting minimum national standards and also believe that national as well as state resources must be increased in order to support these standards. This is a fundamental disagreement about the role of government in health care, and debates are occurring in many states as they choose how to participate in the SCHIP program.

The Medicaid program continues to change rapidly. Eligibility requirements are changing in many states as a result of the implementation of new state children's health insurance programs under the Balanced Budget Act of 1997, and managed care is expected to play a major role in the delivery of care under SCHIP. State decisions about Medicaid expansions involve a complex and often difficult process of weighing competing priorities, resolving political and policy disagreements, and making decisions about the allocation of financial and other resources. The new programs will need to be evaluated carefully to determine their long-term impact on access and health status for all children, and particularly for those with special health care needs.

REFERENCES

AAP (American Academy of Pediatrics) Committee on Child Health Financing. 1993. Scope of Health Care Benefits for Infants, Children, and Adolescents Through Age 21 Years. *Pediatrics* 91(2):509.

Baxter RJ, Mechanic RE. 1997. The Status of Local Health Care Safety Nets. *Health Affairs* 16(4):7–23.

Coughlin TA, Liska D. 1997. *The Medicaid Disproportionate Share Hospital Payment Program: Background and Issues*. Washington, D.C.: Urban Institute. [http://newfederalism.urban.org/html/anf14.html]

DHHS (US Department of Health and Human Services), 1997a. *Medicaid Managed Care and EPSDT*. (Report No. OIE-05–93–00290). Washington, D.C.: Office of the Inspector General, May 15, 1997.

DHHS, 1997b. *Comparison of Prior Law and the Personal Responsibility and Work Opportunity Reconciliation Act of 1996 (P.L. 104–93)*. [http://aspe.os.dhhs.gov/isp/reform.htm]

Epstein AM. 1997. Medicaid Managed Care and High Quality: Can We Have Both? *Journal of the American Medical Association* 278(19):1617–1621.

Fox HB, McManus MA. 1996. *Medicaid Managed Care for Children With Chronic or Disabling Conditions: Improved Strategies for States and Plans*. Washington, D.C.: Fox Health Policy Consultants.

GAO (US General Accounting Office). 1996. *Health Insurance for Children: Private Insurance Coverage Continues to Deteriorate*. GAO/HEHS–96–129. Washington, D.C.: GAO.

GAO, 1997a. *Medicaid: Sustainability of Low 1996 Spending Growth is Uncertain*. GAO/HEHS–97–128. Washington, D.C.: GAO.

GAO, 1997b. *Medicaid Managed Care: Challenge of Holding Plans Accountable Requires Greater State Effort*. GAO/HEHS–97–86. Washington, D.C.: GAO.

Gauthier A, Schrodel SP. 1997. *Expanding Children's Coverage: Lessons From State Initiatives in Health Care Reform*. Washington, D.C.: Alpha Center.

HCFA (Health Care Financing Administration). 1995. *Medicaid 2082 Statistical Report on Medical Care: Eligibles, Recipients, Payments, and Services, Fiscal Year 1995*. [http://www.hcfa.gov/medicaid/mstats.htm]

HCFA. 1996. *Health Care Financing Review: Medicare and Medicaid Statistical Supplement 1996*. Pub. No. 03386. Baltimore, MD: US Department of Health and Human Services.

HCFA. 1997a. Data provided to IOM by the Division of Information Distribution.

HCFA. 1997b. *Overview of the Medicaid Program*. [http://www.hcfa.gov/medicaid/mover.htm]

HCFA. 1997c. *Medicaid Statistics*. [http://www.hcfa.gov/medicaid/hstats96]

Holahan J. 1997. *Expanding Insurance Coverage for Children*. Washington, D.C.: The Urban Institute.

Holahan J, Wiener JM, Liska D. 1997. *The Medicaid Reform Debate in 1997* Washington, D.C.: The Urban Institute. (URL http://newfederalism.urban.org)

Howell EM. 1996. Medicaid Managed Care Encounter Data: What, Why and Where Next? *Health Care Financing Review* 17(4):87–96.

Kaiser Commission on the Future of Medicaid. 1997. *Medicaid Facts: Medicaid's Role for Children*. Washington, D.C.: Author.

Koppelman J. 1993. *State Efforts to Improve Health Care Access for Low-Income Children: EPSDT Today and Under Health Reform. Issue Brief* 639. Washington, D.C.: National Health Policy Forum.

Landon BE, Tobias C, Epstein AE. 1998. Quality Management by State Medicaid Agencies Converting to Managed Care: Plans and Current Practice. *Journal of the American Medical Association* 279(3):211–216.

Lipson DJ. Medicaid Managed Care and Community Providers: New Partnerships. *Health Affairs* 16(4):91–107.

Mann C. 1997. *Why Not Medicaid? Using Child Health Funds to Expand Coverage Through the Medicaid Program*. Washington, D.C.; Center on Budget and Policy Priorities [http://www.cbpp.org/1119mcaid.htm]

NASBO (National Association of State Budget Officers). 1997. *Medicaid*. [http://www.nasbo.org]

NIHCM (National Institute for Health Care Management). 1996. *Assuring Quality of Care for Children in Medicaid Managed Care—EPSDT in a Time of Changing Policy*. Washington, D.C.: NIHCM.

Newacheck, P, Hughes, D, and Stoddard, J. 1996. Children's Access to Primary Care: Differences by Race, Income, and Insurance Status. *Pediatrics* 97(1):26–32.

Overpeck MD, Kotch JB. 1995. The Effects of U.S. Children's Access to Care on Medical Attention for Injuries. *American Journal of Public Health* 85(3):402–404.

Prospective Payment Assessment Commission (ProPAC). 1992. *Optional Hospital Rates for Private Payers Based on Medicare's Methods*. Washington, D.C.: Author.

Rosenbaum S, Shin P, Smith BM, Wehr E, Borzi PC, Zakheim MH, Shaw K, and Silver. KA Johnson, Ed. 1997. *Negotiating the New Health System: A Nationwide Study of Medicaid Managed Care Contracts*. Washington, D.C.: The George Washington University Center for Health Policy Research.

St. Peter RF, Newacheck PW, Halfon N. 1992. Access to Care for Poor Children: Separate and Unequal? *Journal of the American Medical Association* 267(20):2760–2764.

Schneider A. 1997. *Overview of Medicaid Provisions in the Balanced Budget Act of 1997, P. L. 105–33, Rev. 9/8/97*. Washington, D.C.: Center on Budget and Policy Priorities. [http:/www.cbpp.org/908mcaid.htm]

SSA (Social Security Administration). 1997. *The Definition of Disability for Children*. SSA Publication No. 05–11053, July 1997. [http://www.ssa.gov/pubs/11053.html]

Summer L, Parrott S, Mann C. 1997. *Millions of Uninsured and Underinsured Children are Eligible for Medicaid*. Washington, D.C.: Center on Budget and Policy Priorities.

U.S. House of Representatives, Committee on Ways and Means. 1996. *1996 Green Book: Background Material and Data on Programs within the Jurisdiction of the Committee on Ways and Means*. Washington, D.C.: US Government Printing Office.

Zuckerman S, Evans A, Holahan J. 1997. *Questions for States as They Turn to Medicaid Managed Care*. Washington, D.C.: Urban Institute. [http://newfederalism. urban.org/html/anf_a11.htm]

6

State and Private Insurance Initiatives

For more than a decade, many states have had public and/or private programs to provide health insurance coverage for low-income children. These programs have taken three general approaches: Medicaid expansions beyond mandatory levels, state-financed subsidy programs, and private initiatives (Gauthier and Schrodel, 1997; Gehshan, 1997; Johnson and McDonough, 1998).

The State Children's Health Insurance Program (SCHIP) of the Balanced Budget Act of 1997 was designed to build on these state experiences and to give states flexibility in expanding children's health insurance coverage for low-income, uninsured children. Under SCHIP, states will be designing and implementing new programs, as well as expanding Medicaid programs, in the years ahead.

As of April 1, 1998, the six-month anniversary of the program, eight states had federally approved SCHIP plans. Four plans were Medicaid expansions, two were state-designed programs, and two were combination approaches. SCHIP plans had been submitted for federal approval by 15 states, and 22 states were still in the planning phase. Two of the four states with approved Medicaid expansions (Alabama and South Carolina) were planning a second, later expansion through a state-designed program (National Economic Council, 1998; NGA, 1998). The variety in responses suggests that states are taking advantage of the flexibility in SCHIP design.

This chapter begins with a general discussion of the kinds of decisions that are involved in designing and implementing children's health insurance programs, with an emphasis on the factors involved in state-level decision making. The chapter continues with some profiles of state-financed, non-Medicaid children's insurance programs that were implemented before the national SCHIP legislation was passed, including information on the financing and design of the programs, eligibility requirements, covered benefits and services, cost-sharing, and the numbers of children served. Some of these programs are likely to be expanded or replicated under SCHIP.

The chapter also gives examples of private sector initiatives undertaken by insurers and health plans across the country. In summary, the chapter describes some of the key lessons learned from previous experiences in implementing state and private children's health insurance programs.

BACKGROUND

In the early to mid-1990s, the most frequent children's health insurance expansion strategy (in 30 states) was broadening the criteria for Medicaid eligibility to cover children 1 year of age and older. Eight states had developed state-financed subsidy programs for non-Medicaid-eligible, uninsured children

TABLE 6.1 State Initiatives to Expand Coverage to Children (as of May 1997)

Individuals Covered	Subsidy Programs for Children and Families			Subsidies to Employers	Other
	State Only	State and Local	State and Private		
Children	California	Florida	Iowa		
	Massachusetts	Colorado	Kansas		
	Minnesota		Michigan		
	New York		Montana		
	Pennsylvania		North Carolina		
	Vermont		New Hampshire		
Families	Massachusetts (2)			Florida	Iowa [a]
	New Jersey			Maine	New York[b]
	New York (2)			New York	Oregon[c]
	Washington			Washington	

[a] Tax deduction
[b] Pilot voucher program
[c] Tax credit to small employers

SOURCE: Gauthier and Schrodel (1997, p. 7).

living in low-income families. Four states had developed subsidy programs for families. In addition, private programs were operating in 25 states (Gauthier and Schrodel, 1997) (see Table 6.1).

As of May 1997, only six states (Alaska, Illinois, Indiana, Nebraska, Nevada, and South Carolina) had no public or private subsidized insurance programs and had not expanded Medicaid eligibility to children over age 1. Eight states (Alabama, Idaho, Louisiana, Mississippi, Ohio, Oklahoma, Texas, and Wyoming) had only private Blue Cross and Blue Shield Caring Programs for Children and provided no state assistance (Gauthier and Schrodel, 1997; Gehshan, 1997).

Many of the states choosing Medicaid expansions have considered the relative administrative and fiscal advantages of altering an existing program when compared with designing and implementing new state programs (Mann, 1997). Medicaid already has an administrative structure in place in every state, and its administrative costs are low. Medicaid's contracts and rates have already been negotiated and provider networks, payment systems, and benefit packages have been established. In addition, the federal matching payments provide an incentive to expand Medicaid by reducing the amount of money that states need to provide from their own budgets (Dorn et al., 1998; Mann, 1997).

However, some states have preferred to sponsor separate, independent programs that are distinct from Medicaid. Several states have funded programs that subsidize coverage for children through selected commercial insurance or managed care plans. The level of the subsidy typically varies on a sliding scale, with full subsidies for children from families with the lowest income levels and higher premium levels and copayments for children from families with higher levels of income. Some states have relied primarily on private initiatives and have provided some financial support through special taxes on tobacco or alcohol (see Table 6.1). Some programs have focused on children, whereas others include families.

The most frequently mentioned advantages of separate state programs are that they avoid the stigma of the traditional welfare system and allow the states to experiment according to local economic and social needs, preferences, and resources (Lipson and Schrodel, 1996). State-based programs also are not subject to federal requirements about eligibility, the benefit package, provider payment rates, copayments, and other regulations that accompany the use of federal funds for Medicaid.

DESIGNING CHILDREN'S INSURANCE PROGRAMS

For more than a decade, states have been funding programs that provide insurance for children who are not eligible for Medicaid and who do not have private insurance. State-designed, non-Medicaid insurance programs typically develop contracts with private-sector health plans and providers at market rates, so that the subsidized children and families receive the same coverage as the privately insured groups in their communities (GAO, 1996).

State-sponsored programs may be administered by the state or by a nonprofit agency or corporation that agrees to administer the benefits, determine eligibility, and oversee the contracts with health plans that contract to deliver the care to the enrolled population. By acting as the purchaser on behalf of a pool of subsidized children and families, states can negotiate better rates than small employers or parents are likely to be able to receive on their own (Nichols et al., 1997).

For low-income working parents, these subsidized programs offer an attractive alternative to being uninsured or paying a substantial portion of their earnings to buy their own insurance. Coverage offered through public programs may of course differ from the coverage offered to individuals with employer-sponsored or private individual coverage. In fact, private health benefit policies purchased by employers or individuals do not always cover the scope of benefits covered through the Medicaid program. However, some parents prefer a private program because it is not associated with welfare, even if it offers a reduced benefit package (McDonough, 1997).

The design and implementation of programs for children's health insurance involve a complex set of questions. As described in the following sections, these include decisions about the eligibility for the program, the scope of benefits to be provided, sources and extent of financing, impact on the insurance market, and procedures for outreach and enrollment once the program is implemented.

The traditional public health model is to throw money at certain institutions and let them take whoever comes through their doors. We have used that model in Massachusetts, where we have a very sophisticated and deep network of community health centers. But we have found that people are more likely to avail themselves of preventive and other services when they have a sense that they are covered under an insurance plan. Holding an insurance card is an essential piece of people's dignity that gets them to appropriate services.

John McDonough
Massachusetts Legislature, Boston, MA
Public Workshop, June 2, 1997

Levels of Eligibility

The decision about who will be included in the population that is eligible for the program is usually one of the first to be addressed in designing a children's insurance program. In general, uninsured children are the target group, but each state needs to determine the maximum income limit for eligibility (see Table 6.2).

This decision involves determinations about how far existing resources will stretch, including whether additional resources can be generated if there is a shortfall or whether enrollment will simply be closed or capped when it reaches a certain point. In most cases, states try to work from their Medicaid eligibility criteria and to prevent gaps in coverage, so that children up to a certain income level will be eligible for one of the two programs.

Other questions about eligibility concern the age ranges of eligible children and whether individual children or families will be served. States that have age limits on eligibility because of resource limitations may have difficulty explaining to parents why one child in the family is eligible for a program and another is not. Thus, a state might choose to limit its program to certain cities, counties, or regions to avoid the problem of seemingly arbitrary age limits.

A few states have chosen to target entire families for their programs. For example, Health Access New Jersey is a statewide program for children and adults, and the Massachusetts Medical Security Plan provides subsidized coverage for families whose wage earners are unemployed. However, because of resource constraints, the majority of state-sponsored insurance programs focus on children, and some also extend eligibility through adolescence (see Table 6.2).

> Whether or not you limit eligibility based on income, do you cap your program out, for instance, where people over 400 percent of poverty are simply not eligible for your coverage? Or do you design the program such that people over 400 percent of poverty are eligible, but they pay the full premium and you have a sliding scale below it? States have had very different responses to that question.
>
> *Jane Horvath*
> *National Academy for State Health Policy, Portland, ME*
> *Public Workshop, June 2, 1997*

The question of eligibility also involves fundamental views about the nature and purpose of insurance. The higher the parents' income, the greater the likelihood that children will be covered by their parents' employer. If a state program offers generous benefits and subsidizes the cost, there is potential that employers will drop existing coverage or that parents will switch to the new state plans. This is described by different terms, including *substitution* or *replacement* of coverage, or *crowd-out* (Chollet et al., 1997; Cutler and Gruber, 1997; Dubay and Kenney, 1997).

There are a variety of opinions on the likelihood, nature, and extent of coverage replacement. Some of the presenters in the committee's public workshop believe that any replacement of private coverage by public funds should be avoided, whereas others believe that a certain amount of substitution of coverage is reasonable if it reduces the burden of out-of-pocket expenses, improves children's access to care, and reduces the overuse of emergency rooms, with their associated higher costs of care.

As part of the SCHIP accountability process, state program plans are required to describe their intended strategies for preventing substitution of coverage (IOM, 1998). Based on evidence that substitution becomes more likely as levels of income increase beyond the poverty level, the SCHIP legislation set the highest eligibility level at 200 percent of the federal poverty level, which is an annual

TABLE 6.2 Eligibility Criteria for Programs Providing Health Care Coverage For Children (as of May 1996)

Name of the Program	Year Started	Maximum Income[a]	Age of Eligibility
Florida Healthy Kids	1992	No limit	1-19
Massachusetts' Children's Medical Security Plan	1994	No limit	0-18
New Hampshire's Healthy Kids	1995	No limit	0-20
New York's Child Health Plus	1991	No limit	0-18
Tennessee's TennCare	1994	No limit	0-64
Washington's Basic Health Plan	1989	No limit	0-64
Massachusetts' Medical Security Plan (MSP)	1990	400%	0-64
California's Access for Infants and Mothers (AIM)	1992	300%	Pregnant women and children <2
Hawaii QUEST	1994	300%	0-64
MinnesotaCare	1992	275%	0-64
Health Access New Jersey	1995	250%	0-64
Rhode Island's RIte Care	1994	250%	0-17
Pennsylvania's Children's Health Insurance Program	1993	235% ages 1-5 185% ages 6-15	1-15
Vermont's Dr. Dynasaur	1989	225%	0-17
New York's Regional Pilot Projects	1989	200%	0-64
Colorado's Child Health Plan	1992	185%	0-12
Michigan's Caring Program for Children	1991	185%	1-18
North Carolina's Caring Program for Children	1987	185%	0-19
Montana's Caring Program for Children	1992	150%	0-19
Iowa's Caring Program for Children	1989	133%	0-18
Kansas' Caring Program for Children	1989	133%	0-18

SOURCE: Gauthier and Schrodel (1997, p. 18).

[a] Percent refers to percentage of the federal poverty level

gross income of $32,100 for a family of four. The legislation allowed an exception to this eligibility requirement for states that as of June 1997 provided Medicaid to children with family incomes above 150 percent of poverty. Those states may use SCHIP funds to cover children whose family incomes are above 200 percent of poverty, up to 50 percentage points above the state's Medicaid eligibility level.

When you think about the crowd-out issue, you have to look at the parents' insurance status. What you see is that parents don't have insurance and they delay their own care, because they are busy taking care of their children. Forty-six percent of our children were uninsured for six or more months. That is an important thing to factor into this question. If they have been uninsured for six months, they didn't come into our program from some other source of coverage. And 12 months later, only 61 percent of our kids were still in our program. So we're not here building a generational entitlement program.

Charles LaVallee
Western Pennsylvania Caring Program for Children, Pittsburgh, PA
Public Workshop, June 2, 1997

There has been a lot of talk about crowd-out, but there is very limited evidence that at the lowest end of the income spectrum, you are crowding out private insurance. Private insurance largely does not exist for the parents in these working families.

Diane Rowland
Kaiser Commission on the Future of Medicaid, Washington, DC
Public Workshop, June 2, 1997

There is a lot of pressure and debate on the question of when public coverage should let off and when private coverage should begin. Where is that transition area in which you might be providing some public subsidy, but not a full public subsidy? It's a gray area, and there is going to be heavy debate about where the cut-off point should be.

Kay Johnson
George Washington University, Washington, DC
Public Workshop, June 2, 1997

There is a notion in social insurance that if we are going to create safety nets for people, then somebody has to pay. There is a notion of equal justice or horizontal equity, which argues that if you and I both make $30,000 a year and you buy insurance but I don't, then I rely on the safety net, and you end up paying for me. This is the argument we use in requiring everyone to pay some Social Security tax. We say that people making $20,000 or $25,000 a year can't afford to buy insurance, but most of them *are* paying for health insurance in the form of lower cash wages. To say then that other people who don't pay for insurance through lower cash wages cannot afford it is part of the dilemma. If we say they can't afford it and we resubsidize them, that causes substitution, and we end up in a netherworld. There is still a gap between the tax system and the welfare system.

Eugene Steuerle
The Urban Institute, Washington, DC
Public Workshop, June 2, 1997

Scope of Benefits

Questions about the scope of benefits are more often about how generous a benefit package the state can afford than about what kinds of benefits are recommended by experts in children's health. Given a limited amount of resources, does a state choose to cover more uninsured children with a minimal set of benefits, or does the state choose to provide more comprehensive services, in which case fewer children will be covered? Most states have decided on a comprehensive benefit package rather than catastrophic coverage (see Table 6.3), but there often are limitations or restrictions on coverage for mental health, dental care, inpatient hospitalization, disabilities, or chronic conditions.

Some states believe that offering a generous benefit package will encourage employers and families to drop employer-based coverage, particularly when the existing scope of private coverage is limited, as is typically the case with small employers. States with benefits exclusions have been motivated primarily by budget constraints and less by concerns about crowd-out, although the limited packages do seem less likely to attract working families who already have coverage (Chollet et al., 1997).

Program Financing

State programs derive their funding through a variety of financing streams. These may include state general funds, special taxes on tobacco or alcohol, taxes on providers or employers, funds generated from the sale or conversion of not-for-profit hospitals, contributions from employers or insurers, and donations from philanthropic organizations. Some states, such as Florida, are considering using funds from a tobacco settlement for their SCHIP, and other states with budget surpluses may use some of those funds for expansion of children's health insurance coverage (NGA, 1998). Successful competition for funding depends on the prominence of support for children's health insurance in the state, the proportion of uninsured children in the state, the nature of the provider networks, the involvement of children's health advocates, the views of the governors and legislatures about public insurance, and many other factors (Dorn et al., 1998).

One of the major financing questions is whether the families will pay premiums and copayments and, if so, what the amounts will be. Many state-subsidized health insurance programs require that participants share in the cost of their insurance, which not only reduces the public costs of the program

TABLE 6.3 Scope of Benefits of Programs Providing Health Care for Children

Name of the Program	Benefit Level	Number of Contracting Plans	Annual Cost Per Child (dollars)
California's Access for Infants and Mothers (AIM)	Comprehensive	9	NA[a]
Florida Healthy Kids	Comprehensive	8	612
Hawaii QUEST	Comprehensive	5	NA
MinnesotaCare	Comprehensive	8	792
New Hampshire's Healthy Kids	Comprehensive	1	804
Health Access New Jersey	Comprehensive	6	NA
New York's Child Health Plus	Comprehensive	15	432-678
New York's Regional Pilot Projects	Comprehensive	4	NA
Pennsylvania's Children's Health Insurance Program	Comprehensive	5	636
Rhode Island's RIte Care	Comprehensive	4	840
Tennessee's TennCare	Comprehensive	10	505
Vermont's Dr. Dynasaur	Comprehensive	2	446-533
Washington's Basic Health Plan	Comprehensive	18	492-720
Massachusetts' Children's Medical Security Plan	Basic/standard	1	NA
Colorado's Child Health Plan	Limited	0	350
Iowa's Caring Program for Children	Limited	1	350
Kansas' Caring Program for Children	Limited	1	204
Massachusetts' Medical Security Plan	Limited	2	450-540
Michigan's Caring Program for Children	Limited	1	615
Montana's Caring Program for Children	Limited	1	360
North Carolina's Caring Program for Children	Limited	1	312

SOURCE: Gauthier and Schrodel (1997, p.15).

[a] NA = not available.

but also makes the programs seem less like welfare for the families who participate (Ku and Coughlin, 1997).

States vary significantly in their subsidy structures and in the use of sliding-scale premiums (see Table 6.4). Massachusetts uses three broad income levels to determine the level of cost-sharing (200, 300, and 400 percent of the federal poverty level). Other states have more income categories with smaller ranges of income, so the share of the premium is a similar percentage of income across all income levels (Gauthier and Schrodel, 1997).

A recent Urban Institute study examined the relationship of premium levels and program participation in three states with subsidized insurance programs (Minnesota, Tennessee, and Washington). The study found that when families were charged one percent of their income, 57 percent would join a program; when the charge was 3 percent, 35 percent would join; and when the charge was 5 percent, only 18 percent would participate (Ku and Coughlin, 1997). Florida Healthy Kids found that families stayed in the program when the premium was increased from $5 to $10 per month, but an increase from $10 to $15 a month caused more families to drop out.

Some states have provided state tax relief for individuals who purchase insurance or enroll in a health plan in the private market. For example, Iowa has allowed self-employed residents to deduct 100 percent of the cost of their health insurance, and Oregon offered a tax credit to small businesses to provide health insurance for their employees (Gauthier and Schrodel, 1997). These strategies can give more responsibility and flexibility to consumers, but they are difficult to implement because of the lack of a structure or mechanism for providing information about the programs or helping consumers make their own decisions. Also, because state tax levels are low, the financial incentives are relatively limited (see Appendix A). There has been a great deal of discussion about vouchers to allow individuals to purchase their own insurance, but only one state—New York—has passed legislation to implement a voucher pilot program (Gauthier and Schrodel, 1997).

Another important issue for states to consider is the possible impact on the insurance risk pool if they design a separate program for children only. Children are relatively healthy, so the average costs they impose on risk pools are less than the average costs for other individuals. Although many in the children's health community believe that it is appropriate to focus attention on children's access to health care, there may be far-reaching and long-term consequences affecting other sectors of the population if children are "carved out" of risk pools.

Key Outreach and Enrollment Issues

Once eligibility and scope of benefits have been defined and financing has been made available, the outreach and enrollment strategies will determine the program's success in reaching the intended groups of children and families. For example, is there one enrollment process for all programs, or does each program have a separate process? Are families expected to come to a central location for information, do outreach workers visit day-care centers and clinics, are mail-in applications distributed to schools and businesses, or can families apply by telephone? The easier it is for applicants to enroll, the more likely it is that Medicaid-eligible children will be identified. States that want to cap Medicaid enrollment may be reluctant to do outreach or to streamline their application procedures.

PROFILES OF STATE-SPONSORED PROGRAMS

This section describes some of the state-sponsored programs that were developed in the early 1990s: Florida Healthy Kids, Massachusetts' Children's Medical Security Plan, MinnesotaCare, New York's Child Health Plus, and TennCare. These programs were chosen because of their variety of approaches to eligibility, financing, and outreach and enrollment and because their experiences can provide guidance for other states in developing and modifying SCHIP in the years ahead. Although TennCare was based

TABLE 6.4 Premium Subsidy Structure for State-Subsidized Insurance Programs

State	Program	<100% FPL	<100-200 FPL %	200-300% FPL	300% + FPL
CA	AIM	Not eligible	Not eligible	Partial subsidy	Not eligible
CO	Child Health Plan	Partial subsidy	Partial subsidy/Not eligible as income nears 200% FPL	Not eligible	Not eligible
DE	Diamond State Health Plan	Full subsidy	Not eligible	Not eligible	Not eligible
FL	Florida Healthy Kids	Partial subsidy	Partial subsidy/ No subsidy as income nears 200% FPL	No subsidy	No subsidy
HI	Hawaii QUEST	Full subsidy	No subsidy	No subsidy	Not eligible
MA	MSP-Direct Coverage	Full subsidy	Full subsidy	Not eligible	Not eligible
MA	MSP-Premium Assistance	Partial subsidy	Partial subsidy	Partial subsidy	Partial subsidy
MA	Children's MSP	Full subsidy	Full subsidy	Partial subsidy	Partial subsidy
MN	MinnesotaCare (Families)	Partial subsidy	Partial subsidy	Partial subsidy/Not eligible as income nears 300% FPL	Not eligible
MN	MinnesotaCare (Adults)	Partial subsidy	Partial subsidy/Not eligible as income nears 200% FPL	Not eligible	Not eligible
NJ	Health Access	Partial subsidy	Partial subsidy	Partial subsidy/Not eligible as income nears 300% FPL	Not eligible
NY	Child Health Plus	Full subsidy	Full subsidy/Partial subsidy as income nears 200% FPL	No subsidy	No subsidy
NY	Regional Pilot Projects	Partial subsidy	Partial subsidy	Not eligible	Not eligible
OR	Oregon Health Plan	Partial subsidy	Not eligible	Not eligible	Not eligible
PA	Children's Health Insurance Program	Full subsidy	Full subsidy/Not eligible as income nears 200% FPL	Not eligible	Not eligible
TN	TennCare	Full subsidy	Partial subsidy	Partial subsidy	Partial subsidy
VT	Health Access Plan	Full subsidy/Partial subsidy as income nears 50%	Not eligible	Not eligible	Not eligible
WA	Basic Health Plan	Partial subsidy	Partial subsidy	No subsidy	No subsidy

NOTE: FPL = federal poverty level.
SOURCE: Gauthier and Schrodel, 1997, Table 6.

on a Medicaid waiver, it is included because the Tennessee implementation experience has been so instructive for other states.

Florida Healthy Kids

The Florida State Legislature established the Florida Healthy Kids Corporation in 1990 in response to data indicating that both child health and school performance were declining while the number of uninsured children was continuing to grow. Recognizing the relationship between child health and illness and school performance, Healthy Kids provides comprehensive care to children ages 5 to 19 by offering insurance through the schools. The program uses the income criteria of the National School Lunch Program to set sliding premium rates (Shenkman et al., 1996). The only eligibility requirement is that the child have no other medical insurance coverage.

The Healthy Kids program officially began enrolling children from the Volusia County school district in February 1992. By 1997, the program had expanded to five additional counties and covered more than 45,000 children (Gauthier and Schrodel, 1997). It has helped to provide comprehensive health care coverage to more than 20,000 children in 11 school districts across the state, and further expansions are planned under the state's proposed SCHIP.

The $26 million program is funded through a combination of sources, including state funding (50 percent), family premiums (33 percent), and contributions from school districts, hospital authorities, children's services councils, and community organizations (17 percent) (Shenkman et al., 1996). Limited provider networks offer the covered services, which include immunizations, primary and specialty physician visits, inpatient and outpatient hospital care, vision and hearing care, prescription drugs, rehabilitation, organ transplants, preexisting conditions, and certain mental health services. Copayments are charged for certain products or services: $3 for prescription drugs, $25 for nonemergency use of an emergency room, $10 for mental health services, and $10 for eyeglasses. There is a lifetime cap of $1 million dollars on these services (Hill et al., 1993).

Another distinctive trait of the program is that it is not just for low-income families. All children enrolled in school may join if they do not have any other health insurance. Families with incomes under the federal poverty level pay nothing toward the cost of coverage; families with incomes of between 101 and 135 percent of the pay $3 per child a month; families with incomes between 136 percent and 185 percent pay $16 per child a month; and families with incomes above 185 percent of poverty can purchase coverage for the full monthly premium of $57 per child (Hill et al., 1993). The program's full premium stands at $684 annually. As of 1997, 98 percent of program enrollees received some form of subsidy, and almost two thirds did not pay a premium.

According to an evaluation done by the Institute for Child Health Policy at the University of Florida, the Healthy Kids program saved taxpayers and hospitals more than $13 million in health care costs in 1996. Hospitals reported a 30 percent decrease in pediatric charity cases and a 70 percent decrease in emergency room visits during the first year after a Healthy Kids program was implemented in a community. Uninsured children were found to be eight times more likely to seek care in an emergency room than those enrolled in the Healthy Kids program. The level of family satisfaction with the program has been reported to be higher than 90 percent (Shenkman et al., 1996).

The Balanced Budget Act of 1997 allowed Florida to use its 1997 Healthy Kids benefit package as an approved SCHIP program. With funding from the Robert Wood Johnson Foundation, several other states are planning to replicate the Healthy Kids program in the near future.

Massachusetts' Children's Medical Security Plan

The Massachusetts legislature created the Children's Medical Security Plan (CMSP) in 1994 in response to the state's growing Medicaid costs and the growing number of uninsured children. At that time, the Medicaid program had been increasing by 22 percent annually for the previous 4 years. In the late 1980s, an estimated 90,000 children were uninsured, and by 1995, that number had grown to 160,000 despite Medicaid expansions for children (Greenberg and Zuckerman, 1997).

In 1996, the Massachusetts legislature passed the Access to Health Law, expanding Medicaid coverage for children and modifying CMSP to reach low-income children not covered by Medicaid. Previous legislation mandating that employers provide coverage or contribute to a state fund was scheduled for implementation in August 1996, and pressure from businesses had generated interest in either repealing the mandate or replacing it with an alternative, more limited program (Greenberg and Zuckerman, 1997).

Children's health insurance expansions in Massachusetts have been financed through a reallocation of the state's pool of money for uncompensated care and through a 25-cent increase in the cigarette tax (Greenberg and Zuckerman, 1997). In Massachusetts, the Medicaid program is available to uninsured children and adults with incomes up to 133 percent of the federal poverty level. All other children are eligible for CMSP, which provides a limited package of primary and preventive care services. Inpatient hospital care is not covered, and coverage for prescription drugs and mental health is limited.

We found extraordinary political salience in linking children's health and tobacco taxes. People generally look at tobacco taxes differently than any other kind of tax, and most of the public generally like raising cigarette taxes. When you link it with using the funds to buy health care for children, the support just simply goes through the roof.

John McDonough
Massachusetts House of Representatives, Boston, MA
Public Workshop, June 2, 1997

CMSP is partly supported by participant cost-sharing. For families with incomes of up to 200 percent of the poverty level, participation is free. Families with incomes of between 200 and 400 percent of the federal poverty level may buy into CMSP for a monthly premium of $10.50 per child. Families with incomes higher than 400 percent of the federal poverty level pay the full cost of about $52.50 per month (Johnson and McDonough, 1998).

Through 1997, CMSP had covered 31,000 children up to age 19. The program is administered separately from the Medicaid program, and the application, enrollment determination, and outreach staff are different. Because families must apply to different agencies to enroll in the two programs, it is difficult for families to make transitions between the programs when their financial circumstances change. However, the separation of programs has made CMSP more appealing to families who prefer to avoid a welfare program, even though the Medicaid benefits are much more extensive and cost-sharing is greater with CMSP (McDonough, 1997).

MinnesotaCare and Children's Health Plan

Minnesota's Children's Health Plan was one of the first state-financed programs to subsidize coverage for children. In 1987, the Minnesota legislature allocated a 1-cent increase in the cigarette tax to help finance the development of the Children's Health Plan. The program was implemented in July 1988, and in 1992, it was incorporated into MinnesotaCare, the state's subsidized health insurance program for individuals who are not eligible for Medicaid. As of March 1997, MinnesotaCare covered 53,000 children under the age of 21, or approximately 40 percent of the uninsured children in Minnesota (Gauthier and Schrodel, 1997).

The Children's Health Plan originally limited program eligibility to children ages 1 through 8 in families with incomes below 185 percent of the federal poverty level and provided a restricted benefit package of ambulatory, preventive, and primary care services. The intent of the program was to ensure that the greatest possible number of children had at least some kind of basic coverage (Hill et al., 1993). After various Medicaid eligibility expansions, the Children's Health Plan raised its upper age limit. In January 1991, the program began to cover all children under age 18 in families with incomes below 185 percent of the federal poverty level.

MinnesotaCare funding comes from a 2 percent excise tax on hospitals and health care providers and from monthly enrollee premiums, which are based on a sliding scale. Families with incomes greater than 275 percent of the federal poverty level are not eligible for a subsidy, on the assumption that other policies will be available to these families in the private market (Call et al., 1997). The program pays a monthly capitation to contracted health plans for a comprehensive array of services, and enrollees choose their health plan at the time of enrollment. There are no copayments for children. The program's one-page, mail-in application forms are available from schools and health and social services agencies, and applications can also be completed by telephone.

In addition to meeting the income guidelines, there is a 4-month waiting period after losing insurance coverage from another source. This provision is intended to discourage those who seek to replace private coverage with the state-subsidized plan. The Minnesota Department of Health estimates that MinnesotaCare saves the state and federal government $1.8 million each month by meeting the state's cost-containment goals and growth limits (Minnesota Health Information Clearinghouse, 1996).

> **The programs have different benefit packages. Most of the programs have started out with a prevention and primary care program, i.e., not a lot of mental health coverage, not a lot of inpatient coverage. As these programs become more popular and as people understand what they are paying for and what the insurance risks are, the programs have been expanding.**
>
> *Jane Horvath*
> *National Academy for State Health Policy, Portland, ME*
> *Public Workshop, June 2, 1997*

New York's Child Health Plus

In September 1991, the state of New York introduced Child Health Plus, a plan that uses state funds to purchase private health insurance for eligible low-income children. Child Health Plus is financed through the state's system of reserving funds for uncompensated hospital care, supplemented by enrollment fees and premium payments. With an enrollment approaching 160,000 by the end of 1997, Child Health Plus is the largest of state children's insurance programs. New York still has one of the highest rates of uninsured children: about 557,200 children still have no coverage, and state officials plan to double the number of children enrolled in Child Health Plus over the next 3 years (Johnson and McDonough, 1998).

Based on legislation that was enacted in 1996, all children aged 2 to 19 whose family income is below 120 percent of the federal poverty level are eligible for comprehensive benefits, and those with incomes from 120 to 222 percent of the federal poverty level are eligible with a sliding scale. Families with incomes above 222 percent of the federal poverty level pay the full cost of the premium. Premiums range from $477 to $656 per year depending on the region and specific health plan (Hill et al., 1993).

The Child Health Plus benefit package covers a wide array of ambulatory, preventive, and primary care services but excludes more costly benefits such as mental health, nursing home, and home health care services. Although inpatient services were originally excluded, they were added to the list of covered benefits in 1997. At the same time, the state extended eligibility in the Child Health Plus program to children up to age 18, thus more than doubling the number of eligible children (Gehshan, 1997).

Among the advantages of New York's Child Health Plus program are its simple application process, which makes it easy for families to enroll in the programs. In contrast to the Medicaid program, providers are reimbursed at private insurance rates established by the plans. In addition, children and families covered under this program are able to avoid the stigma and the administrative burdens that are often associated with the Medicaid program (Hill et al., 1993).

TennCare

On January 1, 1994, the state of Tennessee replaced its Medicaid program with a comprehensive health care reform plan called TennCare. This program extended health care coverage to approximately 1 million people in the Medicaid population and to 400,000 uninsured people through a system of managed care. To implement the program, the state government contracted with 12 managed care organizations to deliver all Medicaid services and to handle claims processing in exchange for a monthly payment per enrollee.

TennCare initially had an enrollment cap of 1.3 million, which was later raised to 1.4 million. By January 1, 1995, TennCare reached 90 percent of its target enrollment and closed enrollment to uninsured individuals (The Commonwealth Fund, 1996). It reopened to children in April 1997, and state officials anticipate that about three fourths of the 68,000 eligible children will be enrolled in the program (Gauthier and Schrodel, 1997).

Criticism of TennCare has been focused on the inadequacy of the provider networks and the implementation process. According to a 1995 report of the U.S. General Accounting Office, providers receive 20 to 50 percent less than Medicaid payments for some forms of surgery and X-rays, although fees for visits and consultations are slightly higher than those paid by Medicaid. As a result of low levels of state payments, almost half of the managed care companies participating in TennCare reported losing money in the first year of the program. The largest participant, Blue Cross/Blue Shield, reported a loss of $8.8 million (GAO, 1995).

After its initial problems with implementation, the proportion of the population with insurance in Tennessee is among the highest of any state. The overuse of emergency rooms and inpatient hospitalization has dramatically decreased. Patients report that it is easier to develop a relationship with their physicians because they now have a regular primary care provider. Some estimates suggest that TennCare has saved as much as $1 billion compared with the projected Medicaid costs, which were increasing at an annual rate of 20 percent (Gauthier and Schrodel, 1997).

PRIVATE PROGRAMS

Privately sponsored programs have been developed by health plans across the country. Among the plans that have been involved in children's health programs are Aetna Health Plan, Atlanta; Blue Shield Plans in California, Colorado, Georgia, North Carolina, and Ohio; Group Health Cooperative of Puget Sound; Harvard Pilgrim Health Plan; Kaiser Permanente in California, Colorado, Maryland, Virginia, and the District of Columbia; Physicians Health Plan of Greater St. Louis; Prudential Health Care Plan of the Mid-Atlantic; US Healthcare; and others (AAHP, 1998). These programs have included school-based health centers and fitness programs, immunization programs, disease management programs for inner-city asthmatic children, teen substance abuse programs, and AIDS education programs.

This section profiles two private-sector approaches to providing health care coverage for children. Blue Cross and Blue Shield Caring Programs operate in several states and together provide subsidized coverage for more children than any other private program. "Kaiser Permanente Cares for Kids," which was started in California in 1997, is part of a national subsidy program for uninsured people that will be expanded by Kaiser Permanente in the next few years.

Caring Programs

Blue Cross and Blue Shield Caring Programs offer subsidized coverage for primary and preventive services for low-income children in 25 states. Although the particular designs of each program vary slightly, most Caring Programs cover outpatient care, well-child visits, immunizations, primary care for illnesses and accidents, emergency services, laboratory and X-ray services, and outpatient surgery. Caring Programs serve uninsured children who are under age 19, live in low-income families, and do not qualify for Medicaid.

Caring Programs receive the majority of their funding from the private sector, although Pennsylvania and Massachusetts have provided additional support for children's health benefits by increasing the state cigarette tax. In Iowa, Kansas, Missouri, Montana, and North Carolina, the state also provides some subsidies. Local businesses, foundations, religious organizations, civic groups, schools, unions, and individuals sponsor children in the Caring Programs. Many community contributions are matched by the participating Blue Cross and Blue Shield plans. All administrative services are donated by Blue Cross and Blue Shield, so every dollar contributed is used towards providing health care coverage for children. The annual premium across all of the programs averages about $270 (Hill et al., 1993).

Determining eligibility is straightforward and simple. The applications are never more than one page, no restrictions are imposed on assets, no income verification is required, and families pay no enrollment fee. Also, because Caring Programs were created to supplement Medicaid, their plans require that potentially eligible children first apply for Medicaid. When outreach, public education, and enrollment efforts identify children who are eligible but not enrolled in Medicaid, children are referred to the Medicaid program (Hill et al., 1993; LaVallee, 1997).

Despite their continued growth, most Caring Programs still remain relatively small. The Western Pennsylvania Caring Program has the largest enrollment of all the plans, and, in cooperation with the state, provides health insurance for 60,000 children. Yet together these two programs reach only 21 percent of the children currently eligible in that service area (Gauthier and Schrodel, 1997).

The dependence on charitable donations limits the expansion possibilities of the Caring Programs. Presently, most of the programs have waiting lists for coverage. However, Caring Programs have assisted thousands of families who otherwise would have been unable to access health care for their children (Lief, 1997).

Kaiser Permanente Cares for Kids

A total of 1.8 million children in California are uninsured. About 84 percent of the uninsured children in California come from working families, including 60 percent with parents who work full-time (Brown et al., 1997). Medi-Cal, the state's Medicaid program, covers 25 percent of the children in California, but 835,000 children who live in low-income, working families are ineligible for Medi-Cal. California's health insurance rates are among the highest in the country, making them unaffordable for low-income families.

In June 1997, Kaiser Permanente announced that it would donate $100 million over five years ($20 million annually) to subsidize health care coverage for up to 50,000 children a year in California. Children in California who are eligible for "Kaiser Permanente Cares for Kids" (between 200 and 275 percent of the federal poverty level) will be identified through a collaboration with schools as well as through a partnership with the Health Insurance Plan of California (HIPC).

The program's outreach will be conducted in conjunction with state enrollment efforts for "Healthy Families" and Medi-Cal. Kaiser Permanente will refer children who are not eligible for its program to other sources of coverage. Children enrolled in "Kaiser Permanente Cares for Kids" will receive a comprehensive benefit package, including inpatient and outpatient services, prescription drugs, and vision care. Families will pay a sliding scale premium. Two demonstration projects will be established to explore models of collaboration between schools and Kaiser Permanente to enhance health service delivery for children. Coverage is expected to begin in September 1998.

To enhance its initiative in California, Kaiser Permanente has assembled a statewide coalition to provide a coordinated policy forum to address the problem of the remaining uninsured children in the state. Other businesses and health plans are being approached to participate, and long-term plans include working with legislators to develop and secure the passage of legislation to expand access to coverage.

The "Kaiser Permanente Cares About Kids" initiative is part of a broader national effort by Kaiser Permanente to provide subsidized health care for low-income children. In Denver, Colorado, Kaiser Permanente has committed to covering up to 1,300 low-income children through a pilot program called "School Connections," in which eligible children will be able to receive health care at school-based health centers or at Kaiser Permanente's medical offices. In Maryland, Virginia, and the District of Columbia, Kaiser Permanente has developed partnerships with county government, hospitals, and other providers to cover up to 3,200 low-income uninsured children, with Kaiser Permanente providing the majority of the subsidy. Beginning in 1999, Kaiser Permanente will increase its funding for subsidized care, including an additional $10 million allocated to covering uninsured children in other Kaiser Permanente divisions, for a total of $30 million being devoted to covering uninsured children.

Children's Programs in Other Health Plans

In addition to Caring Programs and Kaiser Permanente, several other insurers and health plans across the country have smaller children's health initiatives (AAHP, 1997). Many of these initiatives involve partnerships with state departments of health, hospitals, advocacy groups, and other health plans. They include immunization campaigns, programs designed to improve access to care, health education, and child safety and violence prevention programs.

Among the initiatives are the following:

- Medica, a subsidiary of Allina Health System, uses multidisciplinary teams to help diagnose and treat children with chronic illnesses and disabilities, and allows pulmonologists to be designated as gatekeepers for children who are under their care.
- Mercy Health Plan, Pennsylvania's largest network model health plan for Medicaid beneficiaries, has an educational program for children with asthma to improve routine and primary care and reduce emergency room use.
- OmniCare Health Plan has developed a partnership with the Detroit Department of Health and a school-based health program to provide primary care examinations, health education activities, and immunization fairs for students and their families.
- UniHealth in southern California provides vaccinations at community-based clinics and in schools and churches.
- United HealthCare of Ohio provides free immunizations to children living in Franklin County, Ohio.

SUMMARY AND IMPLICATIONS

During the past decade, states and private insurers have taken a variety of steps to extend health insurance coverage to low-income children. These strategies have included expansions of Medicaid, the development of state-sponsored programs involving subsidies for private coverage, state support for privately sponsored programs, and privately sponsored initiatives designed by private insurers and health plans. Although the majority of these programs have not been evaluated systematically, they have helped to reduce the number of uninsured children. Yet more than 11 million children are still uninsured.

With the new SCHIP legislation, some of these programs may be replicated, and several new and innovative programs also may be designed and implemented. One of the most fundamental questions for each of these programs concerns eligibility. As these and other state programs continue to be implemented and modified in the years ahead, it will be important to monitor the extent and impact of coverage as well as of coverage substitution (IOM, 1998).

Even with full subsidies for coverage, whether Medicaid or another type of program, there are still eligible children who do not enroll in any program. Much more needs to be learned about the ways in which families make decisions about health insurance coverage and about the financial and nonfinancial factors that influence their decisions about how to spend the family's financial resources. Along with more research about families, there is a need for better outreach strategies, more widespread and culturally sensitive public education efforts, streamlined enrollment processes, and other approaches that will support families and caretakers and help them to make the best decisions about their children's health care.

In the child health area, states have undertaken a variety of projects to improve their services and promote "best practices" in the healthy development of children. In recent years, states also have taken many steps to improve their accountability to their citizens, including providing better public information on the performance of state programs. SCHIP offers states flexibility in program design. In return for that flexibility in design, the committee believes that states have the responsibility to implement the program as fully as possible, to provide as much public information as possible about the program, and to coordinate SCHIP with other state and private programs in the states to maximize children's opportunities to receive access to care.

REFERENCES

AAHP (American Association of Health Plans). 1997. *AAHP Fact Sheets: Chronic Care*. Washington, D.C.: AAHP.

AAHP. 1998. *Health Insurance for Children*. Washington, D.C.: AAHP.

Brown ER et al. 1997. *1.6 Million California Children Have No Health Insurance; Most Come from Families with at Least One Working Parent*. [http://www.ph.ucla.edu/sph/pr/wr97119.html]

Call KT, Lurie N, Jonk Y, Feldman R, Finch MD. 1997. Who is Still Uninsured in Minnesota? Lessons From State Reform Efforts. *Journal of the American Medical Association* 278(14):1191–1195.

Chollet DJ, Birnbaum ML, Sherman MJ. 1997. *Deterring Crowd-Out in Public Insurance Programs: State Policies and Experience*. Washington, D.C.: Alpha Center.

Commonwealth Fund. November 1996. Academic Health Centers: The TennCare Experience. *Briefing Note from Karen Davis*. New York: Commonwealth Fund.

Cutler DM, Gruber J. 1997. Medicaid and Private Insurance: Evidence and Implications. *Health Affairs* 16(1):194–200.

Dorn S, Teitelbaum M, Cortez, C. 1998. *An Advocate's Tool Kit for the State Children's Health Insurance Program*. Washington, D.C.: Children's Defense Fund.

Dubay L, Kenney G. 1997. *Lessons From the Medicaid Expansions for Children and Pregnant Women: Implications for Current Policy*. Statement for the United States House Committee on Ways and Means, Subcommittee on Health, Hearing on Children's Access to Health Coverage. April 8, 1997. [http://www.urban.org/TESTIMON/dubay.html]

Gauthier A, Schrodel SP. 1997. *Expanding Children's Coverage: Lessons from State Initiatives in Health Care Reform*. Washington, D.C.: Alpha Center.

GAO (U.S. General Accounting Office). 1995. *Medicaid: Spending Pressures Drive States Toward Program Reinvention*. Washington, D.C.: GAO. GAO/HEHS–95–122.

GAO. 1996. *Health Insurance for Children: State and Private Programs Create New Strategies to Insure Children*. Washington, D.C.: GAO. GAO/HEHS–96–35.

Gehshan S. 1997. *State Options for Expanding Children's Health Insurance: A Guide for Legislators*. Washington, D.C.: National Conference of State Legislatures.

Greenberg J, Zuckerman B. 1997. State Health Care Reform in Massachusetts: How One State Expanded Health Insurance for Children. *Health Affairs* 16(4):188–193.

Hill I, Bartlett TL, Bostrom MB. 1993. State Initiatives to Cover Uninsured Children. *The Future of Children* 3(2):149–151.

IOM, 1998. *Systems of Accountability: Implementing Children's Health Insurance Programs*. Washington, D.C.: National Academy Press.

Johnson K, McDonough JE. 1998. *Expanding Health Coverage for Children: Matching Federal Policies and State Strategies*. New York: Milbank Memorial Fund.

Ku L, Coughlin TA. 1997. *The Use of Sliding Scale Premiums in Subsidized Insurance Programs*. Washington, D.C.: Urban Institute. [http://www.urban.org/entitlements/premium.htm]

LaVallee C. 1997. *The Caring Program*. Presentation to the Committee on Children, Health Insurance, and Access to Care. Public Workshop, June 2, 1997, Institute of Medicine, Washington, D.C..

Lief L. Kids at Risk. *U.S. News and World Report*, April 28, 1997.

Lipson DJ, Schrodel SP. 1996. *State-Subsidized Insurance Programs for Low-Income People*. Washington, D.C.: Alpha Center.

Lurie N, Pheley L, Finch M. 1995. *Is MinnesotaCare Hitting Its Target?* Minneapolis, MN: Institute for Health Services Research, University of Minnesota School of Public Health and Hennepin County Medical Center.

Mann C. 1997. *Why Not Medicaid? Using Child Health Funds to Expand Coverage Through the Medicaid Program*. Washington, D.C.: Center for Budget and Policy Priorities. [http://www.cbpp.org/1119mcaid.htm]

McDonough JE. 1997. *The Massachusetts Children's Medical Security Plan*. Presentation to the Committee on Children, Health Insurance, and Access to Care. Public Workshop, June 2, 1997, Institute of Medicine, Washington, D.C..

Minnesota Health Information Clearinghouse. 1996. *What is MinnesotaCare?* St. Paul, MN: Minnesota Department of Health.

National Economic Council and Domestic Policy Council. 1998. *Implementation of the Children's Health Insurance Program: Six-month Progress Report*. Washington, D.C.: The White House.

NGA (National Governors Association). 1998. *National Governors Association Center for Best Practices, State Implementation Plans of Title XXI, The State Children's Health Insurance Program, as of March 12, 1998*. [http://www.nga.org/MCH/StateImplementation.htm]

Nichols LM, Blumberg LJ, Acs GP, Uccello CE, Marsteller JA. 1997. *Small Employers: Their Diversity and Health Insurance*. Washington, D.C.: Urban Institute. [http://www.urban.org/health/smemployers.htm]

Shenkman E, Pendergast J, Reiss J, Walther E, Bucciarelli R, Freedman S. 1996. The School Enrollment-based Health Insurance Program: Impact on Health Care Use of Low-income Children. *American Journal of Public Health* 86:1791–1793.

7

Children's Health Care Needs

Most American children—approximately 70 percent, or about 50 million children—are generally healthy. To help them stay healthy, these children need age-appropriate immunizations, regular preventive care, and professional treatment for acute illnesses and injuries (Ireys et al., 1997; Lozano et al., 1997; Neff and Anderson, 1995; Newacheck and Taylor, 1992). The expenditures for healthy children using the health care services, outlined above, account for about 10 percent of the total childhood medical expenditures (Neff and Anderson, 1995) (see Table 7.1).

Twenty percent of American children—about 14 million children—have mild to moderate chronic problems such as persistent ear infections, respiratory allergies, asthma, eczema and skin allergies, and speech defects (Neff and Anderson, 1995). These conditions may place significant limitations on their ability to function effectively in school and at home. Children with these chronic conditions require more frequent visits to primary care physicians, are more likely to visit emergency rooms, are more likely to need care from specialists, have greater needs for medications, and may also need hospitalization during acute episodes. Their expenses, on average, are two to three times higher than those for the average healthy child.

Another 10 percent—about 7 million children—have one or more severe chronic conditions, such as congenital heart defects, neural tube defects, juvenile diabetes mellitus, sickle cell disease, or HIV infections. Expenditures for this group account for 70 to 80 percent of all medical expenditures for children (Neff and Anderson, 1995).

Some of these children require high expenditures, primarily early in life (e.g., for surgical procedures). Others with severe medical conditions may require lifelong, intensive case management or enhanced medical care from primary care practitioners; regular consultations with pediatric subspecialists; and services from allied health professionals to maintain or to improve their functioning. They may require long-term medications or special equipment and supplies for home care. On average, the cost of care for this group of chronically ill children is five to six times higher than costs for the average healthy child (Neff and Anderson, 1995).

This chapter describes the health care needs of children, including children with chronic medical conditions and special health care needs. The chapter begins with a description of the epidemiology of acute childhood illnesses. It then turns to the health care needs of the most prevalent chronic conditions—dental conditions, mental health and substance abuse problems, and developmental disabilities—and then discusses the needs of children with severe medical problems. The chapter continues with a description of financial and nonfinancial access barriers for children with special health care

TABLE 7.1 Children's Needs for Health Care, United States, 1992

	Percentage of Population	Number (millions)	Percentage of Total Expenses
Healthy	70	50	10
Mild or Moderate Chronic Conditions	20	14	10-20 (2-3 times)
Severe Chronic Conditions	10	7	70-80 (5-6 times)

SOURCE: Neff and Andersen, 1992. Data are from the National Health Interview Survey as cited by Newacheck and Taylor, 1992.

needs, and then discusses some of the committee's concerns associated with managed care and its effects on access to health care for these children.

Certainly when we talk about children's health care status, we need to recognize how different children are, and how different their health care needs are from adults. Children face many obstacles in health care, but one of the hardest to overcome is the way most people view child health issues. When considering therapeutic interventions, medicines must be more finely calibrated, and diagnostic procedures may be more difficult. Young children, who have only a limited ability to communicate, must be examined more closely to diagnose and monitor illnesses.

Steve Edwards
American Academy of Pediatrics, Raleigh, NC
Public Workshop, June 2, 1997

EPIDEMIOLOGY OF ILLNESSES IN CHILDREN

Acute Illnesses

For most healthy children, a pediatrician, family physician, or other primary care practitioner (e.g., nurse practitioner or physician assistant) is usually the main source of preventive and acute medical care. Depending on the setting for care and the availability of allied health professionals on staff, these primary care practitioners also provide health education for parents and children, refer them for specialty consultations, and coordinate their care, as appropriate. Expanded services such as behavioral counseling, nutrition education, and parenting skills training also may be provided in a primary care setting.

Table 7.2 compares the frequency of acute illnesses and injuries for children with the general population. Infections are the most common acute illnesses of children, especially respiratory infections. Young children (ages 1 to 5 years) have significantly higher rates of acute illnesses than older children (ages 5 to 17 years) or than the general population.

TABLE 7.2 Number of Acute Conditions Per 100 Persons Per Year, for Children and All Ages, United States, 1994.

	Children		
Type of acute condition	Under Age 5	Ages 5-17	All ages
	Number per 100 persons		
Infective and Parasitic Diseases	**54.7**	**41.9**	**20.9**
Viral infections, unspecified	20.7	11.7	6.6
Common childhood diseases	8.6	2.9	1.5
Intestinal virus, unspecified	8.3	9.5	4.6
All other	17.1	17.8	8.2
Respiratory	**153.8**	**103.4**	**80.5**
Common cold	68.5	29.4	25.4
Other acute upper respiratory infections	25.1	20.3	11.9
Influenza	37.3	46.3	34.8
Acute bronchitis	11.3	4.3	4.7
All other	11.6	3.1	3.7
Digestive system	**10.6**	**8.3**	**6.1**
Indigestion, nausea, and vomiting	4.1	6.0	3.2
Dental conditions	3.4	0.7	1.1
All other	3.1	1.5	1.8
Injuries	**25.6**	**26.0**	**23.8**
Fractures and dislocations	1.9	4.6	3.0
Sprains and strains	0.8	4.9	5.5
Open wounds and lacerations	5.9	5.7	4.2
Contusions and superficial injuries	5.2	5.5	4.7
All other	11.8	5.3	6.5
Selected other acute conditions	**90.3**	**30.3**	**27.5**
Acute ear infections	62.7	13.6	9.3
Fever, unspecified	10.5	4.6	2.1
Skin conditions	5.9	2.7	2.4
Acute urinary conditions	2.8	1.2	3.1
Acute musculoskeletal conditions	0.8	1.5	3.5
All other	7.6	6.7	7.1
Other Acute Conditions	**23.7**	**10.2**	**12.7**
ALL ACUTE CONDITIONS	**358.7**	**220.1**	**171.5**

SOURCE: NCHS, 1995, p. 12. Data are from the 1994 National Health Interview Survey.

People come to the pediatric emergency department when their children are sick. Our triage nurses have determined that about 40 percent of the children who present to our facility have non-urgent issues. Parents who look at a young child with an earache or a sore throat don't say, well, we don't have authorization to be seen tonight in the emergency department. They don't want to wait two weeks to get in to the clinic. They perceive their child's pain as a family and social emergency. These people may be treated as though they don't belong in the emergency department. But a cough and a fever can be a sore throat and a viral upper respiratory infection, or it can be the beginning of a serious pneumonia or an asthma exacerbation.

Julius Goepp
Johns Hopkins Hospital, Baltimore, MD
Public Workshop, June 2, 1997

Chronic Conditions

This section describes the distinguishing features of the most prevalent chronic conditions: dental conditions, mental health and substance abuse problems, and developmental disabilities. Figure 7.1 indicates the total number of American children with selected chronic illnesses and conditions.

Concern about the costs of treatment for chronic conditions leads some employers and public officials to choose not to provide coverage for these conditions, or to provide only very restricted coverage. Although certain chronic conditions such as epilepsy or diabetes can be expensive to treat, the incidence of these conditions is limited.

Better risk adjustment methodologies are needed in order to adjust payment rates to reflect the expected costs of care for children with a variety of conditions. With better pricing systems, large employer-based dependent coverage pools and publicly-funded programs (especially those being designed under the authority of the new SCHIP legislation) may be better able to cover expensive conditions or diseases without depleting resources as much as may have been thought in the past.

Children with Dental Conditions

Tooth decay is the single most common chronic disease of children. It affects half of 5- to 9-year-olds in their first teeth and 84 percent of 17-year-olds in their permanent teeth (Kaste, Selwitz, Oldakowski et al., 1996). Untreated tooth decay results in pain, swelling, infection, dysfunction, and poor appearance. The National Health Interview Survey reports that children experience hundreds of thousands of "bed-days" and "low-activity days" because of tooth decay (NCHS, 1997b).

Dental services for children have been part of publicly funded child health programs for more than 60 years, both through direct service programs and through Medicaid. Medicaid offers dental coverage to more than 20 million children, one of every four U.S. children. Still, approximately 80 percent of decay is found in only 25 percent of children, and most often these children are from low-income families (DHHS, 1996).

The *Healthy People 2000* oral health indicators have not improved since the 1986 benchmark. The percentage of children with cavities and the percentage of unfilled cavities in children have not declined. At the same time, the percentage of children who visit a dentist before kindergarten has decreased. Among parents who report that their children have unmet health care needs, 57 percent report that the need is for dental care (NCHS, 1996).

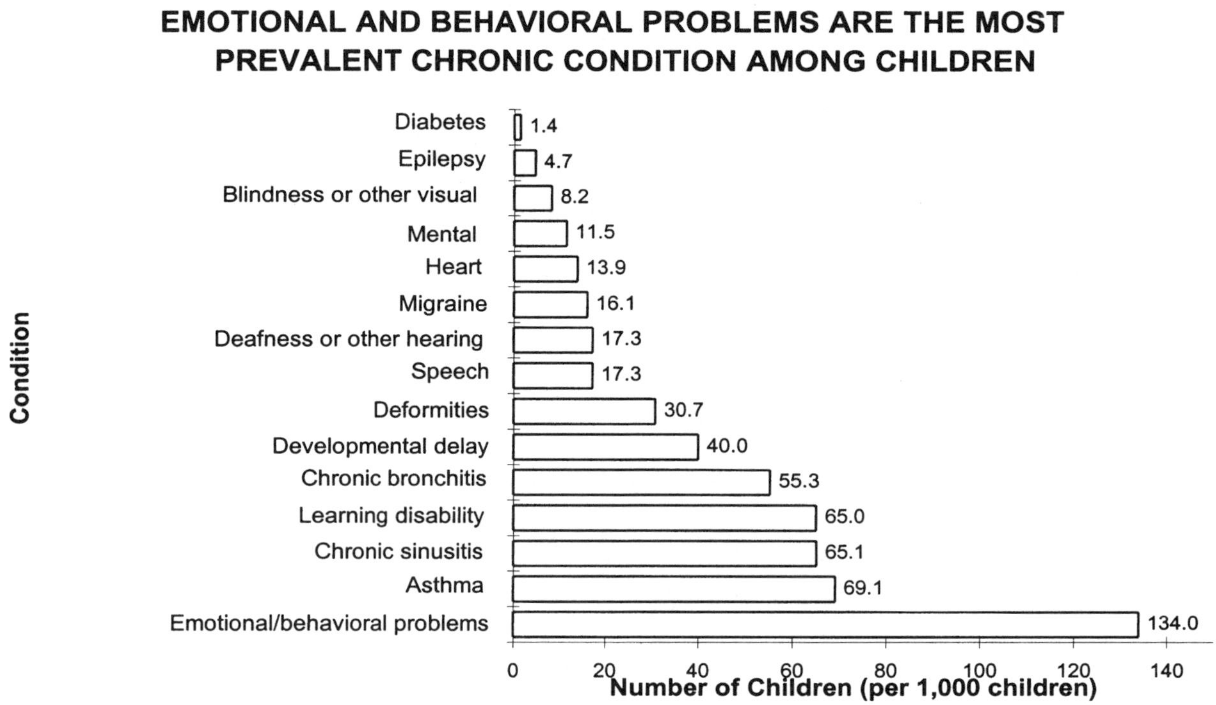

FIGURE 7.1 Number of children, ages 0-17[1], with selected chronic conditions, United States. SOURCE: NCHS, 1997a; NCHS, 1995; NCHS, 1994. NOTE: Data are from the the 1988 National Health Interview Survey, Child Health (learning disability, developmental delay, and emotional/behavioral problems); National Health Interview Survey, 1990-92 (nervous system and respiratory conditions); and National Health Interview Survey, 1994 (physical impairments).

[1]Data for learning disability, developmental delay, and emotional/behavioral problems, from the 1988 survey, cover children ages 3-17 only.

Children with Mental Health and Substance Abuse Problems

Approximately 12 million children, or 20 percent of all children, experience some type of mental health problem (e.g., attention-deficit-hyperactivity disorder, severe conduct disorder, and depression) or substance abuse problem (alcohol and other drug abuse or dependence) during childhood or adolescence (CMHS, 1996). An estimated 3.5 million children have serious emotional disturbances (CMHS, 1996). Compared with healthy children, children with physical health problems are more than twice as likely to have a mental health problem as well (Alliance for Health Reform, 1997).

Only about one third of children with severe mental health problems receive appropriate services from specialists (IOM, 1997a). Pediatricians and other primary care practitioners may be the first and only health care professionals to be consulted for childhood behavioral and emotional problems. Although some of these practitioners may be willing to provide appropriate care and referrals for these children, others may not have adequate training or time to do so.

A variety of sources—including community mental health centers, the mental health and substance abuse block grant, and state and local funding for mental health services—support services for these children and their families. National policies set by the National Institute of Mental Health and the Substance Abuse and Mental Health Services Administration promote "systems of care" for children with serious emotional disturbance, with an emphasis on case management, care coordination, individualized treatment plans, and active involvement of family members and other caregivers (IOM, 1997a). Block grant funds are often used to help states organize and coordinate these services.

Although these principles of case management and coordination have been used to develop children's mental health programs in many states, the programs have rarely been evaluated, and data on the implementation and success of the programs have not been collected. Still, this approach may provide a model for comprehensive approaches that could also be applied to other children with special health care needs.

Children with Developmental Disabilities

The Personal Responsibility and Work Opportunity Reconciliation Act of 1996 defines disability as a physical or mental condition or conditions that can be medically proven and that result in marked and severe functional limitations (SSA, 1997a). Children with developmental disabilities have chronic conditions that manifest as single physical, psychological, self-care, language, cognitive, or speech impairments or combinations of these conditions (e.g., cerebral palsy, spina bifida, hearing impairment, visual impairment, and mental retardation). Partly because of differences in definitions and range of severity, estimates of the prevalence of developmental disabilities among children vary from 3 to 17 percent (Boyle et al., 1994; Newacheck and Taylor, 1992).

Data from the National Health Interview Survey indicate that disabled children have 1.5 times more visits to physicians and 3.5 times more hospital days than other children. They miss twice as many school days and are 2.5 times more likely than children without these conditions to repeat a school grade (Boyle et al., 1994).

Children with developmental disabilities have unique and special needs. In addition to the usual health care needs, such as immunizations or care for acute respiratory infections, they often require the assistance of physicians and nonphysician specialists, such as nutritionists or physical therapists. For example, they may require specialized diets, surgical interventions, and specific therapies to prevent complications and to relieve or reduce symptoms.

Although children with disabling conditions may benefit from care provided by specialists in terms of improved health and longevity, several of the committee members believe that increased use of specialists and specialty services can lead to fragmentation of care unless there is an explicit treatment plan that designates responsibilities for care coordination among primary care providers, specialists, parents, and adjunctive practitioners. Care coordination decreases the likelihood of the need for crisis care, reduces duplication and gaps in services, and helps to increase the likelihood that a child will be referred for appropriate medical and adjunctive services to maintain as high a level of independent functioning as possible.

Children with Special Health Care Needs

Although there are many different definitions of children's disabling or chronic conditions, for the purposes of this discussion the committee believes that special health care needs fall into distinct subgroups. The first includes children with severe conditions that are initially costly but whose use of resources decreases over time (e.g., infants with congenital heart defects requiring surgery or premature infants requiring neonatal intensive care). The second group includes chronically ill children who need repeated episodes of care throughout life to maintain or improve functioning, including those with asthma, diabetes, malignancies, sickle cell disease, cystic fibrosis, and neurodevelopmental disabilities such as cerebral palsy, and visual and hearing impairment.

Naturally, children's health care and medical needs—and thus their medical expenses—vary by the diagnosis and the severity of their illnesses. The prospects for medical improvement and improved functioning vary significantly among children and may change over time with the developmental course of the illness.

I tried my best to do everything to have a healthy baby. I did not drink. I did not smoke. I took vitamins. I took prenatal exercise classes. The doctor assured me that I did nothing wrong, that these things just happen. We are grateful that Courtney is now stable. However, as long as she is on this earth she will continue to have medical needs. She takes several cardiac medicines in the hope of keeping her from going into congestive heart failure. Her heart cannot sustain very much stress, and she must be constantly monitored.

Karen LaPlante
Parent, Dublin, VA
Public Workshop, June 2, 1997

In general, however, appropriately designed early interventions and disease management strategies can help to improve a child's ability to function, can slow the progression of illness, and often can decrease the long-term costs associated with the condition (Neff and Anderson, 1995). Access to these interventions depends in large part on the structure of the child's health insurance benefit package and on the availability of services and providers in a community. Traditionally, more of the case management services and other expanded approaches have been more likely to be financed by the public sector than by private insurers and health plans (IOM, 1997a).

Whether it is children or adults, I don't think we have reached a national agreement on what we do for someone with a very expensive illness. When you pick up tomorrow morning's *Washington Post* Health Section, it will predictably have some story on a very expensive, new, beneficial treatment, and nobody is willing to say what they are going to ante up for that.

James Bentley
American Hospital Association, Washington, DC
Public Workshop, June 2, 1997

Traditional indemnity insurance coverage typically has very limited coverage of the supportive or supplemental therapies (speech, physical, etc.) required for children with severe chronic disease. Most managed care plans provide a core set of preventive and primary care benefits for children, but they differ in the extent to which specialty pediatric services are covered (McManus, 1998).

In recent years, health plans have begun to implement programs specifically for children with special health care needs, often in partnership with public health clinics (AAHP, 1997). Current initiatives include:

- The Blue Cross and Blue Shield Association working in partnership with the National Cancer Institute to refer children to nationally recognized treatment centers after being diagnosed with cancer;

- "ZAP Asthma," in which seven Atlanta-area health plans and local public health clinics will train community health workers to work with 200 families of children with asthma;
- Health Services for Children With Special Health Needs, Inc., a Washington, D.C.-based organization coordinating health care services for Medicaid recipients, including transportation, social services, respite care, and limited-use telephones for families without phone service; and
- HealthPartners in Minneapolis working with a local parent advocacy coalition to develop a streamlined referral process and a flexible benefits package for children with chronic conditions.

Although these initiatives are certainly worthwhile, they are only available in a few communities. Evaluations of these programs could yield useful information that can help in the design and development of programs in other communities.

Although we have private insurance, there are many charges that our insurance company is refusing to pay. We have an annual out-of-pocket deductible of $2,000 before they begin paying at 100 percent. This 100 percent is for "usual and customary charges." The medical providers bill us directly for the remainder of the charges.

Karen LaPlante
Parent, Dublin, VA
Public Workshop, June 2, 1997

PUBLIC COVERAGE FOR SPECIAL HEALTH CARE NEEDS

Historically, the public sector has taken the lead role in financing care for low-income and vulnerable populations. The services needed by families with children with special needs are funded by a mixture of federal, state, and local sources. The services are typically administered at the state and local levels, with significant variation in eligibility, availability of services, coordination among programs, and outreach and public education efforts.

Medicaid pays for health care services for low-income children with and without disabilities and is the major source of federal funds for medical services for special needs children. Medicaid generally covers health and related services for children who receive Supplemental Security Income (SSI), a cash benefit for low-income families with disabled children. It also covers services for children who are institutionalized. States may provide services for children with special health care needs under the Maternal and Child Health Services Block Grant (Title V) of the Social Security Act. This section gives a brief overview of the role of these programs with regard to special-needs children.

Medicaid

Because the benefit package in the Early and Periodic Screening, Diagnosis, and Treatment (EPSDT) program was specifically designed to address the needs of special-needs children (NIHCM, 1995), these expanded services—usually provided by nonmedical agencies or by other professionals such as advanced practice nurses or clinical nutritionists—are more likely to be covered by Medicaid than by private plans.

On a national basis, the average cost of EPSDT benefits for healthy children is typically about $1,000 to $1,500 per year, whereas the cost for special-needs children can approach $5,000 to $6,000 per year (NIHCM, 1995, p. 17). State-specific estimates of costs are generally not available, but average costs are likely to vary significantly by state, region, health care market, as well as by diagnostic and procedural categories.

One of the few states with published cost breakdowns is Washington State. In Washington State's Medicaid program, the average annual cost of care was $3,800 for children with selected chronic conditions, compared with an average of $955 for all enrolled children (Ireys et al., 1997). The proportions of payments for various categories of care (e.g., inpatient, outpatient, home care, drugs, durable medical equipment, and other providers) varied substantially by diagnosis. For example, inpatient costs ranged from 25 to 71 percent of the total. Durable medical equipment accounted for 24 percent of the costs of care for children with cerebral palsy, compared with 12 percent for children spina bifida and 5 percent or less for children with asthma, chronic respiratory disease, and diabetes (Ireys et al., 1997).

The Medicaid program is increasingly using managed care approaches in the delivery of services, most often through contracts with private health plans. An estimated 2.5 million children with chronic special health care needs are enrolled in the Medicaid program, but data are limited to evaluate the impact of Medicaid managed care on these children (Newacheck et al., 1994). Moreover, state Medicaid data tends to be aggregated, and without individual-level encounter data it is difficult to track or evaluate the types or quality of services used by any individual enrollee over time (GAO, 1997; Howell, 1996). The committee's general concerns about managed care are discussed in a later section of this chapter.

Supplemental Security Income

In 1996, approximately 955,000 children with disabilities received SSI payments that made them eligible for Medicaid (Alliance for Health Reform, 1997). SSI benefits are used to preserve the ability of families to take care of disabled children at home by providing cash assistance to help them meet some of their disability-related expenses, to help compensate for lost income, and to help meet basic expenses for food, clothing, and shelter (National Academy of Social Insurance, 1996).

As a result of the welfare reform legislation enacted in 1996, the definition of disability and the process for determining eligibility were tightened for children with behavioral problems (see Box 7.1), thus changing their Medicaid eligibility. The loss of SSI benefits could mean an increased financial burden for parents of disabled children, decrease their access to appropriate services, and ultimately have a significant impact on the children's level of functioning. However, there was controversy about the level of behavioral dysfunction that would merit a monthly federal cash payment and concern that the diagnostic criteria were too generous, as well as difficult to interpret (Koppelman, 1998).

In response to concerns expressed by the disability and children's health communities, the Balanced Budget Act of 1997 mandated Medicaid coverage for all disabled children who lost their eligibility due to changes in the welfare law or who were receiving SSI as of the date of the law's enactment (August 22, 1996). The Social Security Administration is reevaluating the determination criteria and reviewing appeals filed by families who have lost their benefits (see Box 7.1).

Maternal and Child Health Services Block Grant

Title V of the Social Security Act authorizes the Maternal and Child Health Services (MCH) Block Grant, a public health program that allows states to develop model, community-based health programs to improve the health of mothers and children. States are required to match $3 for every $4 that they receive from the federal government, and many states provide funds beyond the required match. More than $1.7 billion was generated in fiscal year 1997 for services at the state and local levels (MCHB, 1997).

The majority of MCH block grant funds are spent on preventive public health services to help meet the *Healthy People 2000* national health objectives of the Public Health Service Act. The funds are used to pay for services for children and pregnant women not covered by Medicaid. These include programs offered by local health departments, community and migrant health centers, and HIV prevention and treatment programs; some also are offered at Women, Infant, and Children (WIC) sites. Title V programs directly operate programs or fund local providers for services, including immunizations and well-child examinations, treatment or referral, school health services and education programs, and others.

State Title V programs are required to coordinate with other federal health, education, and social services programs. As a result, MCH block grant funds typically are used to strengthen linkages among programs and to fill gaps, creating and supporting community-based systems of care for children and their parents. States are required to use at least 30 percent of Title V funds on services for children with special health care needs, and 900,000 children with chronic illnesses and disabilities receive services supported by the block grant (AAP, 1997). These include case management, care coordination, and family support services and a limited number of home-visiting services, supported by the block grant.

FINANCIAL BARRIERS ASSOCIATED WITH SPECIAL NEEDS

Even for families with comprehensive benefits provided through traditional private health insurance, out-of-pocket expenses for copayments and deductibles for the required medical services, occupational and physical therapy, and durable medical equipment can be quite substantial (Leonard et al., 1992). Some estimates suggest that expenses for children and families with special health care needs can be as high as 9 to 12.5 percent of the total family income (Leonard et al., 1992).

According to testimony heard in the committee's public workshop, families with these kinds of expenditures may quickly approach an insurance policy's lifetime limit on benefits, perhaps while the child is an infant, leaving the possibility of several decades without reasonable coverage. Families may be forced to choose between medical care and such basic needs as food, shelter, and long-term economic survival.

To the best of my knowledge, there is not a single state in this country where a family with severe medical needs doesn't have to wind up with poverty as a definition of when it can get access to some broad scale public program. I don't know of any state or any national program that really gets around that.

James Bentley
American Hospital Association, Washington, DC
Public Workshop, June 2, 1997

Caregivers of children with special health care needs must devote significant amounts of their time to coordinating care, often among several agencies and providers. Transportation and related costs can become significant, and frequently one or both parents must miss work to keep appointments (Leonard et al., 1992) (see Box 7.2).

NONFINANCIAL BARRIERS FOR SPECIAL NEEDS CHILDREN

Children with chronic health conditions and special health care needs and their families face the same nonfinancial barriers to health care as other segments of society: transportation barriers, racial and cultural barriers, scheduling problems, lack of day care, and other difficulties. However, because of their complicated medical status, these children need more frequent visits to physicians and other health care

BOX 7.1
Supplemental Security Income Program

Authorized by Title XVI of the Social Security Act of 1965 and begun in 1974, the Supplemental Security Income (SSI) Program replaced state-administered adult assistance programs to provide uniform federal income support to the needy aged, blind, and disabled who were not covered by Social Security, or for those who were only minimally covered. The program is administered by the Social Security Administration (SSA).

Eligibility

To be eligible for the SSI Program, individuals must meet income and resource requirements, and must satisfy one of the following categorical requirements:

- elderly—65 years of age or older;
- blind—defined as those people whose vision is 20/200 or less with a correcting lens in the better eye, or those with tunnel vision 20 degrees or less; or
- disabled—defined as those people who cannot "engage in any substantial gainful activity because they have a medically-determined physical or mental impairment that is expected to result in death or that has lasted, or is expected to last, for a continuous 12-month period."
- spouse or child of a disabled worker.

Children less than 18 years of age (or less than 22, if a full-time student) are also eligible to receive SSI payments, if they are blind or disabled, unmarried, and if their family meets the income and resource requirements.

Benefits

SSI was designed as a program of last resort; beneficiaries must file for all entitled benefits before SSI payments are determined. (It should be noted, however, SSI beneficiaries may not receive TANF payments. See Table 5.1). SSI payments are adjusted annually to reflect the cost of living (COLA). As of September 1997, the average payment was about $436 per month (Vobejda and Goldstein, 1997).

The rationale for the benefits is to help families meet the disability-related costs of raising a disabled child, such as medical supplies and equipment; to help compensate parents for lost income when they stay

professionals (Leonard et al., 1992). In short, children with special needs face even greater challenges to access of appropriate health care and other needed services.

We take all children. In fact, let's be clear about it—we look for the sick children, because in my opinion, those who have a special health care need, who are in a low-income family, these are the children who are most at risk.

Charles LaVallee
Western Pennsylvania Caring Foundation for Children
Public Workshop, June 2, 1997

---

home to care for a disabled child; and to help pay for basic needs such as food, clothing, and shelter. Thus, the purpose is to help support families that choose to care for their disabled children in their own homes.

Childhood Disability—Welfare Reform Changes

In August 1996, the Personal Responsibility and Work Opportunity Reconciliation Act of 1996 (P.L. 104-193) mandated that the Social Security Administration change its definition of childhood disability and make the definition comparable to that for adults. The revised definition requires a child to have a physical or mental condition or conditions that can be medically proven and which result in marked and severe functional limitations, and requires that the conditions must last or be expected to last at least 12 months or to result in death. Before the law was changed, a child with a condition not listed on the medical listing of impairments could be eligible for SSI if he or she was not functioning at an age-appropriate level as measured by the Individual Functional Assessment and evaluated by SSA. (A child with serious attention deficit disorder, for example, would be eligible under this definition.)

As a result of the new law, SSA began to review the cases of 260,000 children, more than one quarter of the one million enrolled in the program in 1996. As of September 1997, 120,000 children had lost their benefits, and as many as 65,000 more, or about quarter of all SSI children, were expected to lose their benefits when the review has been completed. Families that are denied benefits may appeal, and almost half of them have done so. Of 2,200 cases that were appealed and had reached the first stage of review before September 1997, 67 percent were overturned and benefits restored.

The new Commissioner of SSA, Kenneth Apfel, agreed in his Senate confirmation hearing on September 10, 1997, to re-evaluate the implementation of the new eligibility rules within 30 days of his swearing-in. The re-evaluation would be intended to determine whether the problems were due primarily to variations in interpretations of the definitions by states or with the procedures for conducting reviews.

On December 17, 1997, Commissioner Apfel released a report reviewing the implementation of the childhood disability provisions of the welfare reform law. After an examination of quality assurance data and other oversight activities, the accuracy of determination decisions was found to vary by state and by impairment. The Commissioner directed the agency to review the cases of 45,000 children who had lost their benefits during the redetermination process. In addition, families whose eligibility for SSI was ceased under the new law were given another opportunity to appeal.

SOURCES: SSA, 1997a, 1997b; Pear, 1997; Vobejda and Goldstein, 1997.

For children who are dependent on such technology as respirators, specially trained nurses may be required. It is often very difficult to obtain skilled day care for such children, and it can be difficult to obtain reimbursement for day care. As a result, parents lose days from work or give up their jobs to meet ongoing needs or as a result of intercurrent illnesses and disease relapses (Leonard et al., 1992). Because data on the impact of children with special needs on the parents' productivity in their places of work are not available, it is difficult to estimate the number of parents affected.

Although the treatment needs for each child and the treatment protocols for each chronic illness differ, children with chronic conditions and special health care needs typically see a wide range of practitioners. They are clinically managed by primary care pediatricians or family physicians, typically with an extensive amount of family and community involvement and referrals to specialists as needed. Alternatively, their care may be managed and coordinated by a pediatric specialist associated with a children's hospital or a pediatric specialty center within a larger community or academic health center (Neff and Anderson, 1995). More extensive research is needed to compare the relative effectiveness of

BOX 7.2
Caregivers' Time Costs

- personal care (helping with the child's bathing, grooming, eating, and so forth);
- providing medical care (i.e., medications, tube feedings, treat wounds);
- preparing special or extra meals and cleaning up afterward;
- extra or special shopping and running errands (i.e., buying clothes, picking up medications);
- extra household chores (cleaning home, snow shoveling, yardwork);
- escorting this child to get health care;
- escorting this child to nonmedical functions beyond what you would have to do if he or she were healthy (i.e., social activities, entertainment)
- managing this child's medical conditions (scheduling appointments with physicians, nurses, and social workers);
- managing this child's finances (dealing with insurance companies, finding special programs, filling out forms);
- waiting in physician's offices; and
- monitoring medical equipment (cleaning, making sure it is in working order).

SOURCE: Leonard et al., 1992.

these strategies. Such studies should take into account the severity of the child's illness, the family's skills and capacity for caretaking, and a variety of other factors.

> I am sad that there are no state and federal programs that assist middle class families in a way that allows them to continue to be middle class families. I have been told many times in the past that our family would have been much better off if we did not work or if we did not have insurance. Then our child would have qualified for assistance. It has been suggested that we get a divorce, place our child into an institution, or put our child in foster care in order to receive assistance toward her medical bills. Caring for an ill child is stressful enough without the sense of financial responsibilities, even when we have insurance.
>
> *Karen LaPlante*
> *Parent, Dublin, VA*
> *Public Workshop, June 2, 1997*

Pediatric subspecialists and intensivists tend to be located in regional medical centers. In many areas, children with complicated health care needs are referred to regional pediatric specialty centers even for routine care because locally available primary care providers may not be able to deliver the needed specialized care or the necessary case management and care coordination may not be not available locally (Schlesinger and Mechanic, 1993). In addition to the travel time and the rearrangement of work and child care schedules, out-of-pocket expenses for transportation and hotel bills can be significant.

INFORMATION TECHNOLOGY

The use of information technology holds significant promise for increasing access to health care when consumers and their providers live and work in different communities. For example, electronic consultations using computer-based patient records can reduce the need for families to travel long distances to consult specialists. The term "telemedicine" is generally applied to the use of information technology when there is geographic separation or distance between the participants. Telemedicine applications include clinical evaluations, consultations, and supervision of providers in other locations (IOM, 1996).

Computer-based patient records can help to facilitate provider access to records, make transfer of records easier, and increase the availability of clinical information for research (IOM, 1997b). Many other uses of information technology are developing in medicine and health care, including some that are consumer-oriented. For those parents and providers who are able to use computers, an extensive variety of patient education materials are available through the Internet. Electronic parent-support groups, children's advocacy groups, and others are becoming increasingly common.

To provide readers with some examples of the uses of information technology by specialty providers, Box 7.3 includes some scenarios based on the actual clinical experiences of one of the committee members, a pediatric gastroenterologist. Research and evaluation have not caught up with the rapid diffusion or variety of uses of information technology in health care, and standard protocols and guidelines have not been developed, with the exception of the standards for electronic transmission of clinical data that are mandated by the Health Insurance Portability and Accountability Act of 1996.

Medical information systems can cost from $500,000 to several million dollars, depending on their features (Ciotti and Zodda, 1996). The expense of installing new administrative software has slowed its implementation, particularly in public clinics. In the past, insurers and health plans have restricted payments for telemedicine consultations and other electronic applications, such as patient education (IOM, 1996). However, the committee believes strongly in the potential of information technology to improve access and quality in health care for children and their families, and the committee urges insurers and health plans to explore its use further.

ACCESS UNDER MANAGED CARE

As of the summer of 1997, 36 states had mandated managed care arrangements for at least some children with special needs (Alliance for Health Reform, 1997). Some providers and researchers have expressed serious concerns about the potential for incorporating patients with chronic illnesses and serious medical conditions into the typical capitated managed care model (Hughes et al., 1995; Newacheck et al., 1994). Most managed care organizations (MCOs) have traditionally served working adults, who are generally healthy. Thus, MCOs have not tended to have much experience with low-income, chronically ill, or low-income individuals, although some are gaining experience through Medicaid managed care contracts and through developing programs specifically for these groups (AAHP, 1997).

There are few existing studies of children's access to care under managed care and they show many gaps and inconsistencies, making the evidence difficult to interpret. For example, a few studies have compared access to preventive services for low-income children with managed care and traditional coverage. They have found that children enrolled in Health Maintenance Organizations (HMOs) are more likely than children with traditional coverage to receive preventive medical care such as immunizations, vision and other screening tests, as well as more frequent and complete check-up visits compared with children with traditional coverage (Carey et al., 1990; Szilagyi et al., 1990).

A study comparing immunization rates for inner-city infants in Los Angeles found that they were more likely to have current immunizations if they received care in public health clinics rather than in

BOX 7.3
Scenarios Demonstrating Increased Access to Care Via Information Technology

Scenario 1

J.R. is a 4-year-old child who has always been somewhat slow in his development. He didn't walk until nearly age 3-years and at age 4 he only has a few words in his vocabulary. He has always seemed very clumsy, and since beginning to walk, his parents have noticed that he walks on his toes. The child has otherwise been healthy without any serious illnesses. Because of his good health, he has not been seen by a physician since he was 2.

He is brought to the family physician for a routine school physical. During that visit, the physician expresses concern about the child's development, and after examining the child, the physician explains to the mother that the child probably has cerebral palsy. The mother is extremely distraught and uncertain as to the significance of this diagnosis.

The family physician suggests that it would be appropriate for the child to be seen and evaluated at a child development center. However, the family lives in a rural region and the nearest child development center is nearly 5 hours away. The physician provides the mother with the appropriate phone numbers and the mother calls the child development center to schedule an appointment. After a preliminary interview over the phone, the mother is directed to an interactive site on the World Wide Web that describes the services provided by the child development center. The website also contains an interactive multimedia tutorial about cerebral palsy that describes what it is, what some of its symptoms are, what can cause it, and some forms of therapy. Built into the tutorial are links to other educational materials, United Cerebral Palsy (UCP), and several moderated discussion groups.

While on-line, the mother fills out a series of interactive forms on which she details her child's medical and developmental history. Based on the information provided on the forms, the coordinator at the child development center tailors a multidisciplinary evaluation for the child that includes assessments by a speech and language pathologist, a physical therapist, an educational specialist, a developmental psychologist, and a developmental pediatrician. The coordinator phones the mother and provides her with an outline of the planned evaluation and points her back to the web-site for a complete description of all the services planned for the child.

On the day of the assessment, the mother not only comes prepared for the assessment but is also armed with lots of information and many well-informed questions. In this scenario, information technology helps educate and empower the "consumer" as well as optimize the use of resources both from the family's perspective and from the healthcare system's perspective.

Scenario 2

R.W. is a 12-year-old female with severe spastic cerebral palsy. She has been followed by her local family physician for routine health care, but receives specialized care at a large child development clinic affiliated with a children's hospital. During the past 2 years, feeding R.W. has become increasingly difficult.

The parents often spend 6 hours each day trying to get her to eat. Despite all these efforts, her intake has declined over the past 6 months and she has lost several pounds.

At the suggestion of their family physician, the family schedules an appointment at the child development clinic. During that visit, it is suggested that the family consider having a feeding gastrostomy tube placed to improve R.W.'s nutrition. The family members are quite resistant to this intervention but at the conclusion of their visit, they are provided with the address to the child development clinic's website, which contains a multimedia tutorial on feeding through gastrostomy tubes.

Over the weeks following their visit to the child development clinic, the family visit the website several times and review the tutorial on gastrostomy tubes. The tutorial describes the actual procedure of placing the gastrostomy tube including diagrams, videos, and a short virtual tour of the operating and recovery suites. The tutorial also provides links to published follow-up studies concerning the use of a feeding gastrostomy tube in children with cerebral palsy, a link to a moderated listserve run by parents with children with gastrostomies, and the e-mail addresses of several parents who have agreed to serve as lay consultants. The tutorial also includes a direct e-mail link to the developmental pediatricians and pediatric gastroenterologists at the child development clinic to facilitate exchange of information. The family takes advantage of this e-mail consultation service to ask the gastroenterologist several questions concerning the actual operative procedure.

After a great deal of soul-searching and deliberation, the family concludes that a gastrostomy is a good choice for their daughter. In this scenario, information technology helps the family make an informed decision concerning the care of their daughter by helping the family assimilate the available information about the proposed treatment as well as helping them communicate with other families that have gone through similar experiences.

Scenario 3

K.T. is a 6-year-old female with severe spastic cerebral palsy who had a feeding gastrostomy and Nissen fundoplication (anti-reflux procedure) approximately eight months ago. Two months after her surgery, K.T. began experiencing frequent gagging and retching, and her ability to eat by mouth dramatically decreased. K.T.'s pediatrician and surgeon try a number of different medications without substantial change in her symptoms.

The family becomes increasingly frustrated and performs a search on the Internet about gastrostomies. They find a moderated listserve run by parents of children with gastrostomy tubes and post a question on the listserve describing their daughter's symptoms. A number of parents respond stating that most likely K.T. is suffering from "post-Nissen dumping syndrome." These parents offer K.T.'s mother and father several references as well as the web address of a pediatric gastroenterologist who has written about this disorder. K.T.'s parents electronically consult this gastroenterologist, who makes a number of conservative therapeutic recommendations. K.T.'s parents return to their pediatrician and pediatric surgeon armed with information including several references.

In this actual case history, parents used information technology to influence physicians and improve the care of their child. This type of exchange reinforces the concept that health care professionals and parents must be collaborators when caring for children with complex needs.

private physician offices or HMOs (Wood et al., 1994). A national study found, however, that infants were more likely to receive well-child visits and immunizations in private physician offices or HMOs than in public health clinics (Mustin et al., 1994). There is tremendous variation from community to community in the provision of care for low-income groups (Baxter and Mechanic, 1997), and it is very difficult to generalize from the existing studies.

It is well-known that the cost savings under managed care are derived from the increased use of primary care and decreased utilization of specialty and inpatient care. Although this pattern of utilization may be appropriate for children who are generally healthy, its potential impact on children with chronic conditions and special health care needs causes concern (Schlesinger and Mechanic, 1993). Some children's health advocates fear that managed care has an inherent disincentive to provide treatment, although there is little scientific evidence to substantiate this claim. Because the actual costs of inclusion of children with chronic conditions and special needs in managed care plans and networks have not been systematically reported or studied, the issue remains controversial.

Another concern about managed care is that many health plans do not include pediatric specialists in their approved provider networks. As a result, children with complex illnesses may be seen by adult specialists who are trained to care for adults with similar illnesses but who lack the knowledge of the specific manifestations of disease in children and the differences between children and adults (Cartland and Yudkowsky, 1992).

Because at least 36 states now have some form of mandated managed care for at least some children with special needs, several strategies have been proposed to increase the likelihood that their medical needs will be met. These include ensuring that there are a significant number of local pediatric specialists in networks before contracts are negotiated (Newacheck et al., 1994); setting up separate payment systems for children with certain medical conditions or "carving out" these groups (Neff and Anderson, 1995); and developing quality assurance measures that assess quality of care for children with chronic conditions, including clinical practice guidelines and practice parameters, and consumer protections, such as written policies concerning grievances and availability of services (IOM, 1997a; Newacheck et al., 1994).

Long-term strategies include developing better pricing systems, particularly risk adjustment mechanisms that adjust payment rates to reflect the higher expected costs of care for children with chronic conditions. Although health policy and financing experts have been recommending better risk adjustment mechanisms for several years, much work remains to be done to resolve technical and methodological disagreements among proponents of different approaches (Iezzoni, 1997; IOM, 1996).

Despite these technical difficulties and the need for better information involving risk selection and costs of coverage, there is no question that children with special needs typically have additional, nonmedical needs. These include supplemental or adjunctive therapies; specialized transportation, supplies, and equipment; links with schools and other community-based organizations; and family support, including respite care and assistance with out-of-pocket (noncovered) expenses.

IMPLICATIONS FOR CHILDREN'S INSURANCE EXPANSIONS

Insurance coverage for children is variable and fragmented, and many controversial issues remain unresolved. It is generally agreed that the most comprehensive and child-specific package of benefits is Medicaid, which offers a full range of medically necessary care for children, including children with special needs. In some cases, privately insured children can receive additional assistance from public sources, even Medicaid, to pay for what their private plan does not cover.

Some opponents of Medicaid believe that if private insurers do not guarantee comprehensive coverage, public programs should not do so either. Others take a pragmatic position that it is less expensive for society in the long run to provide preventive services and early interventions for low-income children. Still others believe that it is the responsibility of society to provide medically necessary care for all children regardless of their insurance status.

Broadly speaking, traditional private insurance is primarily designed to provide time-limited coverage for acute episodes, whereas Medicaid also covers treatments which may improve functioning and quality of life, but are not expected to result in a cure. Healthy children, as well as children with special health needs, could benefit from the coordination and management of care that are offered in managed care environments, but some in the children's health community are concerned that managed care does not yet have adequate quality assurance methods for special needs children.

Under the new State Children's Health Insurance Program (SCHIP) legislation, states may choose to expand Medicaid, to create or expand a separate state program for children's health insurance, or to use Medicaid for some uninsured children and a separate program for others. Medicaid expansions must provide the existing Medicaid benefits and must be implemented statewide. Other programs do not need to be statewide but must be based on one of the following three options:

- *Benchmark coverage*. The standard Blue Cross/Blue Shield preferred provider plan for federal employees, or the commercial HMO plan with the largest insured, non-Medicaid enrollment in the state, or a health benefits plan offered and generally available to state employees.
- *Benchmark-equivalent coverage*. This must include hospital services, physician's services, laboratory and X-ray services, well-baby and well-child care, and immunizations. Some coverage of prescription drugs, mental health services, and vision and dental care is required if it is covered under the benchmark plan being used by the state for this purpose.
- *Another benefits package approved by the Secretary of Health and Human Services*.

As of April 1, 1998, six months after the SCHIP program began, 8 states had federally approved plans that are expected to cover more than 1 million additional children. Another 15 states had submitted plans to DHHS for approval; of these, only 2 states (Connecticut and Massachusetts) had specifically included programs for children with special needs.

States developing new children's insurance programs have many options for providing coverage for special needs children. The committee encourages states to take advantage of the new program to improve the availability of insurance programs to meet the needs of all children.

REFERENCES

AAHP (American Association of Health Plans). 1997. *AAHP Fact Sheets: Chronic Care*. Washington, D.C.: AAHP Medical Affairs Department.

AAP (American Academy of Pediatrics). 1997. *Legislative and Regulatory Issue: Maternal and Child Health Block Grant*. Washington, D.C.: Author. [http://www.aap.org/advocacy/washing/maternal.htm]

Alliance for Health Reform. 1997. *Managed Care and Vulnerable Americans: Children With Special Health Care Needs*. Washington, D.C.: Author.

Baxter RJ, Mechanic RE. 1997. The Status of Local Health Care Safety Nets. *Health Affairs* 16(4)7–23.

Boyle CA, Decoufle P, Yeargin-Allsopp M. 1994. Prevalence and Health Impact of Developmental Disabilities in US Children. *Pediatrics* 93(3):399–403.

CMHS (Center for Mental Health Services), Substance Abuse and Mental Health Services Administration, Department of Health and Human Services (DHHS). 1996. *Child, Adolescent, and Family Programs*. Washington, D.C.; National Mental Health Services Knowledge Exchange Network.

Cartland JDC, Yudkowsky M. 1992. Barriers to Pediatric Referral in Managed Care Systems. *Pediatrics* 89:183–188.

Carey T et al. 1990. Prepaid versus Fee-for-Service Medicaid Plans: Effects on Preventive Health Care. *Journal of Clinical Epidemiology* 43:1213–1220.

Ciotti V, Zodda F. 1996. Selecting Managed Care Information Systems. *Healthcare Financial Management*, June, 35–40.

DHHS (Department of Health and Human Services, Office of the Inspector General). 1996. *Children's Dental Services Under Medicaid*: Access and Utilization, OEI-09–00240. San Francisco, CA: US DHHS.

GAO (General Accounting Office). 1997. *Medicaid Managed Care Accountability*. Washington D.C.: GAO/HEHS/97–86.

HIAA (Health Insurance Association of America). 1997. *Source Book of Health Insurance Data*. Washington, D.C.: HIAA.

Howell EM. 1996. Medicaid Managed Care Encounter Data: What, Why, and Where Next? *Health Care Financing Review* 17(4):87–95.

Hughes D.C., Newacheck PW, Stoddard JJ, Halfon N. 1995. Medicaid Managed Care: Can It Work for Children? *Pediatrics* 95(4):591–594.

Iezzoni LI. 1997. The Risks of Risk Adjustment. *Journal of the American Medical Association*, 278:1600–1607.

Institute of Medicine (IOM). 1989. *The Future of Public Health*. Washington, D.C.: National Academy Press.

IOM. 1993. *Employment and Health Benefits: A Connection at Risk*. Washington, D.C.: National Academy Press.

IOM. 1996. *Telemedicine: A Guide to Assessing Telecommunications in Health Care*. Washington, D.C.: National Academy Press.

IOM. 1997a. *Managing Managed Care: Quality Improvement in Behavioral Health*. Washington, D.C.: National Academy Press.

IOM. 1997b. *The Computer-Based Patient Record: An Essential Technology for Health Care. Revised Edition*. Washington, D.C.: National Academy Press.

Ireys HT, Anderson GF, Shaffer TJ, Neff JM. 1997. Expenditures for Care of Children With Chronic Illnesses Enrolled in the Washington State Medicaid Program, Fiscal Year 1993. *Pediatrics* 100(2):197–204.

Kaiser Commission on the Future of Medicaid. 1997. *Medicaid Facts: Medicaid and Managed Care*. Washington, D.C.: Kaiser Commission on the Future of Medicaid.

Kaste LM, Selwitz RH, Oldakowsky RJ, et al. 1996. Coronal caries in the primary and permanent dentition of children and adolescents, 1988–91. *Journal of Dental Research* 75(Special Issue):631–641.

Koppelman J. Personal communication to Institute of Medicine. February 1998.

Leonard B, Burst JD, Sapienza JJ. 1992. Financial and Time Costs to Parents of Severely Disabled Children. *Public Health Reports* 107:302–312.

Lewit EM, Monheit AC. 1992. Expenditures on Health Care for Children and Pregnant Women. *The Future of Children* 2(2):95–114.

Lozano P, Fishman P, VonKorff M, Hecht J. 1997. Health Care Utilization and Cost Among Children with Asthma who were Enrolled in a Health Maintenance Organization. *Pediatrics* 99(6):757–764.

McManus M. 1998. *Evaluating Managed Care Plans for Children With Special Health Care Needs: A Purchaser's Tool*. [http://www.ichp.edu/mchb/center/policy/index.htm]

MCHB (Maternal and Child Health Bureau), Health Resources and Services Administration, DHHS. 1997. *Maternal and Child Health Bureau - Overview*. [http://www.os.dhhs.gov/hrsa/mchb/overview.htm]

Moore CM, Ahmed I, Mouallem R, May W, Ehlayel M, Sorensen RU. 1997. Care of Asthma: Allergy Clinic Versus Emergency Room. *Annals of Allergy, Asthma, and Immunology* 78:373–380.

Mustin HD et al. 1994. Adequacy of Well-Child Care and Immunizations in U.S. Infants Born in 1988. *Journal of the American Medical Association* 272:1111–1115.

National Academy of Social Insurance. 1996. *Restructuring the SSI Disability Program for Children and Adolescents*. Washington, D.C.: Author.

NCHS (National Center for Health Statistics). 1994. Health of Our Nation's Children. *Vital and Health Statistics* 10 (191). Hyattsville, MD: US Department of Health and Human Services.

NCHS. 1995. Current Estimates from the National Health Interview Survey, 1994. Prepared by PF Adams and MA Marano. *Vital and Health Statistics* 10 (193). Hyattsville, MD: US Department of Health and Human Services.

NCHS. 1996. *Healthy People 2000 Review 1995–96*. DHHS Publication No. PHS 96–1256. Hyattsville, MD: US Public Health Service.

NCHS. 1997a. Prevalence of Selected Chronic Conditions: United States, 1990–1992. *Vital and Health Statistics* 10 (194). Hyattsville, MD: US Department of Health and Human Services.

NCHS. 1997b. Priority Area 13, Oral Health. *Healthy People 2000 Review 1997*. Hyattsville, MD: US Department of Health and Human Services.

Neff JM, Anderson G. 1995. Protecting Children With Chronic Illness in a Competitive Marketplace. *Journal of the American Medical Association* 274:1866–1869.

Newacheck PW, Taylor WR. 1992. Childhood Chronic Illness: Prevalence, Severity, and Impact. *American Journal of Public Health* 82:364–371.

Newacheck PW, Hughes D, Stoddard JJ, Halfon N. 1994. Children With Chronic Illness and Medicaid Managed Care. *Pediatrics* 93:497–500.

NIHCM (National Institute for Health Care Management). 1995. *Assuring Quality of Care for Children in Medicaid Managed Care–EPSDT in a Time of Changing Policy*. Washington, D.C.: NIHCM.

Pear R. 1997. 135,000 Children to be Struck From Disability Benefit Rolls. *The New York Times*, February 7, 1997.

Schlesinger M, Mechanic D. 1993. Challenges for Managed Competition from Chronic Illness. *Health Affairs Supplement*. 1993:123–137.

SSA (Social Security Administration). 1997a. *The Definition of Disability for Children*. SSA Publication No. 05–11053, July 1997. [http://www.ssa.gov/pubs/11053.html]

SSA. 1997b. *News Release: Statement by Kenneth S. Apfel, Commissioner of Social Security, on SSI Childhood Disability Reviews*. [http://www.ssa.glv/press/childhood_statement.html]

Szilagyi PG et al. 1990. The Effect of Independent Practice Association Plans on Use of Pediatric Ambulatory Medical Care in One Group Practice. *Journal of the American Medical Association* 263(16):2198–2203.

Vobejda B, Goldstein A. 1997. Quick Review Promised for SSI Rules: Thousands of Children Have Lost Benefits. *The Washington Post*, September 11, p. A9.

Wood D et al. 1994. Access to Infant Immunizations for Poor, Inner-City Families: What is the Impact of Managed Care? *Journal of Health Care for the Poor and Underserved* 5(2):112–23.

Zuckerman S, Evans A, Holahan J. *Questions for States as They Turn to Medicaid Managed Care. Number 11 in Series, "Issues and Options for States*." Washington, D.C.: Urban Institute. [http://newfederalism.urban. org/html/anf_a11.htm]

Appendixes

A

Market-Based Approaches to Insurance Reform

Robert B. Helms[1]
American Enterprise Institute, Washington, DC

Although 26 percent of the American population have health coverage through public programs, the majority of Americans, approximately 61 percent in 1994, are covered by health insurance arranged through their place of employment.[2] The private sector is especially important when it comes to the coverage of children, because in 1995 approximately 59 percent of children were covered by their parents' employer-based plans. Eighty-three percent of the 9.8 million children who are not presently covered are dependents of working Americans.[3] This appendix will look at the history and present characteristics of private sector health insurance and the pros and cons of several policy proposals designed to increase health insurance coverage for children.

A BRIEF HISTORY OF EMPLOYER-BASED HEALTH INSURANCE

The history of health insurance in the United States has always been tied to the development of modern medicine. There was little reason to buy health insurance until medicine created the ability to affect medical outcomes. The cost of these new forms of medical care created a desire to spread the risk of a relatively large medical expenditure among a large number of individuals, any one of whom would face a low probability of an expensive medical condition.[4] Although the development of modern scientific medicine can be traced to the 19th century, several developments during and after World War II were most important in shaping the unique form of health insurance in the United States.[5]

---

[1]This appendix was prepared at the request of the Committee on Children, Health Insurance, and Access to Care as background material about private sector health insurance coverage of children. The views expressed are the author's and are not necessarily shared by any other member of the committee, the Institute of Medicine, or the American Enterprise Institute.

[2]Employee Benefit Research Institute, *Sources of Health Insurance and Characteristics of the Uninsured*, EBRI Issue Brief No. 170, February 1996.

[3]Alliance for Health Reform, *Health Coverage: Insuring America's Children*, March 1997, Figure 2.

[4]For readable explanations of the basic economics of insurance, see Mark A. Hall, *Reforming Private Health Insurance*. (Washington, D.C.: The AEI Press, 1994), especially Chapter 2; and Mark V. Pauly, "Overinsurance: The Conceptual Issues," in Pauly, ed., *National Health Insurance: What Now, What Later, What Never?* (Washington, D.C.: American Enterprise Institute, 1980), pp. 201–219.

[5]For reviews of the history of American medicine and health care delivery, see Paul Starr, *The Social Transformation of American Medicine*. (New York: Basic Books, Inc., 1982); Herman M. Somers and Anne R. Somers, *Doctors, Patient, and Health Insurance*. (Washington, D.C.: The Brookings Institution, 1961); and Marilyn J. Field and Harold T. Shapiro, eds., *Employment and Health Benefits*. (Washington, D.C.: National Academy Press, 1993), pp. 49–86.

Health insurance in this country is unique in two ways. First, unlike most other developed countries, the United States relies on the private sector rather than the public sector to provide health insurance for most of the population. Second, health insurance is unlike most other forms of insurance because it is provided through a person's employer rather than being purchased directly by an individual, as is commonly the case with casualty, automobile, and life insurance. This unique development is primarily the result of unintended employment and tax policies that had their origin during World War II.

In an effort to control wartime inflation and reduce the cost to the government for war materials and services, the government established a system of wage and price controls during the early 1940s. Unable to compete for scarce labor by raising wages, employers began to expand their use of fringe benefits as a way to attract and hold employees. The value of these benefits, including employer-based health insurance, was not considered by the IRS to be part of taxable income. This principle of excluding the value of employer-based health insurance from taxable income became part of established tax law following the war. The economic effect of this policy was to give a preference for health insurance obtained through an employer rather than purchased individually with after-tax dollars. This part of tax law was established at a time when marginal tax rates were relatively low and the cost of health insurance was a relatively small part of the total cost of compensation. This situation was not to last.[6]

In addition to the growth of modern scientific medicine, the 20 years following World War II were a period of unusually rapid growth of population and personal income. These factors combined to increase the demand for health insurance to protect against the cost of expensive medical events. This had two effects: the growth of employer-based health insurance relative to individually-purchased insurance and an expansion in types of coverage offered.

To contrast the period before and after World War II, Somers and Somers point out that in 1930 only two percent of the labor force (1.2 million workers and about 2 million of their dependents) had any form of health coverage[7] although in 1958, 123 million Americans had hospital insurance and 75 percent of these individuals obtained this coverage through their employer.[8]

The tax treatment of health insurance created strong incentives for unions and employees to bargain for tax-free health insurance relative to taxable wages and to expand both the completeness of insurance (reduced cost sharing) and the range of medical coverage to be included in the employer's plan. In addition, tax policy may also be partially responsible for extending coverage to dependents, because providing coverage for an employee's family was an additional way to purchase insurance with tax-free dollars.

THE EFFECTS OF HEALTH INSURANCE

The private sector health insurance industry has grown to become a major sector of our economy. The latest figures indicate that there are approximately 2,900 insurance companies providing individual

[6]For a more complete history of the tax treatment of health insurance with numerous references, see Robert B. Helms, "The Tax Treatment of Health Insurance: Early History and Evidence, 1940–1970" in Grace Marie-Arnett, ed., *Health Care Reform: Solutions for a New Century*. (Ann Arbor, MI.: The University of Michigan Press, forthcoming); Ronald J. Vogel, "The Tax Treatment of Health Insurance as a Cause of Overinsurance," in Mark V. Pauly, ed., *National Health Insurance: What Now, What Later, What Never?* (Washington, D.C.: American Enterprise Institute, 1980), pp. 220–249; Congressional Budget Office, *The Tax Treatment of Employment-Based Health Insurance*, March 1994; Sherry Glied, *Revising the Tax Treatment of Employer-Provided Health Insurance*. (Washington, D.C.: The AEI Press, 1994); Walter M. Cadette, *Prescription for Health Care Policy: The Case for Retargeting Tax Subsidies to Health Care*. Annandale-on-Hudson, New York: The Jerome Levy Economics Institute of Bard College, Public Policy Brief No. 30/1997, 1997.

[7]Somers and Somers, *Doctors, Patients, and Health Insurance*, p. 230.

[8]Somers and Somers, *Doctors, Patients, and Health Insurance*, p. 228.

and group policies to about 164 million Americans who have private health insurance coverage.[9] This growth of insurance has had both positive and negative effects on the performance and efficiency of the health care sector. A partial description of some of these effects follows.[10]

- Health insurance has provided financial protection to a majority of the American work force and their dependents. The special tax treatment of health insurance has increased both the absolute number of people covered and has extended the range of medical services provided in a typical policy.
- This insurance coverage has been provided by a relatively large number of diversified firms, which has increased the choices of types of coverage and the efficiency and adaptability of the insurance industry.
- The business firm has provided a convenient method of spreading risk and efficiencies in the administration of the insurance plan. From the health insurance company's point of view, it is cheaper to insure an employer group than a similar number of individual policies for three reasons: (1) there are economies of scale in the administration of a group of employees, resulting in lower loading factors; (2) on average, working individuals are younger and healthier than individuals who are not working;[11] and (3) if the group is large enough, the insurer can be relatively sure that the employees did not accept the job to obtain health insurance (the probability is low that the group has attracted individuals who are sicker than average).[12]
- Because individuals with health insurance use more health care services than uninsured individuals, the special tax subsidies for employer-based health insurance have increased the demand for health care above the amount that would have existed without the subsidy. As research by Martin Feldstein and others has shown, this increase in the demand for health care resulted in higher health care prices and higher rates of growth in health care expenditures than would have existed without the subsidies.[13]
- Tax policy has also contributed to the health cost problem by reducing the extent of consumer cost sharing in health insurance plans. During the period of a rapidly increasing demand for health insurance, health insurance companies competed for business by offering policies with lower deductibles and copayments. Such policies were more expensive than policies with more cost sharing, but because the extra cost was partially subsidized by the tax exclusion, the average amount of cost sharing declined in health insurance policies for most of the 1960s, 1970s, and into the 1980s. Since the mid-1980s, there has been some retrenchment on cost sharing as employers have attempted to control the rapidly rising cost of their plans. Because the purpose of cost sharing is to control the insurance-induced consumption

[9]*Statistical Abstract of the United States*, 1996, Table 767; EBRI, *Sources of Health Insurance and Characteristics of the Uninsured*, Issue Brief No. 179, November 1996. Not all employer-based insurance coverage is provided through insurance companies because the current ERISA law gives firms strong incentives to self insure, that is, instead of paying premiums to an insurance company, they set aside funds to directly pay the medical costs occurred by their employees and their dependents. Some firms who self insure may contract with insurance companies to provide administrative services for their plan without paying an insurance company to assume risk.

[10]For more on the effects of insurance, see Mark V. Pauly, "Taxation, Health Insurance, and Market Failure in the Medical Economy," *Journal of Economic Literature*, vol. 24 (June 1985), pp. 629–675; Field and Shapiro, *Employment and Health Benefits*.

[11]Self-employed individuals may be just as healthy as individuals working for an employer, but the cost of determining their health status is greater. In addition, insurance companies face higher risks to the extent that the self-employed and small employers have incentives to include relatively unhealthy dependents in their group policies.

[12]The health insurance industry has been accused of "redlining," that is refusing to cover some employers in certain locations or occupations where they perceive that the employer group may have attracted employees with a high risk of having an expensive disease (e.g., AIDS) or who may engage in work activities (e.g., a tree surgeon) with a high risk of injury. Almost all states have some regulations that attempt to control unfair discrimination.

[13]Martin Feldstein, *Hospital Costs and Health Insurance*. (Cambridge, Massachusetts: Harvard University Press, 1981).

of health services, the principal effect of lower cost sharing has been to further reduce the incentives of individual consumers with insurance to be cost-conscious in their use of health care services. Individuals with insurance have little incentive to shop for cost-effective providers because they typically do not pay for services directly and cannot share in any savings that may result from their actions.

• The tax treatment of health insurance has also exacerbated the problems of those without health insurance. The uninsured are individuals and their dependents who are not eligible for public programs, who are unemployed, self-employed, or working for an employer who does not offer health insurance. All of these individuals face a higher cost of purchasing individual or small group policies because current tax policy has artificially inflated the cost of health care and the cost of all health insurance. The cost of individual policies could be reduced if it were possible to purchase catastrophic policies with higher deductibles and cost sharing, but the availability of these policies is limited due to the dominance of low deductible policies in the group market and state regulations that inhibit the sale of such policies in some states.

• The tax treatment of health insurance has also contributed to a very regressive distribution of tax subsidies. Because the value of a benefit that is excluded from taxable income increases with one's marginal tax rate, the result of the present tax policy is to distribute the value of the tax subsidies more to higher income individuals who work for employers offering health insurance than to lower income workers. For taxpayers in the 28 percent federal tax bracket (Adjusted Gross Income in a joint return beginning at $38,000), their marginal tax rate can easily exceed 40 percent considering the 7.65 percent payroll tax for Social Security and Medicare and state income taxes. For such a worker, a dollar spent on health insurance is worth approximately 40 percent more than a dollar spent on taxable wages. This advantage can go as high as 60 percent for some high-income individuals in some high-tax states. By contrast, an individual purchasing an individual policy must use after-tax dollars and thus receives no tax subsidy.

• The Congressional Budget Office uses the 1987 National Medical Expenditure Survey (NMES) and its own tax model to estimate the distribution of tax benefits for the year 1994. For families with employment-based health insurance (61 percent of the population), they estimate that the tax subsidy averages 26 percent of health insurance premiums (which average $4,310). This subsidy increases with income, going from 11 percent of premiums for those with family incomes under $10,000 to 33 percent for those with incomes over $200,000.[14] When the tax subsidy is compared to after-tax income, they find that the tax subsidy averages 2.4 percent of after-tax income for families with employment-based health insurance but only 1.9 percent when those taxpayers who do not have health insurance provided by their employer are added in.[15]

• Current tax policy also contributes to the difficulties of welfare recipients attempting to make the transition from public assistance to productive employment in the private sector. The high cost of health insurance is one of the principal reasons that many businesses do not offer health insurance to their employees. Surveys indicate that the incidence of uninsurance in the private sector is greater in the southern states and in the service sector of the economy, exactly the places where most welfare recipients seek jobs as an alternative to welfare. The welfare reform legislation in 1996 attempted to ease this transition from welfare to work by extending the ability of working parents to keep their dependents on Medicaid, but these benefits are limited, so that the number of uninsured children can be expected to increase as more welfare recipients are forced to accept jobs in firms that cannot afford to offer health insurance. The unavailability of low-cost group or individual policies will continue to make this problem worse, especially for children.

---

[14]Congressional Budget Office, *The Tax Treatment of Employment-Based Health Insurance*, March 1994, Table 4, p. 30.

[15]CBO, *The Tax Treatment of Employment-Based Health Insurance*, Table 4, p. 31.

OPTIONS FOR EXPANDING HEALTH INSURANCE FOR CHILDREN

The desire to expand access to health care for children through health insurance has been a central part of the health policy debate for most of this century. The following section presents several basic policy options that have been, or might be, considered as ways to expand health insurance coverage for children. The organization of this analysis into discrete policy options does not mean that other options and variations of these options could not be considered. The objective here is to present a range of realistic policy options and illustrate the tradeoffs that must be made among conflicting objectives.[16]

Federal Preemption of State Insurance Laws and Regulations

One option is to establish federal requirements that forbid state laws and regulations that interfere with the coverage of children. Such an approach is controversial because it goes against the Constitutional and legal tradition of granting maximum autonomy and flexibility to states. However, many state laws and regulations have been established at the behest of special interests, thereby raising the cost of health insurance and making it more difficult for the uninsured to buy affordable health insurance. Mandated benefits increase the cost of offering health insurance, making it more difficult for small firms to offer group policies or for individuals to buy insurance directly.

Several studies have documented the growth of state laws affecting the health insurance and managed care markets. Gail Jensen presents data showing that state mandates increased from 37 in 1970 to 854 in 1990.[17] She also reports on studies showing that these mandates significantly raise the cost of health insurance, which has especially strong effects on the ability of small firms to offer health insurance to their employees.[18] More recent studies indicate that the nature of state legislative action is changing, with more laws now being passed to regulate the activities and coverage of managed care plans.[19] And, as shown by recent activity by Congress to mandate mental health parity and regulate maternity coverage, the legislative urge to mandate benefits and regulate health insurance is not limited to state legislatures. Numerous proposals for new mandates are continually being debated at both the federal and state levels.

One factor making the federal preemption of state laws so controversial is the difficulty of distinguishing between the benefits and costs of the mandates. Some children may benefit from mandating coverage for some preventive and screening services or for the coverage of children with special needs. But there is a trade-off in the design of any insurance plan: the higher costs of the mandated benefits will make it more difficult for the uninsured to purchase health insurance either individually or through their employer. This is further complicated by special interest politics at the federal and state levels. Mandates and other provisions may be promoted by groups of providers as a way to increase the demand for the services they provide or to reduce the ability of other providers to effectively compete in the market.[20] Any federal legislation to preempt state laws that are detrimental to the coverage of children would face

---

[16]For detailed descriptions of state and federal proposals, see U.S. Library of Congress, Congressional Research Service, *Health Insurance for Children: Legislation in the 105th Congress*. CRS Report for Congress 95-385 EPW, May 6, 1997; Kay Johnson, et al., *Children's Health Insurance: A Comparison of Major Federal Legislation*. Washington, D.C.: Center for Health Policy Research, The George Washington University, May 1, 1997; and, Shelly Gehshan, *State Options for Expanding Children's Health Insurance: A Guide for Legislators*. Washington, D.C.: National Conference of State Legislatures, May 1997.

[17]Gail Jensen, "Regulating the Content of Health Plans," in Robert B. Helms, ed., *American Health Policy: Critical Issues for Reform*. Washington, D.C.: The AEI Press, 1993, p. 169.

[18]Jensen, pp. 180–187.

[19]Patricia A. Butler, "Public Oversight of Managed Care Entities: Issues for State Policymakers," *National Governors Association*, 1996; Susan S. Laudicina, et al., *State Legislative Health Care and Insurance Issues*. BlueCross BlueShield Association, December 1996.

[20]James F. Blumstein, "Health Care Reform and Competing Visions of Medical Care: Antitrust and State Provider Cooperation Legislation," *Cornell Law Review*, Vol. 79, No. 6, September 1994, pp. 1459–1506.

two rather difficult problems: identifying the set of state laws that are harmful and overcoming the efforts of special interests to maintain these provisions.

The task might be more politically feasible if the objective of the federal preemption were to create a broader range of choice among health insurance plans rather than trying to force all plans in all states to adhere to federal standards. By eliminating state requirements that have little or no benefit for children and requiring preventive and catastrophic benefits that are cost effective, it might be possible to give employers and individuals choices of types of policies that would be cheaper than existing policies. Catastrophic coverage is a lower-cost form of insurance because it covers the high-cost, low-probability events and lets the insured bear the risk of low-cost and predictable health events. The relatively high deductibles in catastrophic plans give consumers incentives to avoid unnecessary care, pick more cost-effective providers, and not to file numerous small claims. Prevention and screening services that are cost-effective can be excluded from the deductibles so the insurance plan gets both kinds of savings: more use of cost-saving activities and less use of cost-increasing activities.

To avoid the criticism of federal micro-management, as well as to reduce the cost of enforcement, any such federal legislation would have to allow for insurance companies to compete in benefit design rather than try to specify exactly what benefits should be offered. If federal preemption to create more cost-effective insurance for children were combined with one of several inducements for such coverage (discussed below), this approach has the potential to offer attractive choices to many of the presently uninsured.

Federal Mandates for Employer-based Coverage of Children

A more direct approach than altering state laws is a federal mandate that all employers must provide health insurance to their workers and their dependents. Variations of federal mandates have been proposed in past years, the most recent in the Clinton Administration's Health Security Act. Although several states have provided state insurance plans for children or subsidies for private coverage, Hawaii is the only state so far to use a mandated benefits approach.[21] Most of the actual proposals have included exemptions for small employers as a way to reduce the economic effects of mandates or to phase in the new coverage.

To be enforceable, any mandate for coverage must provide some definition of the benefits that must be included in the mandated plan. Again, this presents two difficult obstacles to such legislation, one medical and one political. Ideally, if we had definitive knowledge of the medical benefits of alternative types of procedures and coverage, it would be relatively straightforward to design a mandated insurance policy that included effective treatments and excluded ineffective treatments.

But that is not the case, which leads to the political problem. If Congress attempts to mandate a set of benefits that must be provided by all employers, it becomes vitally important for every component of health care, every specialty, every type of provider, to be included in the plan. This creates a difficult situation for the Congress (or any state legislature) attempting to define a mandated set of benefits. The

[21]The Hawaii mandate is for employees only and excludes dependents, agricultural workers, and part-time workers. For a study questioning the ability of the Hawaiian approach to reduce the number of uninsured, see Andrew W. Dick, "Will Employer Mandates Really Work? Another Look at Hawaii," *Health Affairs*, Vol. 13, No. 1, Spring (I) 1994, pp. 343–349.

[22]Despite the usual contention that the cost of mandates is imposed on employers, economists have shown that the cost of employment-based health insurance is borne by the employees. For discussions of the cost of health insurance, see Michael A. Morrisey, "Mandated Benefits and Compensating Differentials—Taxing the Uninsured," in Robert B. Helms, ed., *American Health Policy: Critical Issues for Reform*. Washington, D.C.: The AEI Press, 1993, pp. 133–151; Mark A. Pauly, *Health Benefits at Work: An Economic and Political Analysis of Employment-Based Health Insurance*. Ann Arbor: The University of Michigan Press, 1997.

result is likely to be an expansive set of benefits that will be expensive and have detrimental effects on employment and business growth.

The major criticism of mandated benefits is that they impose large economic costs on employees.[22] That is why the employment effects of mandated benefits are concentrated in small firms where the incidence of uninsurance is relatively high and why most mandated benefit proposals have some exemption for small firms. This creates an especially difficult dilemma for attempts to increase insurance coverage for children through federal mandates. Because a large proportion of uninsured children are dependents of adults that work for small firms,[23] any exemption of small firms reduces the ability of a mandated benefit law to increase insurance coverage for children. If small firms are not exempted, the higher costs of insurance will likely decrease the number of parents employed and thereby force more children to become uninsured or to turn to Medicaid or other public programs for coverage.

Another variation of mandated benefits is for the federal government to require states to provide private sector health insurance for families or just for children. States would be required to provide choices of plans similar to those provided to federal employees for all families who are not on Medicaid and who have incomes less than a fixed amount (e.g., $75,000) or less than a percentage of the poverty level (e.g., 200 percent of poverty, the income category where 45 percent of the uninsured children are situated).[24] Such proposals could come with or without federal subsidies or be tied to various tax provisions, as discussed below. They are likely to impose lower costs on the states because they allow for less benefits than are required in state Medicaid programs. Their disadvantage is that they require the states to administer a new health benefit plan without using their existing Medicaid program to administer the benefit.

Federal Vouchers to Individuals or Families

Another mechanism to increase the health coverage for children is a federal voucher that could be used by an individual or family to purchase a private insurance plan.[25] A voucher is a means of providing a subsidy to specific recipients that restricts the purposes for which it can be used. An example is food stamps that are given to qualified poor people to subsidize food purchases without allowing them to spend on other items.[26] Educational vouchers are often proposed as a more efficient way than public schools to subsidize education.

As with any other federal subsidy program, a federal voucher program designed to subsidize health insurance would have to target the population and specify the type of policy that the voucher could be used for. As a standard for benefits, the federal government could adopt the minimum federal Medicaid benefits or a plan that would meet the standard for federal employees (the FEHBP). Alternatively, the federal government could leave the design of a qualifying plan to the states or attempt to establish minimum deductibles and standards for prevention and screening. As is done with Medical Saving Accounts, establishing a minimum deductible, say $4,000 per year for a family policy, is an attempt to

---

[23]EBRI estimates based on the 1996 Current Population Survey indicate that in 1995, 45 percent of the parents of uninsured children worked in firms employing 99 or fewer workers. Eighteen percent of such parents were self-employed. Employee Benefit Research Institute, "Expanding Health Insurance for Children: Examining the Alternatives," Issue Brief Number 187, July 1997, Chart 9.

[24]U.S. Library of Congress, Congressional Research Service, *Health Insurance for Children: Legislation in the 105th Congress*. CRS Report for Congress 95-385 EPW, May 6, 1997, Table 1.

[25]The voucher could also be used to purchase Medicaid coverage or a state health insurance plan. This discussion concentrates on the purchase of insurance from the private sector.

[26]Restricting an individual's purchases to one specific purpose is not completely possible because the increased income from the voucher may allow the individual to spend more for other purposes. The substitution effects of vouchers are explained in Kenneth W. Clarkson, *Food Stamps and Nutrition*. Washington, D.C.: American Enterprise Institute, 1975.

assure that the voucher would go to subsidize catastrophic coverage with high lifetime maximums rather than first-dollar coverage.

The voucher could be made available on the basis of income by extending the percent of poverty standards now in place for Medicaid, but excluding children currently on Medicaid. This would be an additional administrative burden on the states, but a system for determining income eligibility already exists for Medicaid and could be expanded. A more complicated procedure would be to try to make the voucher available only to those children who were uninsured. It is more complicated because it creates strong incentives for employers and employees currently paying for dependent coverage to drop such coverage, the so-called crowding out problem. Establishing regulations to prevent crowding out would be difficult in the absence of some inducement to maintain coverage.

Enforcement problems associated with vouchers could be reduced to the extent that the federal subsidy did not cover the entire cost of the insurance plan. With a partial subsidy, the individual who would bear some of the cost of the insurance would have an incentive to use the voucher wisely and to purchase a plan that would provide them with the most value. Allowing an eligible employee to use the voucher to buy into his or her employer's group policy might be a way to reduce the danger of crowding-out.

Federal Tax Policy to Encourage Additional Coverage

Proposals to expand health insurance through the use of tax policy are based on the notion that it is better to offer a positive incentive rather than direct subsidies or mandates. Tax policy proposals to reform health care markets are supported by a number of economists and health policy experts, but are probably the least understood by politicians and the public.[27] In addition to being misunderstood, any change in tax policy creates winners and losers, so the losers can be expected to strongly oppose the change. Scholars of tax policy have also criticized any use of the tax system to achieve any social objective because such proposals complicate the tax system, create distorting incentives, and interfere with the objective to create an efficient and fair system of raising revenue.[28] Any attempt to use tax policy to encourage more coverage of children will not be immune to that criticism. However, if properly designed, a tax policy proposal could increase children's coverage while removing some of the present complications and distortions of tax law.

Any attempt to use tax policy as a positive incentive to expand health insurance for children would face two administrative problems. First, the current federal income tax system is administered by the Internal Revenue Service (IRS), an agency that many feel is already overburdened by the complexity of the tax law. Adding any new provisions to encourage health insurance for children would add to this complexity and to the enforcement and administrative problems faced by the IRS.

Keeping any new provision relatively simple would reduce the problems faced by the IRS, but would likely reduce the ability to target new health coverage to the presently uninsured or to assure that private insurance contained the features that would be deemed best for children. For example, if the desire of Congress was to subsidize the purchase by low-income people of catastrophic policies that included good prevention and screening services, the IRS would have to take on some of the functions of a welfare or insurance regulatory agency to assure that the benefit design of the qualifying plans met some federal standard and that only eligible people received the subsidy. The alternative is to have the IRS work

[27]For some of the health reform proposals based on tax policy, see Mark Pauly, Patricia Danzon, Paul Feldstein, and John Hoff, *Responsible National Health Insurance*. Washington, D.C.: The AEI Press, 1992; Stuart M. Butler, ed., *Is Tax Reform the Key to Health Care Reform?* The Heritage Foundation, 1990; C. Eugene Steuerle, "Beyond Paralysis in Health Policy: A Proposal to Focus on Children," *National Tax Journal*, Vol. 45, No. 3, September 1992, pp. 357–368.

[28]Joint Economic Committee, "The Inefficiency of Targeted Tax Policies," United States Congress, April 1997.

closely with state welfare and regulatory agencies, institutions that have not traditionally worked closely with either federal or state taxing authorities.

The second administrative problem involves using the tax system to target children, who are not typically taxpayers. The IRS deals with taxable units that are usually families. Because children are almost always the dependents of adult taxpayers, it adds a layer of complexity to target any tax incentive only to children. In addition, on the insurance side, most children receive coverage through a family policy that is purchased by at least one of the parents, either through that parent's employer or directly from an insurance company. The practical solution to this problem is to realize that most uninsured children are dependents of parents who are also uninsured, so that any tax policy to subsidize the purchase of family policies will increase the level of coverage of children and adults alike. Because children on average use less health services than adults, a less targeted subsidy that includes more adults will cost more than a subsidy targeted only to children.

There are several options for the design of a tax subsidy for children's health insurance, but they vary in terms of their ease of administration and their ability to actually increase the level of coverage. For simplicity, the following section considers two methods of providing tax subsidies—tax credits and tax deductions—and two targets for these subsidies—employers and taxpayers.

Tax Deductions

In its simplest form, our income tax system works on the principle of imposing a tax that is a percentage of a taxpayer's or business firm's taxable income. Taxable income may be less than gross income to the extent that the taxpaying unit is able to subtract actual expenditures that are allowable as tax deductions or a fixed amount for each member of the taxpaying unit (called exemptions). Examples for families include standard exemptions based on the number of children in a family, mortgage interest payments, and medical expenditures above 7.5 percent of adjusted gross income. Each of these deductions from income is designed to lower the taxes of families that have children, own their own homes, or experience unusually high medical expenses. Business firms are allowed to deduct from gross income almost all costs of conducting their business including the cost of raw materials, labor costs, and the costs of fringe benefits, including what the firm pays for a group health insurance plan for its employees.

Because the cost to the employer of providing dependent coverage through a family policy is already fully deductible as a business expense, there is no opportunity for using tax deductions as an additional inducement for employers to expand coverage. The use of the deduction for health insurance expenses could be made contingent on providing all employees and their dependents a specified level of benefits, but this becomes equivalent to a mandate and has all the disadvantages discussed above. In addition, if the employer retains the freedom not to provide health insurance at all, any requirement that the tax deduction could only be used when all dependents were covered would create strong incentives for many firms to drop the provision of health insurance. The result would likely be an increase in the number of uninsured children, not the desired decrease.

Using a tax deduction for individual taxpayers is a different story, because the current use of the deduction is so limited that it has very little effect on the purchase of private health insurance. There are two very limited ways that the purchase of health insurance can be deducted from gross income. Self-employed individuals can currently (1998 through 1999) deduct as a business expense 45 percent of the cost of health insurance for themselves and their family. To make this more compatible with the full deductibility of the cost of health insurance for working people who are not self-employed, Congress recently passed provisions to increase the self-employed deduction gradually to 100 percent by the year 2007.[29] The coverage of dependents is allowed but is not required by the tax law. A positive incentive for

[29]Taxpayer Relief Act of 1997, Public Law 105-34, August 5, 1997, Sec. 934.

the self-employed could be created by increasing the portion of the cost of a policy that is deductible when it covers children (or all dependents). But because there are only 12.0 million self-employed workers (9.2 percent of the total labor force), and only 2.6 million self-employed people who take the health insurance deduction, this provision would have only a limited effect on insurance coverage for children.[30]

More children could be affected if an expanded deduction for the cost of health insurance were made available to individual taxpayers regardless of their employment status. This type of tax subsidy would be advantageous to any person purchasing an individual policy directly from an insurance company or any worker whose employer does not provide health insurance or does not cover dependents.

Any amount of deduction from taxable income would lower the net cost of the insurance to the purchaser, but because the deduction lowers a person's taxable income, the amount of the reduction in taxes is determined by the person's marginal tax rate. For example, if a single parent with one child made $20,000 in 1996, her tax would be $1,639. If a $1,000 deduction had been allowed for health insurance, the tax would only go down $150 to $1,489, a reduction that is only 15 percent of the $1,000 deduction because that person is in the 15 percent tax bracket.

In addition, a major disadvantage of using deductibles as a positive incentive is that it is difficult to target this type of tax subsidy to lower-income workers. Under present law, it is usually advantageous for a low income worker to take the standard deduction ($4,000 for a single taxpayer or $6,700 for a couple filing jointly in 1996) rather than itemize deductions. Therefore, to take advantage of the tax deduction, a person must first have an income high enough to require him or her to pay taxes. And even if the person pays income taxes, he or she would have to itemize deductions unless a change in tax law would allow him or her to take the health insurance deduction in addition to the standard deduction. These difficulties making tax deductions effective for low income taxpayers are why most tax subsidy proposals use some form of tax credit as a way to induce a change in behavior.

Tax Credits

The use of tax credits is a more efficient way to subsidize the purchase of health insurance for low-income taxpayers. In addition, by making tax credits refundable, it is possible to use the tax system to subsidize those people who do not currently pay income taxes.

A tax credit is a direct reduction of taxes owed and does not require a taxpayer to itemize deductions in order to qualify for the credit. This is especially important because those who are most likely to qualify for the tax credit and to need it to purchase health insurance are likely to be among those least likely to itemize their deductions.

To illustrate, consider again the single parent with one child earning $20,000 per year and facing a tax bill of $1,639 under current law. If she were allowed a $1,000 tax credit for the purchase of health insurance for herself and her child, her taxes would be reduced by the full amount of the $1,000 tax credit, to $639. The amount of the tax credit could be set to cover most or all of the cost of a defined health insurance benefit for the parent and the child or just for the child.

A tax credit has three other advantages over direct subsidies or tax deductions. First, the amount of the tax credit can be based on an actuarial calculation to cover either a portion of or all of the cost of the desired level of benefits for the people that are to be subsidized. The IRS would still have to assure that the taxpayer actually purchased health insurance, but the federal government would not face the difficult task of defining a complicated benefit package and determining that each person's policy contained those benefits. The purchase of health insurance could be left to the individual consumer, who could choose among alternative plans offered by competing health insurance companies. Insurance

[30]These figures are for 1995. Employee Benefit Research Institute, "Sources of Health Insurance and Characteristics of the Uninsured," November 1996, p. 9.

companies are now subject to the scrutiny of both the federal antitrust agencies and state insurance regulation, which could continue to assure that consumers are offered quality insurance products at fair market prices.

Some educational activities may have to be undertaken with this new population of potential buyers because most of the people who would qualify for the tax credit to purchase health insurance and who would therefore be the most likely to use it are not now insured and therefore have little experience with purchasing health insurance products. Because the great majority of those who are uninsured do not have the option of receiving health insurance through the workplace, they will not typically have an employer helping them with the choice of plans and therefore will need more information about health insurance products.

A second advantage of tax credits is that the size of the subsidy can be relatively easily related to the income of the recipient. For example, if the desire is to give a full subsidy for the coverage of children for taxpayers up to $20,000, but only a partial subsidy for those earning between $20,000 and $40,000, the size of the tax credit could be reduced on a sliding scale for the latter group of taxpayers. In this example, there would be no tax subsidy for any taxpayer earning above $40,000. Instead of an absolute income amount, the starting and stopping incomes of the phase-down of the tax credit could be set as percentages of poverty.

In general, the cost of the tax credit program will be greater and more people will be subsidized if the phase-down begins at a higher income (for example, $25,000) and extends to an even higher income (for example, $60,000) before it is ended.[31]

A third advantage of tax credits is that they can be used to target subsidies to people whose income is so low that they do not owe any taxes. This segment of the near-poor population will likely contain many of the presently uninsured children. To reach people who do not owe taxes requires that the tax credit be made refundable. A refundable tax credit is a cash payment (for health insurance this could be a voucher) from the IRS to the taxpaying family. To qualify, a low-income person would have to file a tax return and show proof of purchase of a qualified health insurance plan.

Because the eligibility for a tax credit is not established until after the taxable year is over, a practical way would have to be found to transfer purchasing power to the recipient of the tax subsidy during the tax year. For wage earners, this could be achieved by decreasing their tax withholdings. Transferring purchasing power to recipients of refundable tax credits may be more difficult because they may not be working or working at jobs not subject to wage withholding. Some system of temporary access to a government insurance plan (Medicaid or FEHBP) or verification that would allow access to short-term credit would have to be developed in order to more rapidly enroll the presently uninsured.

One of the aspects of tax policy that has not been discussed is the effect on government receipts and expenditures. All three of the major ways to use tax policy to encourage health insurance, as well as the direct payments and vouchers discussed earlier, have negative effects on the budget. Tax deductions and tax credits reduce the revenue that would be collected by the IRS. Refundable tax credits, direct payments, or vouchers, would increase direct government expenditures because they involve sending direct subsidies to those who qualify. Finding a funding source for more health insurance for children while meeting the requirements for a balanced budget is a major challenge for the Congress, but this challenge must be met regardless of the kind of policy that is adopted.[32]

---

[31]For some examples of actual tax credit proposals, and a more extensive discussion of design features and probable policy effects, see Pauly, Danzon, Feldstein, and Hoff, *Responsible National Health Insurance*; Stuart M. Butler, ed., *Is Tax Reform the Key to Health Care Reform?* The Heritage Foundation, 1990; C. Eugene Steuerle, "Beyond Paralysis in Health Policy: A Proposal to Focus on Children," *National Tax Journal*, Vol. 45, No. 3, September 1992, pp. 357–368.

[32]Using the arguments that the present exclusion of employer-based health insurance is a major cause of distorted incentives in health care markets and is a regressive public subsidy, two major plans for refundable tax credits propose to include the value of employer-based health insurance in taxable income as the major source of funding. See Pauly, Danzon, Feldstein, and Hoff, *Responsible National Health Insurance*, and Butler, ed., *Is Tax Reform the Key to Health Care Reform?*

Expanding health insurance to children through the use of tax credits would provide more people with options to select the policies that most suit their needs and would allow the competitive market to develop a range of options to attract business. This type of policy would help to bring about more price competition, the kind of competition that has been missing in the American health insurance system. By driving choice and efficiency in the health care marketplace, consumers will begin to reverse the cycle of high costs that has been forcing people without job-based insurance out of the health care marketplace. This type of health care market has advantages for all consumers, not just the children who receive the tax credits.

B

Information for Accountability

BACKGROUND

Public and private purchasers are increasingly accountable for their health care spending. Accountability involves acceptance of the responsibility to balance costs while purchasing health care with reasonable quality, as well as to determine the relative values of a variety of options within the constraints of existing resources (IOM, 1997a and b; 1998). An essential requirement for accountability is information on performance, such as whether a health plan has met conditions of participation or reached targets agreed to receive financial bonuses.

For cost-conscious purchasers and public policymakers, it is difficult to use the existing sources of public information (e.g., national surveys of households and employers and report cards from health plans) to determine the relative values of different insurance purchasing options. A better understanding of the technical limitations and strengths of the currently available data might assist decision makers as they judge performance and make informed decisions, such as whether to continue or modify current oversight processes or contractual relationships with different health care delivery organizations.

This appendix begins with a description of the available sources of public data on health insurance, with an emphasis on information about children's coverage. The appendix then discusses more generally the technical challenges in measuring performance and describes the kinds of capacities and infrastructure that need to be built to support systems of accountability, particularly in the area of health care for children. The appendix profiles sources of publicly collected data, such as federal surveys, as well as privately collected data collected by health plans and reported to consumers.

SOURCES OF DATA ON INSURANCE COVERAGE AND UTILIZATION

Medicaid is the largest single insurance program for American children. One significant limitation encountered in evaluating evidence about Medicaid coverage and services has been the poor history of collecting information within the program. The U.S. Congress and the U.S. Department of Health and Human Services (DHHS) have had minimal reporting requirements, and other than financial reporting, the Health Care Financing Administration has not requested information that can be used to easily evaluate the impacts of the services that Medicaid provides.

For example, although the Omnibus Budget Reconciliation Act of 1989 mandated treatment found to be indicated through Early and Periodic Screening, Diagnosis, and Treatment (EPSDT) program screens, there was no requirement to collect information on whether the children who were referred for treatment actually received any. The law did call for the collection of data on the number of children receiving screens, the number of children referred for treatment, and the number of children receiving dental services.

Under fee-for-service systems, screens and completed referrals could potentially be tracked by examining bills submitted for reimbursement. The EPSDT program reporting process is less reliable under managed care systems. Health plans paid through capitation may not report the encounters as EPSDT program screens if they follow other internal reporting guidelines, and capitated providers are paid whether they deliver the EPSDT program services or not. Consequently, information on the effectiveness of EPSDT as a comprehensive program of services for children is not complete.

Table B.1 summarizes the federal data sources that contain information about rates of health insurance coverage, health care utilization, and health status. The technical issues arising from these sources of data can be summarized as follows:

- Differences in definitions and data collection methods; for example, the Current Population Survey and National Health Interview Survey use different questions in collecting insurance data, making comparisons difficult.
- Limitations and discontinuities in published reports from different sources, for example, lack of statistical breakdowns for racial and ethnic groups, lack of published breakdowns for children or breakdowns for different ages, lack of breakdowns of employer data by size of employer, and lack of standardized categories for employer size.
- Differences in capacity to report current information because of the cycle of reporting requirements, the lag time in collecting large enough samples, a lack of appropriate technical resources to analyze the information, incompatibilities of computer systems, out-of-date computer software, and many other technical factors.

In addition to these technical problems, other obstacles exist. For example, some purchasers do not specify reporting requirements or standards for information collection, whereas in other circumstances different purchasers of services from the same providers may have conflicting requirements and standards (IOM, 1997a). Purchasers may make decisions without analyzing the existing data or information on effectiveness, and systematic information on implementation of new programs and strategies is not collected, so inefficiencies may inadvertently be repeated when new programs are put in place.

In the public sector, technical capacity is generally more limited than in the private sector (IOM, 1989, 1998). For example, a GAO report (GAO, IMTEC, 1993) found that the majority of government-owned software was several years old and could not keep up with the technical demands for the timely analysis of data. In recent years, with the availability of Internet access, most federal agencies have become better able to make public information accessible to researchers, state governments, and the general public.

In the private sector, a great deal of information is proprietary and is not generally available to the public, such as the scope and price of benefits for dependents, provider reimbursement levels, etc. However, the quality movement, with its emphasis on report cards, performance measures, and plan-to-plan standards for data collection and reporting, has greatly improved the level of information sharing. Information sharing is discussed in the following section.

TRENDS IN INFORMATION INFRASTRUCTURE DEVELOPMENT

Private Sector

The de facto standard for health plan performance reporting is the Healthplan Employer Data Information System (HEDIS), now in its third version (HEDIS 3.0) (see Box B.1). This standardized set

TABLE B.1 Federal Data Sources for Information on Health Insurance, Health Care Utilization, and Health Status

Federal Data Source	Department	Agency	Data Type	Data Collection Frequency	Description
Current Population Survey	DOC	Bureau of the Census	Survey, households	Monthly	Primary source of detailed information on income and work experience in the U.S. for the civilian, noninstitutional population ages 15 years and older. Annual March Supplement used to generate U.S. Population Profile and labor market profile and to make employment projections. Data gathered include employment status, income, poverty status, education, and sources of health insurance and noncash income (e.g., food stamps).
Medicaid Data System	DHHS	HCFA	Record	Continuous	The primary sources for Medicaid statistical data are the HCFA 2082 and the HCFA 64 reports. HCFA 2082, or Medicaid program statistics, is the basic source of state-reported data on the Medicaid population characteristics and utilization. HCFA 64, or Medicaid financial statistics, is a statement of actual expenditures for the Medicaid programs that states submit to HCFA each quarter (includes payments to disproportionate share hospitals).
Medical Expenditure Panel Survey	DHHS	AHCPR	Four surveys	Longitudinal, overlapping panel design; new panel each year. Data collected over two-year period.	Four national probability surveys: Household Component, Insurance Component, Medical Provider Component, and the Nursing Home Component. Collects information on health care use, expenditures, sources of payment, insurance coverage, and nursing homes and residents.
National Ambulatory Medical Care Survey	DHHS	CDC	Record	Annual	Provides statistics on the demographic characteristics of patients and the services provided, including information on diagnostic procedures, patient management, and planned future treatment.

Table continued on next page

TABLE B.1 Continued

Federal Data Source	Department	Agency	Data Type	Data Collection Frequency	Description
National Employer Health Insurance Survey	DHHS	CDC (cosponsored by AHCPR and HCFA)	Survey, private and public-sector businesses	Periodic; first collection began in April 1994 and ended in December 1994	Provides national and state-level analyses of private health insurance and examines characteristics of employer-sponsored health insurance. (Released December 1997)
National Health Interview Survey	DHHS	CDC	Survey, households	Annual	Principal source of information on the health of the civilian noninstitutional population. Basic health and demographic information, incidences of acute and chronic conditions, and injuries, the numbers of people with limited activity due to health conditions, data on respondent-assessed health status, the rate of utilization of health care services (physician care and short-stay hospitalizations), and data on other special health topics are provided.
National Health and Nutrition Examination Survey	DHHS	CDC	Survey	Continuous	Collects nationally representative information on the health and nutritional status of the U.S. civilian, noninstitutional population (ages 2 and older) to estimate number and percentage of people and subgroups of the population with selected diseases and risk factors. Data are used to study the relationship between diet and health, and between nutrition and health, and to explore emerging public health issues.
National Health Provider Inventory (NHPI)	DHHS	CDC	Survey	Periodic; last conducted in 1986 (called Inventory of Long-Term Care Places)	A comprehensive national listing of nursing homes, residential care facilities, hospices, and home health agencies. The NHPI serves as a model framework for several sample surveys. Provides national statistics on the number, type, and geographical distribution of health providers in the U.S.
National Home and Hospice Care Survey	DHHS	CDC	Survey	Annual	Provides data on home and health agencies and hospices and their current patients and discharges to assess the availability and utilization of these services. Data include referral and length of service, diagnoses, number of visits, patient charges, health status, reason for discharge, and types of services provided.

National Hospital Ambulatory Medical Care Survey	DHHS	CDC	Record	Annual	Uses visits to hospital emergency departments and outpatient departments to obtain information. Data include demographic characteristics of patients, expected sources of payment, patients' complaints, physicians' diagnoses, diagnostic/screening services, procedures, medication therapy, disposition, types of health care professionals seen, and causes of injury where applicable.
National Hospital Discharge Survey	DHHS	CDC	Record	Annual	Principal source of information on inpatient utilization of hospitals. It includes data on diagnoses, procedures, lengths of stay, expected sources of payment, and patterns of use of care in nonfederal hospitals. Data are used to track specific diseases, the introduction of new technologies, and the impact of changes in the financing systems.
National Immunization Survey	DHHS	CDC	Survey	Continuous	Collects information on the immunization coverage of children 19–35 months of age across the U.S.
National Nursing Home Survey	DHHS	CDC	Survey, providers and patients	Periodic; most recently in 1995	Provides data on nursing homes and their services, staffs, and financial characteristics and data on residents' personal and health characteristics.
National Nursing Home Survey Follow-up	DHHS	CDC	Longitudinal survey	Periodic; last survey February to April 1990 (Wave III)	Follows the cohort of surviving current residents and discharged residents sampled in the 1985 National Nursing Home Survey. The primary purpose is to provide data on the flow of people into and out of long-term-care facilities and hospitals. Data include subjects' vital status, living arrangements, nursing home stays, hospital stays, and sources of payment for stays.
National Survey of Ambulatory Surgery (NSAS)	DHHS	CDC	Record	Annual	Provides information on the use of freestanding and hospital-based ambulatory surgery centers in theU.S. In addition, NSAS provides detailed data on the wide variety of surgical and diagnostic treatments now performed outside the inpatient setting. Other data include expected sources of payment, patient disposition, and region.

Table continued on next page

TABLE B.1 Continued

Federal Data Source	Department	Agency	Data Type	Data Collection Frequency	Description
National Survey of Family Growth (NFSG)	DHHS	CDC	Survey	Periodic; last survey conducted in 1995	Survey of women, ages 15–44, in the U.S. civilian, noninstitutionalized population that is used to examine factors affecting pregnancy and women's health. Some of the information collected includes the number of children born and expected to be born; the number of intended and unintended births; marriage and cohabitation, family planning, smoking, and breast-feeding status; numbers of adopted children; and health insurance coverage.
National Vital Statistics System	DHHS	CDC	Record	Continuous	Responsible for the U.S. official vital statistics: births, deaths (including infant deaths), fetal deaths, induced terminations of pregnancy, marriages, and divorces. Provides annual data for the U.S. and for states, counties, and other local areas and monthly provisional data for the U.S. and each state.
Survey of Income and Program Participation (SIPP)	DOC	Bureau of the Census	Longitudinal survey, households	Periodic; the last survey covered the 1992–1994 period	Collects information on demographic and social characteristics of the U.S. civilian, noninstitutional population ages 15 years and older. Data include many of the same information as data collected for the Current Population Survey; however, SIPP shows changes in characteristics such as age, educational attainment, marital status, federal program participation, and health insurance status.

NOTE: DOC = Department of Commerce; DHHS = Department of Health and Human Services; AHCPR = Agency for Health Care Policy and Research; BLS = Bureau of Labor Statistics; CDC = Centers for Disease Control and Prevention; and HCFA = Health Care Financing Administration.

SOURCES: The information in this table is based on and excerpted from publications and documents from agencies of the federal government.

of performance measures was developed by the National Committee for Quality Assurance (NCQA), an accreditation organization for health maintenance organizations (HMOs), with input from a variety of employers, federal and state agencies, providers, consumer groups, and others.

HEDIS measures cover eight domains:

- effectiveness of care,
- accessibility and availability of care,
- satisfaction with the experience of care,
- cost of care,
- stability of the health plan,
- informed health care choices,
- use of services, and
- descriptive information about health plans.

NCQA has compiled a database with HEDIS data from more than 330 health plans that collectively cover more than 37 million enrollees. Because HEDIS performance data are standardized, they allow comparisons of performance across plans; for example, the percentage of children who have been immunized can be reported for an individual plan, and average immunization rates can be compared for different regions; the national average can also be determined. NCQA has also recognized that improved performance measurement will require more detailed content as well as comparability and connectivity of health data bases.

Later revisions of HEDIS will incorporate these goals into new health plan accreditation standards for information systems capability. In addition, NCQA is in the process of developing HEDIS measures and accreditation standards for provider organizations.

The Joint Commission on Accreditation of Health Care Organizations (JCAHO) is likewise

BOX B.1
Selected Reporting Measures for HEDIS 3.0

Effectiveness of Care	Access/Availability of Care	Use of Services
• Childhood immunization status • Adolescent immunization status • Treating children's ear infections • Prenatal care in the first trimester • Low birth-weight babies • Check-ups after delivery	• Children's access to primary care providers • Annual dental visit • Availability of dentists • Initiation of prenatal care (phased in) • Availability of obstetrical/prenatal care providers (phased in) • Low birth-weight deliveries at facilities for high-risk deliveries and neonates • Availability of language interpretation services	• Well-child visits in the first 15 months of life (phased in) • Well-child visits in the third, fourth, fifth, and sixth years of life (phased in) • Adolescent well-care visit (phased in) • Births and average length of stay, newborns • Frequency of ongoing prenatal care

SOURCE: NCQA (1997).

making efforts to improve monitoring and information structures by integrating outcome and performance measures into its accreditation process. One initiative, entitled ORYX, will require health care providers and, eventually, plans to collect and use performance data and to communicate those data to JCAHO. As part of the ORYX initiative, JCAHO has developed the Indicator Measurement System (IMSystem). The IMSystem will function as a comparative performance measurement system on measures of patient outcomes. This system will allow the Joint Commission to evaluate performance as part of the accreditation process.

Individual purchasers have also created a demand for timely information on health plan performance beyond that of HEDIS or JCAHO. For example, in the late 1980s, Digital Equipment Corporation developed a set of performance standards for HMOs. Digital has 800 facilities, annual revenues of $14 billion, 56,000 employees, and annual health care costs of $150 million.

When negotiating contracts to purchase care for employees, Digital and other large employers using Digital's HMO performance standards began to specify that providers must meet standards in the following six areas:

- access and member services,
- information management,
- behavioral health,
- finance and contracts,
- clinical quality, and
- health education and preventive services.

Box B.2 lists Digital's HMO performance standards that are specific to children's health. The most recent edition of Digital's standards builds on HEDIS 3.0 and Foundation for Accountability measures and reporting requirements, including the format for reporting.

Purchasing coalitions such as the Pacific Business Group on Health (PBGH) have also increased the demand for standardized information from health plans. PBGH conducts a variety of studies to assess and improve the quality of health plans, hospitals, and medical groups, including regular surveys of consumers and providers. PBGH also manages the collection of HEDIS quality measures for all of the larger California health plans serving commercial enrollees. PBGH makes performance information on plans, medical groups, and hospitals available to the public through a web site and published report cards.

A majority of health plans are reporting information on plan performance, although they are meeting different sets of standards. As health plans begin to contract with public agencies to deliver health care financed by Medicaid and state insurance programs, pre-existing data used for performance measurement can be used as a platform for new applications and analyses on coverage, utilization, access, and sources and continuity of care.

Finally, each of the major benefits consulting firms maintains its own national data base on health plans. These include and extend well beyond HEDIS.

Public Sector

In 1979, DHHS initiated a process of setting national objectives and performance measures for health promotion and disease prevention. The initiative, known as *Healthy People 2000*, has evolved to include 300 objectives in 22 priority areas addressing health promotion, health protection, preventive services, and data systems (DHHS, 1995) (see Box B.3).

Public review and comment has involved more than 10,000 individuals from hundreds of national membership organizations, 56 state and territorial health departments, the Institute of Medicine (IOM), and federal agencies (DHHS, 1990, 1992). Regular reports are issued to describe national progress toward meeting the objectives.

In 1995, DHHS began a process of establishing performance measures and objectives in anticipation of block grants legislation in public health, mental health, and substance abuse (NRC, 1997). A national initiative known as performance partnership grants is under way to improve the capacity of health departments and other public agencies to monitor and report on the health status of the U.S. population (NRC, 1997). DHHS also sponsored another IOM effort to examine performance measures for public health, which resulted in the development of prototypical sets of indicators for specific public health concerns that can be used by communities to monitor the performance of public agencies, private organizations delivering personal health services, and others (IOM, 1997b).

SCOPE OF PERFORMANCE MEASUREMENT FOR CHILDREN

The scope of performance measurement on aspects of children's health and health care spans federal, state, and local governments; independent and university-based policy research organizations; provider organizations; and many other sources.

At the federal level, the agencies that follow use, produce, and advance performance measures in their role or responsibility with regard to children's access to care, health status, and health outcomes.

- U.S. Department of Health and Human Services:
  —Agency for Health Care Policy and Research,
  —Centers for Disease Control and Prevention,
  —Food and Drug Administration,
  —Health Care Financing Administration—Medicaid,
  —Health Care Financing Administration—Disabled,
  —Health Resources and Services Administration,
  —Indian Health Service,
  —National Institutes of Health, and
  —Substance Abuse and Mental Health Services Administration;
- U.S. Department of Agriculture (nutrition programs);
- U.S. Department of Commerce (Current Population Survey);
- U.S. Department of Defense (Comprehensive Health and Medical Programs of the Uniformed Services);
- U.S. Department of Labor (employer and workforce statistics);
- U.S. Department of Treasury (tax policy); and
- Social Security Administration—Social Security Income;

At the state level, the following agencies use, produce, or advance performance measures for children's health care, insurance, access to care and for quality assurance:

- Medicaid agency,
- health department (often decentralized to include local agencies),
- human services department (often decentralized to counties),
- insurance department, and
- professional licensure and credentialing boards.

Private-sector organizations with specific interest in performance measures for children's health include:

BOX B.2
Digital HMO Performance Standards

Objectives:

- To ensure that the HMO offers an acceptable level of provider and medical care access for Digital employees
- In addition, the HMO must show a commitment to the development, maintenance, and improvement of efficient processes that effectively support member service activities.

Proximity Requirements

Proximity Requirement/Two Primary Care Practitioners (PCPs)(Pediatrics): Members will have access to at least two available pediatric primary care practitioners (pediatric and/or family practice) within a 15-mile radius and/or 30 minutes in all zip codes in the HMO's service area. This standard may be adjusted in rural areas if appropriate.

Provider Access

The HMO will maintain the following provider-to-member ratios to ensure adequate provider access. These standards will be used as a guide and should *report only those providers with practices that are open to new patients.* Provider network and delivery system differences will be evaluated as needed.

Ratio for Internists/Family Practitioners: The ratio of internists/family practitioners to the enrolled population will not be less than 0 = 0.50:1,000.
Ratio for Pediatricians: The ratio of pediatricians to the enrolled population will not be less than 0 = .25:1,000.

Appointment Availability

The HMO will have a process in place to monitor PCP appointment availability for internal medicine/family practice and pediatrics. In addition, the HMO will have a triage system which is available to members 24 hours a day. This triage system will have established guidelines for directing members to an appropriate level of care.

Nonsymptomatic Office Visits: Members requesting an office visit for nonsymptomatic related conditions will be seen within 30 calendar days. Examples of nonsymptomatic visits include well/preventive care appointments for services such as annual physical examinations, annual gynecological examinations, and pediatric/adult immunizations.
Routine (Follow-up) Office Visits: Appointments will be available within 14 calendar days. Examples of routine appointments include follow-up appointments, blood pressure checks, and suture removal.
Nonurgent, Symptomatic Office Visits: Members requesting an office visit for nonurgent, symptomatic conditions will receive telephone triage including guided self-care the same day and the opportu-

nity for an office visit within 48 hours. Examples of nonurgent, symptomatic office visits include appointments for the diagnosis and treatment of colds, headaches, minor injuries, joint/muscle pain, and similar nonurgent conditions.

Urgent, Symptomatic Office Visits: Members requesting an office visit for urgent, symptomatic conditions will be seen by a physician within 24 hours. Examples of conditions requiring urgent care include persistent diarrhea and/or vomiting and/or high fever (>101°F).

Emergency Care Services: Emergency care services will be available 24 hours per day, 7 days per week. Examples of emergency conditions include the presence of severe symptoms that require immediate medical care and for which a delay in care would be life threatening or would seriously jeopardize health or create permanent disability.

Emergency Access to Medical Provider: On-call coverage or centralized triage by a medical provider will be available 24 hours per day, 7 days per week, for response to medical inquiries.

Change of PCP: The HMO will permit Digital enrollees to change primary care practitioners and/or health care facility locations upon the enrollee's request.

Health Education and Preventive Services

The HMO will provide, upon request, targeted on-site health promotion services. These services may include:

- informational campaigns,
- immunizations,
- health screenings,
- behavior change programs,
- health committee consultations, and
- research on health improvement interventions.

Information Management Objectives

To ensure that the data collection and reporting sources in each HMO represent an acceptable standard of reporting for internal management, including operations management, case and clinical management, financial monitoring and management, as well as external reporting to governmental agencies and employers.

To ensure that each HMO demonstrates an ever improving system to record the reliability and validity of the information needed to manage patient care and the entire health plan.

To ensure that each HMO displays an increasing ability to not only report but also use information to monitor and improve the clinical effectiveness and cost-efficiency of the organization.

To strongly encourage each HMO to effectively use information technology in the delivery of care to enrollees. Examples include clinical workstations, Internet access, and electronic processing of eligibility, referrals, and claims.

SOURCE: Digital Equipment Corporation, 1997.

BOX B.3
Selected *Healthy People 2000* Goals and Objectives

Priority Areas with Objectives Relating to Children's Health Status and Health Services

Nutrition
2.4 Growth retardation among low-income children ages 5 years and younger
2.10 Iron deficiency prevalence

Mental Health and Mental Disorders
6.3 Mental disorders in children and adolescents ages 18 years and younger
6.14 Clinician review of children's mental functioning

Unintentional Injuries
9.3a Motor vehicle crash deaths among children ages 14 years and under
9.5a Drowning deaths for children ages 4 years and under

Environmental Health
11.1 Asthma hospitalizations
11.2 Mental retardation
11.4 Blood lead levels among children
11.17 Children's exposure to smoke at home

Oral Health
13.1 Dental caries in children ages 6–8 years, and adolescents ages 15 years
13.2 Untreated dental caries in children ages 6–8 years and older

Maternal and Infant Health
14.1 Infant mortality
14.4 Fetal alcohol syndrome

- accreditation organizations, particularly the National Committee for Quality Assurance and the Joint Commission on Accreditation of Healthcare Organizations;
- Foundation for Accountability;
- ambulatory certification programs;
- insurers;
- purchasers (e.g., large employers and purchasing coalitions);
- trade unions;
- advocacy organizations; and
- private philanthropic organizations (e.g., Annie E. Casey Foundation, Robert Wood Johnson Foundation).

Given the large number of agencies and organizations with interest in and/or responsibilities for collecting and analyzing information on aspects of performance in children's health, it is not difficult to see why there is no single entity that has taken overall responsibility for assuring efficient, comprehensive performance measurement in children's health care.

14.5 Low birth weight.
14.14 Pregnant women and infants receiving risk-appropriate care.
14.15 Newborn screening and treatment.
14.16 Babies receiving primary care
14.17 Spina bifida and other neural tube defects

Diabetes and Chronic Disabling Conditions

17.15 Clinician assessment of childhood development (visual acuity, hearing, speech, motor development) and treatment/referrals

Immunization and Infectious Diseases

20.11 Immunization (percent immunized)
20.15 Financial barriers to immunization

Clinical Preventive Services

21.2 Receipt of recommended services: immunizations, screening, counseling, chemoprophylaxis, interventions for children with special risk factors (see Box 3.2)

Objectives Relating to Data Systems and Accountability

Surveillance and Data Systems

22.1 Health status indicators: develop, establish use of, monitor, and provide
22.2 National data sources: state-level data for at least two thirds of state objectives
22.3 Comparable data collection procedures for federal, state, and local agencies
22.4 Identify gaps in health data
22.5 Periodic analysis and publication of data
22.6 Number of states with data transfer systems
22.7 Timely release of national data

ASSESSING THE ADEQUACY OF PERFORMANCE MEASUREMENT FOR CHILDREN'S HEALTH CARE

The Balanced Budget Act of 1997 specifies that states applying for funds to establish children's health insurance programs must submit plans that describe the strategic objectives, performance goals, and performance measures that they will use to meet those goals and objectives. These plans will become legal documents, and DHHS will hold the states accountable for implementing them (IOM, 1998).

In early 1998, the Health Care Financing Administration and Health Resources and Services Administration of DHHS began to discuss the development of reporting requirements and other regulatory mechanisms to help monitor the performance of the states in meeting the objectives of the state plans.

In addition to the technical and methodological challenges described above, there are other challenges in developing performance measures and other strategies for monitoring methods of accountability in children's health care. Some of these challenges are not specific to children's health care, such as the fundamental inadequacy of the health care industry's clinical information systems or the lack of an evidence base for most current clinical services. However, special challenges relate to children. These include: (1) the inability to know the maximum potential for each child's physical, mental, and social health status, and therefore to detect and measure shortfalls; (2) ambiguity about the health care system's scope of responsibility for ensuring optimal psychological, cognitive, and environmental inputs to children's health status compared with the responsibilities of parents, communities, and the larger environment; and (3) the embryonic state of reliable and valid outcomes measures for services to children with chronic physical and mental conditions.

Broadly viewed, large knowledge gaps remain in evidence-based medical practice, in the health care industry's information systems, measures of children's health status, as well as in the nature and extent of relationships between children's health status, health care interventions, and other causal factors.

POLICY OPTIONS TO IMPROVE ACCOUNTABILITY

In addition to adequate data sources and measures of performance, meaningful accountability—in children's health and other areas—requires an adequate means of enforcing the performance obligations assumed by each relevant party. In the SCHIP program, relevant parties extend from DHHS to states to health plans to providers to enrollees and their families (IOM, 1998). General methods of enforcement of accountability in these relationships include the following:

- setting minimum conditions for delegation of responsibility through contracting or other means, and
- setting incentives based on performance.

Factors resulting in difficulties in enforcement include the following:

- weaknesses in performance measurements,
- insufficient resources to implement enforcement methods (e.g., inadequate state agency budgets for monitoring health plan performance),
- failure to recognize enforcement methods,
- lack of resources among Medicaid beneficiaries for filing a lawsuit,
- failure to clearly specify enforcement methods in negotiations and/or contract language, and
- failure to implement enforcement methods.

A variety of general policy options for improving accountability are available. These options are not mutually exclusive and can be implemented separately or in a coordinated way.

- Continue to improve the scope and quality of performance measures and underlying data sources.
- Recommend and/or regulate a specific approach to ensuring performance at each link in the chain between public and private funding sources and patients.

As states begin to develop their children's health insurance programs under the SCHIP program, they will be making many decisions. During the decision-making and implementation phases, the accountability systems that will be developed will need to be comprehensive, and efficient, with effective placement of responsibility and authority (IOM, 1998). These systems of accountability should focus on: (1) developing the information infrastructure and capacity to measure coverage (eligibility and enrollment, as well as sources of financing), access (utilization), and quality (technical customer satisfaction); and (2) integrating improved performance information into an approach for ensuring maximum levels of performance by every party on whom the health of American children depends.

REFERENCES

Digital Equipment Corporation. 1997. *HMO Performance Standards*, 3rd ed. Maynard, MA: Digital Equipment Corporation.

DHHS (U.S. Department of Health and Human Services). 1990. *Healthy People 2000*. Washington, D.C.: Public Health Service, U.S. Department of Health and Human Services.

DHHS. 1992. *Prevention 91/92*. Washington, D.C.: Public Health Service, U.S. Department of Health and Human Services.

DHHS. 1995. *Healthy People 2000: Midcourse Review*. Washington, D.C.: Public Health Service, U.S. Department of Health and Human Services.

GAO, IMTEC (U.S. General Accounting Office, Information Management and Technology Division). 1993. *Automated Medical Records: Leadership Needed to Expedite Standards Development* (GAO/IMTEC 93–17). Washington, D.C.: GAO.

IOM (Institute of Medicine). 1989. *The Future of Public Health*. Washington, D.C.: National Academy Press.

IOM. 1993. *Employment and Health Benefits: A Connection at Risk*. Washington, D.C.: National Academy Press.

IOM. 1996. *Telemedicine: A Guide to Assessing Telecommunications in Health Care*. Washington, D.C.: National Academy Press.

IOM. 1997a. *Managing Managed Care: Quality Improvement in Behavioral Health*. Washington, D.C.: National Academy Press.

IOM. 1997b. *Improving Health in the Community: A Role for Performance Monitoring*. Washington, D.C.: National Academy Press.

IOM. 1998. *Systems of Accountability: Implementing Children's Health Insurance Programs*. Washington, D.C.: National Academy Press.

NCHS (National Center for Health Statistics). 1996. *Healthy People 2000 Review 1995–96*. Hyattsville, MD: Public Health Service, U.S. Department of Health and Human Services.

NCQA (National Committee for Quality Assurance). 1997. *HEDIS 3.0* (Health Plan Employer Data and Information Set) [www document]. URL http://www.ncqa.org/hedis.htm

NRC (National Research Council). 1997. *Assessment of Performance Measures for Public Health, Substance Abuse, and Mental Health*. Washington, D.C.: National Academy Press.

C

Public Workshop Agenda and Participants

CHILDREN, HEALTH INSURANCE, AND ACCESS TO CARE
National Academy of Sciences/National Research Council
Public Workshop, June 2, 1997
Washington, DC

Agenda

9:00 a.m. **WELCOME AND INTRODUCTIONS**
Molly Joel Coye, *Committee Chair*
Karen Hein, *Executive Officer, Institute of Medicine*
Margo Edmunds, *Study Director*

9:15 a.m. **PANEL ONE: CURRENT TRENDS AND POLICY IMPLICATIONS**
Moderator: Molly Joel Coye, HealthDesk Corporation, Berkeley, CA

Overview: Federal Proposals for Children's Health Insurance
Kay Johnson, *Center for Health Policy Research, George Washington University, Washington, DC*

Overview: State Proposals for Children's Health Insurance
Jane Horvath, *National Academy for State Health Policy,Silver Spring, MD*

Employers' Views on Insurance Expansion for Children
Kim Monk, *Washington Business Group on Health, Washington, DC*

9:45 a.m. **DISCUSSION: QUESTIONS FROM COMMITTEE AND AUDIENCE**

10:00 a.m. **PANEL TWO: TAX CREDITS AND OTHER FINANCING ISSUES**
Moderator: Carl Schramm, Greenspring Advisors, Towson, MD

Overview: Sources of Health Care Spending
C. Eugene Steuerle, *The Urban Institute, Washington, DC*

Who's Responsible for Children's Health Insurance?
John Goodman, *National Center for Policy Analysis, Dallas, TX*

What Happens to Poor Children?
Diane Rowland, *Kaiser Commission on the Future of Medicaid, Washington, DC*

10:45 a.m. **DISCUSSION**

11:15 a.m. **PANEL THREE: COMMUNITIES AND FAMILIES**
Moderator: Margo Edmunds, Institute of Medicine

A Parent's Perspective on Catastrophic Coverage and Lifetime Caps
Karen LaPlante, *Dublin, VA*

A Parent's Perspective on Being Uninsured
Maureen Ceidro, *Pittsburgh, PA*

Working With High-Risk Families and Communities
Julius Goepp, *Johns Hopkins Hospital and School of Medicine, Baltimore, MD*

12:00 noon **DISCUSSION**

1:00 pm **PANEL THREE: STATE AND LOCAL EXPERIENCES WITH INSURANCE COVERAGE AND ACCESS**
Moderator: Patrick Chaulk, Annie E. Casey Foundation, Baltimore, MD

The Massachusetts Children's Medical Security Plan
Representative John McDonough, *Massachusetts Legislature, Boston, MA*

The Caring Program for Children
Charles LaVallee, *Western Pennsylvania Caring Foundation for Children, Pittsburgh, PA*

Innovations in Serving Medically Homeless Children
Dennis Johnson, *Children's Health Fund, New York, NY*

1:45 p.m. **DISCUSSION**

2:00 p.m. **PUBLIC STATEMENTS**

Steve Edwards, *Pediatrician, Raleigh, NC, and Board Member, American Academy of Pediatrics*

James Bentley, *American Hospital Association, Chicago, IL*

Stan Dorn, *Children's Defense Fund, Washington, DC*

Shelly Gehshan, *National Conference of State Legislatures, Washington, DC*

Kathleen Means, *Health Care Leadership Council, Washington, DC*

Ross Marine, *Jackson County Health Department, Kansas* City, MO, and National Association of City and County Health Officials, Washington, DC

Catherine Hess, *Association of Maternal and Child Health Programs, Washington, DC*

Samuel Flint, *American Academy of Pediatrics, Chicago, IL*

4:30 p.m. **SUMMARY**
J. Michael McGinnis, *Scholar in Residence, National Research Council*

COMMITTEE ON CHILDREN, HEALTH INSURANCE, AND ACCESS TO CARE PUBLIC WORKSHOP, JUNE 2, 1997 WASHINGTON, DC

List of Participants

Irene Aguilar, MD*
Primary Care Physician
Westside Family Health Center
Denver, CO

Brian K. Atchinson, JD*
Superintendent of Insurance
Maine Bureau of Insurance
Augusta, ME

Sheila Avruch, MBA
Senior Evaluator
U.S. General Accounting Office
Washington, DC

John Bartkowski, Dr PH
Chief Executive Officer
Sixteenth Street Community Health Centers
Milwaukee, WI

James Bentley, PhD
Senior Vice President for Policy
American Hospital Association
Chicago, IL, and Washington, DC

Jill Bernstein, PhD
Senior Research Associate
National Academy of Social Insurance
Washington, DC

Stephen Borowitz, MD*
Associate Professor of Pediatrics
Division of Pediatric Gastroenterology and Nutrition
University of Virginia Health Sciences Center
Charlottesville, VA

Richard Bucciarelli, MD*
Professor, Institute for Child Health Policy
Associate Chair, Department of Pediatrics
University of Florida College of Medicine
Gainesville, FL

Maureen Ceidro
Director of Pastoral Care
Jeannette District Memorial Hospital
Jeannette, Pennsylvania

Thomas W. Chapman, MPH*
Senior Associate Vice President for Network Development
The George Washington University Medical Center
Washington, DC

Patrick Chaulk, MD, MPH
Senior Associate for Health
Annie E. Casey Foundation
Baltimore, MD

*Member of the Committee on Children, Health Insurance, and Access to Care.

Brenda Conner, JD
Attorney
Roanoke, VA

Molly Joel Coye, MD, MPH*
Executive Vice President
HealthDesk Corporation
Berkeley, CA

Constance Dellmuth
Director
Washington Business Group on Health
Washington, DC

Stan Dorn
Health Division Director
Children's Defense Fund
Washington, DC

Denise Dougherty, PhD
Senior Policy Advisor
Office of Policy Analysis
Agency for Health Care Policy and Research
Rockville, MD

Faye Drummond
Senate Finance Committee
Washington, DC

Steve Edwards, MD
Pediatrician and Member, Board of Directors
American Academy of Pediatrics
Elk Grove Village, IL

Amy Fine, BSN, MPH
Senior Policy Analyst
Association of Maternal and Child Health Programs
Washington, DC

Samuel S. Flint, PhD
Associate Executive Director
American Academy of Pediatrics
Elk Grove Village, IL

Yvonne Fuller
National Medical Association
Washington, DC

Stephen Garrison
Office of Congresswoman Kay Granger
Washington, DC

Shelly Gehshan
Program Principal
National Conference of State Legislatures
Washington, DC

Julius G. K. Goepp, MD
Assistant Professor, Pediatric Emergency Medicine
Johns Hopkins School of Medicine
Baltimore, MD

María Socorro Gómez
Executive Director
Mary's Center for Maternal and Child Care
Washington, DC

John Goodman, PhD
President
National Center for Policy Analysis
Dallas, TX

Donna Grossman, JD, MPH
Director of Government Affairs
National Association of City and County Health Officials
Washington, DC

Elizabeth Hadley, JD
Associate Counsel for Health Policy
National Association of Insurance Commissioners
Washington, DC

Kris Haltmeyer
Blue Cross Blue Shield Association
Washington, DC

Margaret Heagarty, MD*
Director of Pediatrics
Harlem Hospital Center and
Professor of Pediatrics
Columbia University
New York, NY

Robert Helms, PhD*
Resident Scholar
Director of Health Policy
American Enterprise Institute
Washington, DC

Joan Henneberry
Program Director for Maternal and Child Health
National Governors Association
Washington, DC

Catherine A. Hess, MSW
Executive Director
Association of Maternal and Child Health Programs
Washington, DC

Jane Horvath
Director of Medicaid Projects
National Academy for State Health Policy
Silver Spring, MD

Ed Howard
Executive Vice President
Alliance for Health Reform
Washington, DC

Sally Jagger
U.S. General Accounting Office
Washington, DC

Kay Johnson
Senior Research Staff Scientist
Center for Health Policy Research
George Washington University
Washington, DC

Sarah Lamb
Intern
U.S. General Accounting Office
Washington, DC

Karen LaPlante
Dublin, VA

Charles LaVallee
Vice President and Executive Director
Western Pennsylvania Caring Foundation for Children
Pittsburgh, PA

Cara Lesser, MPP
Health Research Analyst
Center for Studying Health System Change
Washington, DC

Susan Lieberman
Director
CityMatch
Philadelphia, PA

Ross Marine, DHL, MHA
Director of Public Health
Jackson County Health Department
Independence, MO

Rep. John McDonough
Massachusetts State Legislature
Boston, MA

Marty McGeein
President
The McGeein Group
Washington, DC

Kathleen Means
Vice President, Policy
Health Care Leadership Council
Washington, DC

Joy Midman
Executive Director
National Association of Psychiatric Treatment Centers for Children
Washington, DC

Velvet Miller, PhD, RN*
Deputy Commissioner
New Jersey Department of Human Services
Trenton, NJ

Arnold Milstein, MD, MPH*
Managing Director
William M. Mercer, Inc. and
Medical Director
Pacific Business Group on Health
San Francisco, CA

Kim Monk
Manager of Public Policy
Washington Business Group on Health
Washington, DC

Paul W. Newacheck, DrPH*
Professor of Pediatrics
Institute for Health Policy Studies and Department of Pediatrics
University of California
San Francisco, CA

Graham Newson
Senior Assistant Director
Washington Office
American Academy of Pediatrics
Washington, DC

Jackie Noyes
Associate Executive Director
American Academy of Pediatrics
Washington, DC

Annika Olsen
Office of the Assistant Secretary for Planning and Evaluation
U.S. Department of Health and Human Services
Washington, DC

Mary Parke
Project Coordinator
Harvard Center for Children's Health
Harvard School of Public Health
Boston, MA

Wendy Parker
Office of Policy Analysis
Agency for Health Care Policy and Research
Rockville, MD

Gail Perry
Project Director
Community Integrated Service Systems
National Center for Education in Maternal and Child Health
Arlington, VA

Irwin Redlener, MD, FAAP
President, Children's Health Fund and
Director of Community Pediatrics
Albert Einstein College of Medicine-Montefiore Medical Center
New York, NY

Diane Rowland, ScD
Executive Vice President
Kaiser Commission on the Future of Medicaid
Washington, DC

Arthur Safran
Office of Senator Edward Kennedy
Washington, DC

Carl J. Schramm, PhD, JD
President
Greenspring Advisors, Inc.
Towson, MD

Patricia Seliger
Policy Analyst
Kaiser Commission on the Future of Medicaid
Washington, DC

Marjorie Shofer
National Council of State Legislatures
Washington, DC

Barbara Skydell
Office of Senator Edward Kennedy
Washington, DC

Eugene Steuerle, PhD
Senior Fellow
Urban Institute
Washington, DC

Patricia Stroup
Senate Labor Committee
Office of Senator James Jeffords
Washington, DC

David Weiner, MPH*
President and CEO
Children's Hospital and Children's Medical Center
Boston, MA

Marina L. Weiss, PhD
Senior Vice President, Public Policy and Government Affairs
March of Dimes
Washington, DC

Steven Woolf, MD, MPH*
Fairfax Family Practice Center
Associate Clinical Professor of Family Practice
Medical College of Virginia
Fairfax, VA

INSTITUTE OF MEDICINE AND NATIONAL RESEARCH COUNCIL

Drusilla Barnes
Administrative Associate
Board on Children, Youth, and Families

Clyde J. Behney
Deputy Executive Officer
Institute of Medicine

Mike Dombeck
Summer Intern
Division of Health Care Services

Margo Edmunds, PhD
Senior Program Officer
Division of Health Care Services

Robert Epstein, MD
Scholar in Residence
Division of Health Care Services

Karen Hein, MD
Executive Officer
Institute of Medicine

Annice Hirt
Research Assistant
Division of Health Care Services

Marion Ein Lewin, MA
Director
Office of Health Policy Programs and Fellowships

J. Michael McGinnis, MD
Scholar in Residence
Commission on Behavioral and Social Sciences and Education
National Research Council

Tracy McKay
Project Assistant
Division of Health Care Services

Kathleen Nolan
Research Assistant
Division of Health Care Services

Dan Quinn
Office of News and Public Information

Deborah Phillips, PhD
Director
Board on Children, Youth, and Families

Michael Stoto, PhD
Senior Program Officer
Division of Health Promotion and Disease Prevention

D

Members of the Liaison Panel

National Organizations and Associations	Contact Person
American Academy of Family Physicians	Robert Graham
American Academy of Pediatrics*	Steve Edwards Samuel S. Flint Graham Newson Jacqueline Noyes
American College of Nurse Midwives*	Trish Woollcott
American College of Obstetricians and Gynecologists	Ralph W. Hale
American College of Preventive Medicine*	Hazel Keimowitz
American Hospital Association*	James Bentley Bonnie Connors Jellen
American Public Health Association	Mohammad Akhter
American Public Welfare Association	A. Sidney Johnson
Association for the Care of Children's Health	Heather Bennett McCave
Association for Health Services Research	Michael Stafford
Association of Asian Pacific Islander Community Health Organizations*	Stephen Jiang

*Submitted written materials to the committee.

Association of Maternal and Child Health Programs*	Amy Fine Catherine A. Hess
Association of State and Territorial Health Officials	Cheryl A. Beversdorf
Association of Women's Health, Obstetric, and Neonatal Nurses	Joy Grohar
Children's Defense Fund*	Stan Dorn
Families USA*	Geraldine Dallek
Federation of Families for Children's Mental Health	Barbara Huff
National Association of Children's Hospitals and Related Institutions*	Shirley Girouard Lawrence A. McAndrews
National Association of City and County Health Officials*	Donna Grossman
National Association of Community Health Centers*	Dan Hawkins
National Association of Health Data Organizations	Mark Epstein
National Association of Insurance Commissioners*	Elizabeth Hadley
National Association of Psychiatric Treatment Centers for Children	Joy Midman
National Association of Public Hospitals	Dennis Andrulis
National Coalition of Hispanic Health and Human Services Organizations	Jane L. Delgado
National Conference of State Legislatures*	William T. Pound Marjorie Shofer Shelly Gehshan
National Governors Association*	Joan Henneberry Raymond C. Scheppach
National Health Lawyers Association	Marilou M. King
National Medical Association	Yvonne Fuller
National Perinatal Association	Gail J.H. Wilson
Society of Pediatric Nurses	Sheila Q. Rucki

Foundations and Charitable Organizations

Annie E. Casey Foundation*	Patrick Chaulk
Caring Program for Children/BlueCHIP of Pennsylvania*	Charles P. LaVallee
The Children's Health Fund*	Dennis Johnson Irwin Redlener
Kaiser Family Foundation*	Diane Rowland Patricia Seliger
March of Dimes Birth Defects Foundation*	Marina Weiss
Robert Wood Johnson Foundation	Robert Hughes Judith Whang
Women's Health Foundation	Teri G. Fontenot

Policy Research Organizations

Alliance for Health Reform	Ed Howard
Alpha Center*	Ann Gauthier
Brookings Institution	Robert Reischauer
Center for Health Policy Research, George Washington University Medical Center*	Kay A. Johnson Sara Rosenbaum
Center for Studying Health System Change	Cara Lesser
Center on Budget and Policy Priorities	Wendell Primus
Children Now*	Mike Bergmyer Maryann O'Sullivan Lois Salisbury
CityMatch, University of Nebraska*	Magda Peck
Employee Benefits Research Institute*	Paul Fronstin
The Heritage Foundation*	Carrie Gavora
Hudson Institute*	William Styring
Making the Grade*	Jane Koppelman
National Academy for State Health Policy*	Jane Horvath

National Center for Education in Maternal and Child Health	Gail Perry
National Center for Policy Analysis*	John Goodman
National Academy of Social Insurance	Jill Bernstein Pamela Larson
National Health Policy Forum	Judy Miller Jones
National Institute for Healthcare Management	Ed Neuschler
National Perinatal Information Center	David Gagnon
The Urban Institute*	C. Eugene Steuerle

Health Care Industry Groups

American Association of Health Plans*	Ellen Bayer
Blue Cross Blue Shield Association*	Kris Haltmeyer
Foley & Lardner	Ann Langley
Gibbons and Company	Sam Gibbons
Greenspring Advisors, Inc.	Carl J. Schramm
Health Care Leadership Council*	Kathleen Means
Healthy Futures Group	Diane Albrecht
Hewitt Associates LLC, Washington DC Research Office*	Frank B. McArdle
Human Affairs International	David Nace
The McGeein Group	The Honorable Marty McGeein
National Account Consortium, Inc.	Alex Rodriguez
Pfizer Inc., Corporate Strategies	Alison Keith
Washington Business Group on Health*	Constance Dellmuth Mary Jane England Kim Monk

Academic Health Centers

Columbia University School of Nursing	Judy Honig

Georgetown University Child Development Center	Sybil Goldman
Georgetown University, Institute for Health Care, Public Policy, and Research	Judith Feder
Georgia State University Department of Risk Management and Insurance	William Custer
Harvard School of Public Health, Department of Maternal and Child Health	Marie C. McCormick Mary Parke
Harvard School of Medicine, Department of Pediatrics	James Perrin Judith Palfrey
Johns Hopkins School of Medicine, Department of Pediatrics*	Julius Goepp
Johns Hopkins School of Hygiene and Public Health, Department of Maternal and Child Health	Bernard Guyer
Northeastern University School of Business	Charles Baker, Sr.
Stanford University	Annika Olsen
University of California, Los Angeles National Center for Infancy and Early Childhood Health Policy*	Neal Halfon Miles Hochstein
University of California Los Angeles School of Public Health	Janet Currie
University of California, San Francisco Department of Pediatrics	Elena Fuentes-Afflick
University of Connecticut, UCONN Health Center	Jonelle C. Rowe
University of North Texas-Health Sciences Center	Fernando Trevino
University of Pittsburgh Schools of Medicine and Public Health	Kelly Kelleher
University of Rochester School of Medicine	Charles Phelps
University of Washington School of Medicine	Gina Sucato
Wake Forest University School of Law and Bowman Gray School of Medicine*	Mark A. Hall

Health Care Providers

Boston Children's Hospital	Laura Camisa
California Children's Services	Diana Obrinsky
California Pacific Medical Center	George F. Lee
The Children's Hospital of Alabama	Crayton A. Fargason
Children's Hospital of Oakland, Center for the Vulnerable Child	Laurie Soman
Children's Hospital of New Mexico–University of New Mexico Hospital	Robert T. Maruca
Church Health Center*	G. Scott Morris
Columbia Hospital for Women	Amy R. Niles
CURE	Melvin B. Tuggle, II
DMC/Hutzel Hospital	Susan A. Erickson
Howard University Hospital	Sherman P. McCoy
Jeannette District Memorial Hospital*	Maureen Ceidro
Johns Hopkins Hospital, Corporate and Community Services, Office of Community Health	Adrian Mosley
Kaiser Permanente*	Jane Andrews
Magee-Womens Hospital	Irma E. Goertzen
Mary's Center for Maternal and Child Care	Maria Socorro Gomez
Memorial Hospital Southwest	Vicki A. Lukas
Merit Health Care System	Joan Justesen
Northside Hospital	Janis Dubow
Phoenix Children's Hospital	Leland Clabots
Presbyterian Intercommunity Hospital	Margo J. Kaatz
Saint Barnabas Health Care System	Mark D. Pilla

Saint Luke's Hospitals of Kansas City	Ann L. Ropp
Shriners' Hospital for Children	David Wood
Sibley Memorial Hospital	Dietra L. Ford
Sixteenth Street Community Health Centers	John Bartkowski
Strong Memorial Hospital–The University of Rochester	James Woods
University of Kansas Community Health Center	Martin Gerry

U.S. Government Agencies

U. S. Department of Health and Human Services	
Agency for Health Care Policy and Research	Denise Dougherty Wendy Parker
Health Care Financing Administration	Debbie Chang Patricia MacTaggart Richard Strauss
Health Resources and Services Administration, Maternal and Child Health Bureau	Woodie Kessel
Substance Abuse and Mental Health Services Administration, Center for Mental Health Services	Judith Katz-Leavy
Office of Assistant Secretary for Planning and Evaluation	Margaret Hamburg Gary Claxton Cheryl Austein-Casnoff
U.S. Department of Treasury	James E. Duggan Jonathan Gruber
U.S. General Accounting Office	Sheila Avruch Sally Jaggar

U.S. Congress

House Democratic Policy Committee	Melissa Narinf
Office of Congressman Pete Stark	Bill Vaughn
Office of Representative Kay Granger	Stephen Garrison
Office of Senator James Jeffords/ Senate Labor Committee	Karen Guice Patricia Stroup

Office of Senator Edward Kennedy/ Senate Labor Committee	Susan Hammersten Arthur Safran Barbara Skydell
Office of Senator Tom Daschle	Burton Edelstein
Senate Finance Committee	Faye Drummond

State and Local Government

California Department of Health Services*	Robert Isman
California State Senate Insurance Committee*	Richard Figueroa
Florida Agency for Health Care Administration*	Martin Markovich
Jackson County Health Department*	Ross Marine
Massachusetts Department of Public Health	Deborah Kline Walker
Massachusetts Division of Medical Assistance	Annette Hanson
Massachusetts State Legislature*	John McDonough
Philadelphia Health Department	Susan Lieberman
Virginia Department of Medical Assistance*	William J. Lessard, Jr.

Parents

San Mateo, CA	Barbara Lamb
Dublin, VA*	Karen LaPlante

E

Committee and Staff Biographies

COMMITTEE MEMBERS

MOLLY JOEL COYE, MD, MPH (*Chair*) (IOM), is Senior Vice President and Director of the West Coast Office for The Lewin Group, in San Francisco, California. Previously, she was Executive Vice President for Strategic Development at HealthDesk Corporation in Berkeley, California and Senior Vice President of Clinical Operations for the Good Samaritan Health System in San Jose, California. From 1991 to 1993, Dr. Coye was Director of the California Department of Health Services, where she directed Medi-Cal's transition to managed care. She also was the Commissioner of Health in New Jersey and served on the Board of Directors of the Association of State and Territorial Health Officials and the Board of Directors for The Medical Quality Commission, which certifies managed care providers. Currently, Dr. Coye is a member of the Board of Directors of the California Endowment. Her past academic appointments include Head of the Division of Public Health at the Johns Hopkins University of School of Hygiene and Public Health, Professor on the clinical faculty in the Department of Medicine at the University of California at San Francisco and the Department of Community Health at the University of California at Davis, and visiting professor at the School of Public Health at the University of California at Los Angeles. Dr. Coye has served on several IOM committees.

IRENE AGUILAR, MD, is Primary Care Physician at the Westside Family Health Center in Denver Colorado, and Assistant Professor at the University of Colorado Health Sciences Center. Dr. Aguilar is a member and Secretary of the Colorado Board of Medical Examiners, and served on the Health Benefits Advisory Board of the Colorado Division of Insurance. She is also the parent of three children, one of whom has special health care needs.

BRIAN K. ATCHINSON, JD, is Second Vice President, Government Relations, for UNUM in Portland, Maine. He was the Superintendent of Insurance for the State of Maine from June 1992 through August 1997. Previously, he was Legal Counsel for the Maine Department of Professional and Financial Regulation. Mr. Atchinson also served as a member of the Governor's Cabinet Council on Health Care Policy. Mr. Atchinson is a former President of the National Association of Insurance Commissioners.

STEPHEN M. BOROWITZ, MD, is Associate Professor of Pediatrics and Health Evaluation Sciences at the University of Virginia. Dr. Borowitz has a special interest in the use of technology to increase access to care and improve the exchange of information. Dr. Borowitz is developing a computer-based medical record for all pediatric patients, a comprehensive on-line children's immunization database, and a regional medical information system based on the Internet to provide practitioners and consumers with information and electronic consultations. Dr. Borowitz is a Fellow of the American Academy of Pediatrics.

RICHARD BUCCIARELLI, MD, is Professor, Institute for Child Health Policy, and Associate Chair, Department of Pediatrics, at the University of Florida College of Medicine. Dr. Bucciarelli is a former Fellow in the Robert Wood Johnson Health Policy Program and has expertise in neonatology and pediatric cardiology. Dr. Bucciarelli is a Fellow of the American Academy of Pediatrics and of the American College of Cardiology.

PETER BUDETTI, MD, JD, is Professor of Law, Preventive Medicine, and Health Services Management and the Founder and Director of the Institute for Health Services Research and Policy Studies at Northwestern University in Chicago and Evanston, Illinois. Dr. Budetti founded the Center for Health Policy Research at George Washington University in 1990 and served as its Director until 1996. From 1984 to 1990, Dr. Budetti served as Counsel to the Subcommittee on Health and the Environment in the U.S. House of Representatives. Dr. Budetti is a former Associate Professor of Social Medicine in Pediatrics at the Institute for Health Policy Studies at the University of California, San Francisco.

THOMAS W. CHAPMAN, MPH, is Senior Associate Vice President for Network Development and Professor, Health Services, Management and Policy at the George Washington University Medical Center. Mr. Chapman is the former President of Greater Southeast Healthcare System and has a particular interest in urban health initiatives, community outreach, and community-based medicine. He has received several awards for community service, leadership, and innovation.

MARGARET C. HEAGARTY, MD (IOM), is Director of Pediatrics at Harlem Hospital Center and Professor of Pediatrics, College of Physicians and Surgeons of Columbia University, New York, New York. Dr. Heagarty is a Fellow of the American Academy of Pediatrics, Past President of the Ambulatory Pediatric Association, and a former member of the Board of Trustees of the New York Academy of Medicine. She is a former member of the Institute of Medicine Council and has participated on several IOM committees, including the Steering Group of the National Forum on the Future of Children and Their Families, the Committee to Study Outreach for Prenatal Care, and the Committee for the Study of U.S. Health Goals for the Year 2000.

ROBERT B. HELMS, PhD, is a Resident Scholar and director of health policy studies at the American Enterprise Institute in Washington, D.C. Dr. Helms participates in the Consensus Group, an informal task force that is developing market-oriented health reform concepts. An economist, he served as Assistant Secretary for Planning and Evaluation and Deputy Assistant Secretary for Health Policy in the U.S. Department of Health and Human Services from 1981 to 1989. Dr. Helms served on the IOM Committee on Implementation of a National Graduate Medical Education Trust Fund.

VELVET MILLER, PhD, is Deputy Commissioner of the New Jersey Department of Human Services. She is responsible for policy, program, and fiscal oversight of the state Medicaid and welfare programs, including the state's children's health program, KidCare. Her previous positions include Assistant Commissioner, Bureau of Public Health and Hospitals, Associate Commissioner, Division of Health Systems Management in the Commonwealth of Massachusetts, and Assistant Commissioner for the

Division of Medical Assistance in New York State. Dr. Miller is a member of the board of Families USA and has published work on ethnic health issues and health care conflict resolution.

ARNOLD MILSTEIN, MD, directs the national clinical consulting practice at William M. Mercer, Inc., and is the Medical Director of the Pacific Business Group on Health, based in San Francisco, California. His work focuses on evaluating and strengthening managed care programs for providers, large purchasers, insurers, and government. Dr. Milstein is board certified by the American Board of Psychiatry and Neurology and the American Board of Utilization Review and Quality Assurance. Dr. Milstein held positions with the Health Care Financing Administration from 1977 to 1994 and was a member of the IOM Committee on Utilization Management from 1988 to 1990.

PAUL NEWACHECK, DrPH (BYCF), is Professor of Health Policy at the Institute for Health Policy Studies and the Department of Pediatrics at the University of California at San Francisco. He is also a Co-director of the Maternal and Child Health Policy Research Center based in Washington, D.C. and in San Francisco, California. Dr. Newacheck conducts health services research in the areas of utilization and access, Medicaid, and chronic illness in children. He has published widely on the role of insurance as a determinant of access to and use of health services by children. Dr. Newacheck is a member of the Board on Children, Youth, and Families of the National Research Council and Institute of Medicine. He is also a member of the National Committee on Vital and Health Statistics.

DAVID S. WEINER, MPH, is President and Chief Executive Officer of Children's Hospital in Boston, Massachusetts, where he has held several positions since 1967. Mr. Weiner is a Lecturer at the Department of Social Medicine and Health Policy at Harvard Medical School and has received awards from the Massachusetts Health Council and the NAACP Legal Defense Fund. He is a Fellow in the American College of Healthcare Executives and a former Trustee and Chair of the National Association of Children's Hospitals and Related Institutions.

STEVEN H. WOOLF, MD, MPH, is a Family Physician with the Fairfax Family Practice Center and Professor of Family Medicine at the Medical College of Virginia–Virginia Commonwealth University. From 1987 to 1995, Dr. Woolf served as Science Advisor to the U.S. Preventive Services Task Force in the U.S. Department of Health and Human Services. He provides independent consulting to government agencies and specialty societies regarding practice guideline development and is an Associate Editor of the American Journal of Preventive Medicine.

IOM STAFF

MARGARET EDMUNDS, PhD, Study Director and Senior Program Officer, joined the IOM in October 1995 to direct a study of quality assurance in managed behavioral health care. From 1992 to 1995, she directed a multisite, clinical evaluation of integrated delivery systems at the Institute for Health Policy Studies, University of California, San Francisco. Previously, she directed studies relating to national standards for information technology and day care. Dr. Edmunds was a member of the affiliate staff of the Johns Hopkins Hospital from 1986 to 1992 and was a member of the faculty at the Johns Hopkins Medical School from 1989 to 1992. She was a Research and Clinical Fellow at the Johns Hopkins School of Medicine from 1986 to 1989 and a Postdoctoral Fellow at the Johns Hopkins School of Public Health from 1985 to 1986. Dr. Edmunds received her doctoral degree in human development from The Pennsylvania State University. She is a member of the Board of Directors and a Fellow of the Society of Behavioral Medicine.

ELISE LIPOFF, MPP, Program Officer, Office of Health Policy Programs and Fellowships, serves as deputy to the director for the Robert Wood Johnson Health Policy Fellowship program and also served as Research Associate for this study. She is coeditor of the recently published book entitled *Information Trading: How Information Influences the Health Policy Process*. Her previous health policy and research experience includes positions with The Finance Project, the National Center for Education in Maternal and Child Health at Georgetown University, and the Washington Business Group on Health. She received her master's in Public Policy from the University of Maryland's School of Public Affairs and her bachelor of arts from the University of Pennsylvania.

ANNICE HIRT, Research Assistant from March through September 1997, has worked at the IOM for more than 3 years. As a Project Assistant, she worked on a 2-year study to assess the adequacy of nursing staff in hospitals and nursing homes and later worked as Acting Administrative Assistant for the Division of Health Care Services. She has provided research support to two IOM studies: Children, Health Insurance, and Access to Care and Health Services in the U.S.-Associated Pacific Basin. She received her bachelor of science degree in Psychology from Mary Washington College.

KATHLEEN NOLAN, Research Assistant from January through May 1998, came to the IOM in 1996. She has worked on The National Roundtable on Health Care Quality, Implementing a National Graduate Medical Education Trust Fund, and a study on non-heart-beating organ donors. Previously, she worked on regulations and legislation in the Colorado Department of Public Health and Environment. She is enrolled in the master of Public Health program at the George Washington University and received her bachelor's degree in psychology from Carleton College.

TRACY MCKAY, Project Assistant, joined the IOM Division of Health Care Services in January 1997. She also serves as project assistant for the National Roundtable on Health Care Quality. Ms. McKay received her bachelor of arts degree in sociology from Vassar College in May 1996.

JOHN BROTHERS, Graphics Consultant, has held a variety of administrative and technical writing positions with the International Finance Corporation since 1994. His software experience includes Access, Excel, Word, and WordPerfect. Mr. Brothers received a bachelor of arts degree in anthropology from the University of Virginia and studied economics at Davidson College.

CARINA WEI-YEE FUNG, Summer Intern, is a candidate for bachelor of sciences degrees in chemical engineering, biology, and literature at the Massachusetts Institute of Technology (MIT). She was selected for the MIT Washington Summer Internship Program and the Congressional Asian-Pacific American Caucus Institute's Summer Internship Program and spent June and July of 1997 with the IOM Division of Health Care Services working on this report.

MICHAEL DOMBECK, Summer Intern, will graduate from Duke University in May 1998 with a bachelor of science degree in biology, bachelor of arts degree in public policy studies, and a certificate in health policy studies. Previously, he was a summer intern for the intellectual property division of Pfizer Inc. He spent June, July, and August of 1997 with the IOM Division of Health Care Services working on this report and other projects.

Index

D

E

F

N

O

T